THE CROSS: PAYMENT OR GIFT?

True grace requires nothing but the love of the Giver and the grateful receptivity of the receiver.

THE CROSS:

PAYMENT OR GIFT?

RETHINKING THE DEATH OF JESUS

GRACE ADOLPHSEN BRAME

CHARIS ENTERPRISES, WILMINGTON DELAWARE
2010

THE CROSS: PAYMENT OR GIFT?
Rethinking the Death of Jesus
©2010 by Grace Adolphsen Brame. All rights reserved.

No part of this book may be reproduced, stored in a retrieval system, or transmitted in any form or by any means: electronic, mechanical, photocopying, recording or otherwise, without the written permission of Charis Enterprises.

All quotations must bear the author's name, and quotations of more than a paragraph must be requested and affirmed by Charis Enterprises 13 North Cliffe Drive, Wilmington, Delaware 19809

References from the Bible
The Holy Bible: Revised Standard Version
(Camden, New Jersey: Thomas Nelson and Sons, 1952)

The Holy Bible: New Revised Standard Version
(New York: American Bible Society, 1989)

The New Testament and Psalms: An Inclusive Version
(only where noted as NTP-IV)
(New York: Oxford University Press, 1995)

Cover Art and Layout: Alan E. Singles, Singles Design
Cover Picture: "Easter Sunrise Above Rome," Kathy Dempsey, Keep Shedding, Inc.

By Permission. Parts of the fifth to ninth chapters were first published by *Perspectives in Religious Studies,* vol. 32, no. 2, Summer 2005.

Library of Congress Cataloging-in-Publication Data
Brame, Grace Adolphsen
The Cross: Payment or Gift? Rethinking the Death of Jesus /
    Grace Adolphsen Brame
Includes endnotes; quotations; subject, person, and scripture indexes.
ISBN 978-0-9769090-2-6
1. Christology 2. Soteriology. 3. Pneumatology.
    I. Brame, Grace Adolphsen, II. Title.

Books by
Grace Adolphsen Brame

RECEPTIVE PRAYER:
Prayer Which Nourishes, Heals, and Empowers

A MANUAL OF RECEPTIVE PRAYER:
For Study, Practice, and Retreats

FAITH, THE YES OF THE HEART
(A Theology of Spirituality)

Evelyn Underhill's
THE WAYS OF THE SPIRIT
Compiled, Edited, and Introduced

THE CROSS: PAYMENT OR GIFT?
Rethinking the Death of Jesus

DEDICATION

To all you who continuously yearn
to discover more about what matters most of all.

To all who experience
the Spirit who permeates the universe,
moving, felt, awesome, treasured, beloved:
the Spirit whose name is Love,
which is the Life of all,
the Spirit who claims us
now and forever.

What we cannot see, we yet can know.
To that Spirit I commend us all in trust.

IN THANKSGIVING

- To all whose love has nourished and encouraged me and probably will do so to the end of this journey on earth: Ruth, Dana, Ruth Ann, and Kathy.
- To three special spiritual daughters: Pr. Judith Van Osdol, Meg Hardt Brown, and Judith Apy.
- To my fourth spiritual daughter, Kathy Dempsey, for her cover picture: "Easter Sunrise Above Rome."
- To my marvelous cover designer, layout artist, and friend, Alan Singles of Singles Design, Garnet Valley, Pennsylvania.
- To Katherine S. Ward, my faithful editor, not only for her expert editing skills through countless hours of outstanding work, but also for her invaluable advice.
- To lovingly critical friends and associates who edited or read the text: Dr. Ruth Flexman, Pr. Judith Van Osdol, and Robert Heller.
- To advisors Pr. Henry French, whose final reading was invaluable, and to Pr. Brady Faggart, Pr. Fred Melton, and Pr. Garth Thompson whose encouragement has blessed me.
- To Diana Decker for uncommon thoughtfulness and generosity.
- To the consistently faithful, helpful, and cheerful librarians: Ben Prestianni, Rhonda Allende, Renee O'Donnell, Chris Paolini, Louise Glenn, and Tom Morabito of the Wilmington Public Library in Wilmington, Delaware.
- To the Host of Heaven who, I am sure, have watched over this venture, especially to my treasured Ed, my parents and brothers David and John, and my dear friends: Dr. John Yungblut, Argnete Fenger, Dorothy Steere, and Dr. Douglas Steere.

TABLE OF CONTENTS

INTRODUCTION   11
    To My Readers: The Questioning Faithful, Their Pastors, The Disenchanted, and Believers in Other Religions

PROLOGUE   29
    JESUS' PERCEPTION OF GOD, HIMSELF, AND US

CHAPTERS
1. THE CROSS: PAYMENT OR GIFT?   35
    Asking Essential Questions First

2. METAPHOR AND MYTH   56
    Pointers Toward Truth

3. WHO WAS JESUS' GOD?   73
    The God Who Forgives, Heals, and Frees

4. GOD, IN JESUS, ON THE CROSS   91
    God Is Spirit

5. LIFE-GIVING LOVE ON CALVARY   110
    Kenosis and Pouring Out Love as Life

6. TWO KINDS OF SACRIFICE   116
    Destroying Life and Giving Life

7. SALVATION THEOLOGY THROUGH HISTORY   128
    The Devil, God, and Us

8. FROM ANCIENT BLOOD SACRIFICE   139
   TO GIVING THE SELF
   Propitiation to *Gelassenheit*

9. REDEMPTION VERSUS SALVATION   149
   To Purchase or To Heal

10. FROM ANIMISM TO TODAY   163
    Spirits to Holy Spirit

11. THE BIG QUESTION   180
    God's Great Intention

EPILOGUE   187

ENDNOTES   195

QUOTATIONS ON SACRIFICE AND SALVATION   208
FROM RESPECTED AUTHORS

Edward Schillebeeckx • Marcus Borg • Edgar M. Carlson
Theodore G. Tappert • Arthur C. Piepkorn • Douglas John Hall
J. Denny Weaver • Michael Hardin • Karen Armstrong
Darby Kathleen Ray • Rebecca Ann Parker • Leonardo Boff
John Hick • John Shelby Spong • Gary Wills on René Girard
Jaroslav Pelikan • Arnold Toynbee • Garth Thompson

INDEX OF PERSONS   225

INDEX OF SUBJECTS   228

INDEX OF SCRIPTURE QUOTED   237

INTRODUCTION

TO MY READERS

Whether you are reading alone or with others in seminary, college, church, or at home, this book is written to challenge and support inquiry by addressing four types of readers:
1. *Faithful people with many unanswered questions:* those who are seeking a fresh, applicable, contemporary understanding of Christian belief.
2. *Pastors of the questioning faithful:* those who are on the front lines when it comes to dealing with new thoughts about old beliefs and concerns.
3. The *disenchanted* who have given up on Christianity because it seems to be unbelievable or meaningless.
4. *Followers of faiths other than Christianity* who are interested in contemporary dialogue based on scripture.

Caring, Yet Questioning
1. *The Faithful*
This book is for faithful people who find some of the church's teachings to be confusing and even painful at times. They love God, their church family, and the church's mission of compassion to the world, yet they are uncomfortable. As adults, they still question details about the stories and teachings they learned as children in Sunday school, but they have not found resources to help them mature sufficiently in their faith. Not many average church goers have had the opportunity to study ancient cultures; biblical, Semitic forms of expression; the influence of religions upon each other; and the contextual settings of biblical stories. It is rare that average members have noticed or been informed of *the evolution of theology and practice in scripture*.

God, by no means, is perceived in the same way throughout the Bible. The evolution of thought that permeates its pages needs to be made clear and understandable. There is a wide gulf between the ancient perception of Yahweh as the exclusive God of the Israelites – to whom he was the God of creation, the God of both priests and prophets, and, variably, a God of war and peace, of giving and of retribution – and the much later understanding of Jesus who knew him as the Father of Love for all people.

Jesus knew his Father as an immanent God of abundant, life-giving love, forgiveness, inspiration, and healing. But, in earlier times, mired in the concerns of becoming themselves and building a nation, the Israelites only rarely glimpsed what Jesus clearly saw. We who follow, are the same. We grow individually as well as in groups of faith. We have come only gradually to partial intimations of "I AM who and what I am:"[1] the God who, from before the beginning of time, has been fully God, even if only partially perceived. Understandings of worship, of sacrifice and salvation, have shifted as well, for *every theological issue is dependent upon one's view of God.*

Former childhood teaching is not enough for the mature in any field I can think of. Yet most individuals do not grapple with religion after entering high school. As adults, knowing that there have to be some answers we have not yet found, how do we ask our questions? Do questioning people have to "just believe" and do as they are counseled by people who "ought to know"? Do they have to "accept everything on faith" although their brains, and even their hearts, rebel?

Furthermore, shall they put their faith in their teacher or in inerrant scripture or in their own experience and logic? When scripture appears to contradict itself, how should they deal with it? Will they be considered "heretics" and ostracized or bypassed if they ask what is on their minds? Could they already have missed some wonderful, life-giving approaches to understanding the ways of God?

Would it not be exhilarating if our understanding of faith might keep up with our knowledge of science, psychology, politics, and stocks and bonds? They seem important and relevant enough to study seriously and continuously throughout life. Might a more insightful understanding of our faith and that of others positively affect international relations?

INTRODUCTION

The great historian Arnold Toynbee pointed out that religion has affected history more than any other factor.[2] Yet, if we do not mature intellectually and spiritually, how will we affect history? It is imperative that each of us develops an adult faith to face the challenges, temptations, and unbelievable evil found in our world. Creation, though made to be good, has been ransacked, and talents have been twisted by selfish greed. Human beings, though created in the image of God, with the ability to speak and act for God, need more opportunity to learn how to be ever more effective.

It is time for more of us to take a risk, to go deeper than literalism, to understand meaning behind texts and practices, and to assess context. That is, to discover when, to whom, and why each came to be. Then we should not expect them to fit perfectly into our own time and situation.

The time has come to participate in greater dialogue and discussion. Arguing from a stance of righteousness and assumed superiority will be fruitless, but discussion that embraces listening and speaking with respect will help us to learn and to appreciate others' ideas and experiences. Often we will find similarities behind different words. Then our own understanding is enriched. We also will discover concepts that challenge and clarify our own comprehension.

Spirituality is the personal receptive experience of God and consequent commitment to God in life. Theology is the explanation of that experience and an evaluation of the resulting commitment. If we are wise enough to integrate spirituality and theology, experience and explanation, our own faith may become more whole. We will be more genuinely free in spirit. Then we will see that facts and expressions will change, and even teaching varies, but inherent truth will always be true, regardless of how it is expressed.

There is no question about God and life that does not end in mystery. But for some of us, the term *mystery* is a just an evasion. If we were willing to think as far as our brains could take us, there would still be mystery, but we would be much further on than the stage of giving up. And we would have helped countless others, as well as ourselves, in clearing away what stands in the way of truth.

2. *Pastors of the Questioning Faithful*
How fortunate you are to minister to people who continually seek knowledge, who question old beliefs, and who are unafraid to express their doubts! They will enrich your entire congregation by daring to ask deeper questions than others would, by going beyond the obvious, by not taking old, revered thought for granted. I never have considered myself an apologist for the status quo in the practice of tradition, spirituality, or theology. I challenge, inform, and share my own convictions and passions when teaching or pastoring, but make it very plain that I cannot give others *their* faith. It must be their own, or it has little reason for existing except to honor those who taught them. I deeply believe that no one should stand between God and us. I try to help others respect past teachings and practice as well as honor their teachers, but urge them to claim their freedom and responsibilities as individuals. I see their lives today and eternally as depending first upon their own relationship with the Spirit, who is Life.

Pastors make the greatest difference in the Church by helping parishioners mature. You are giving your lives to support and lead your people in worship and prayer, knowledge and service. Both parishioners and you, increasingly, must graduate from milk to the food of spiritual adults as Paul would say (I Cor. 3:2). I encourage you with all my heart, and I offer whatever I can give to support you. Above all, I hope you will feel comfortable in saying to your parishioners that we can live together without having lockstep thinking, but not without large measures of gratitude, sensitivity, and love. You know well that theological explanations always will be incomplete. No one has all the answers and should not be expected to have them. It is wonderfully freeing to find some of those answers together.

3. *The Disenchanted*
This book is just as much for those who have left the traditional church and now stand outside. Perhaps they have discovered another way to worship God, possibly through a religion other than Christianity. Some wistfully desire a way to worship that they could joyfully share with *all* believers in God. They have become disenchanted with arguing about issues rather than discussing them. They are uncomfortable with those

who assume they have all truth and tell others adamantly what it is. Some have found it fruitless to search for those who share *their* truth, even passionately, but with a willingness to listen and to learn more. They are disgusted when they see either hierarchy or members using the church to seek power over others rather than using their power for others.

Many of the disenchanted have lost patience with irrational, unthinking religion that seems unwilling to take on science, politics, and the social questions of the day. Or the reverse may be true. We see people believing that God can do anything and therefore insisting that they will trust *only* in miracles. For them, that would mean that God refuses human "channels of spiritual power."[3] They will not accept God's grace given through professionally trained and committed human beings. They have made religion into something that is "no earthly good." But should not everything we know be offered for God's use? Not to realize this is to miss the greater miracle: God does not work only without our help, but through our help. That is what we are here for. We are each meant to be a tool of God. I believe that it is not only church or charitable work that is our gift to God, but everything we do.[4]

When believers insist that God must work alone, when they see the work of human hearts, brains, and hands as useless human abilities, it is heartbreaking. To the disenchanted, this attitude is irrational. They simply walk away. They feel detached from such naïveté and find it useless to argue.

Something really important has been missing. *Often, the hard questions are not being asked!* We may not even ask ourselves about them privately, let alone dare to address the leaders who should be concerned. Are we too disgusted? Do we lack courage? Are we afraid to "rock the boat" (the symbol of which the church, presumably, is)? *Yet faith is not much of a faith if it cannot exist when confronted by nagging questions.* In fact, questions, asked because we really care about the answers, can open the door to intelligent, deeper faith, strong enough to uphold us in the challenges throughout our lives.

Through the years, I have lived in Russia for more than twelve cumulative months. In my seven trips to the former Soviet Union I have discovered that apparent disbelievers can love God, or wish there were a God, when they don't understand what God might be. The only definition of God that will ever work for anyone is not a definition that others insist on, but one that makes sense to that person. It seems that often people who believe there is no God actually disbelieve a particular *definition* of God, a definition that others claim is the only, the ultimate, truth. Those holding just one definition are thus shutting out others who stand on the edge. And those on the edge may be pointing out something both natural and sensible. God, by nature as well as according to most historic teaching, is *beyond definition*. That does not mean that there is nothing we can say about the God we experience. It does mean that we never can explain in words *all* that God is.

4. *Followers of Other Faiths*

The fourth group for whom I write is those of other religions who reject the exclusivity particular to Christianity. The Christian faith claims it has relationship with the Savior, the Messiah or Christ, long looked for, but not yet found by the Jews or others. The heart of this discussion, which members of other faiths cannot accept, deals with two issues: the divinity of Jesus (and what that really means inside as well as outside Christianity), and the meaning of Jesus' death.

It is the meaning of Jesus death that is exactly the subject of this book. Are all children of God on earth doomed to hell eternally if they do not intellectually believe that Jesus is the only door to eternal life? Must they say so out loud, even if there is hesitancy within? And if they do make that audible claim, in spite of not understanding everything thought necessary, are they safe for eternity?

My own conviction is that intellectual faith is by no means the core of personal relationship with God. Theological affirmations and creedal statements attempt to explain that relationship as adequately as possible, but they can only point to truth. Truth, especially sacred truth or truth presumed to speak of eternal things, cannot be encompassed in words. But truth can be alluded to in words, and it can be felt through poetry or in words set to music. It can be deeply and wordlessly experienced in nature and in art.

Different cultures and even members of one faith group may mean different things when they use similar words to express their faith. Standing side by side and saying the same words, their minds and hearts may be in very different places. And even exterior symbolic actions cannot imprison a relationship with the mystery that many feel, but cannot express.

Conversely, we may use different words and symbols to point to the same thing. Some, trying to be true to themselves, may simply be unwilling to pin down to a prescribed statement all that their hearts may fleetingly experience of the sacred. Even among lifelong Christians, there are great differences in the depth of understanding of the Cross.

If the Cross has a deeper meaning than has been typically ascribed to it, what might that be?

Perhaps some Christians and non-Christians will find the meaning of Jesus' death to be that which this book suggests. Here is the book's essential message:

> The Cross says that God, who is Spirit, will go as far as possible to reveal, through Jesus, God's unconditional love to all humanity, now and forever.
>
> God's life and healing – called salvation – is constantly offered to everyone. We may choose whether to receive it.
>
> Forgiveness, healing, inclusion, reconciliation, and freedom were incarnated by the limitless, self-giving love of God in Christ and made visible through his life and teaching, his death and resurrection.
>
> Whenever human beings receive this gift of love, they instinctively give themselves away as the natural instruments of God.

Defending God from Sacred Story

"Why do you Christians think you have to pay God in order to get into heaven? What kind of God is that?"

When I was a young college freshman, riding a bus home for Thanksgiving vacation, there was a fascinating young man who sat next to me and almost immediately claimed to be an atheist. He challenged me with the words you have just read. I felt shocked, trapped, and defenseless. "That's not really the way I see it," I fumbled, but I knew exactly what he meant. Spoken by a non-believer in Christianity, the words *cut*, yet in some way they were hauntingly justifiable. For the next hours, I tried to put into sensible words what I had never been forced to explain. My new acquaintance was the toughest of challengers, but he became for me an angel, goading me on to further insight. I thank him now, but then ...

I knew my answers were not sufficient. I reached back to my three adolescent years of preparation to join the church in a ceremony we call "confirmation." I remembered long theological conversations with my pastor, who was also my father. He had been asked to teach in a seminary but had declined in favor of the mission field in India. It was he who had taught me, backward and forward, the salvation theology my church still teaches. But it was not enough. There was more! I could not leave the questions alone. They mattered too much! I believed people's understanding of the Cross was one of the most important concerns a human being could consider.

Yet I thought that before either of us could speak about the Cross, there were other, more basic questions. For instance: "Is there really a God? If there is, what is God like? What difference does God make?"

For Christians, the next questions would have to be: "What did Jesus have to do with God, and then, what difference did Jesus make?"

I have spent part of my life responding to that young man, whose face I no longer can see. After deep involvement in a number of satisfying professions, I have become a theologian centered in the field of spirituality. All along the way, I have created a long list of questions regarding Christian theology. I also have found wonderful, positive responses to most of those queries. They are deeper insights than those I previously had been taught, or had grown into, or made my way through. Today I stand in even greater awe of that which is beyond our understanding.

Years after my first attempts at deeper comprehension, I finally wrote the heart of this book, which was published as an article in 2005 in the journal, *Perspectives in Religion*.[5]

Yet even as I wrote the article, an unspoken, indistinct question was gnawing at me. A new insight was beginning to come. I began to think that, in focusing on the Crucifixion, I was starting at the wrong place. *Because the purpose of Jesus' life was to reveal God,* the real issue in the Crucifixion was God, not Jesus. We now bring up the most important question of all.

What Kind of God Was Jesus to Reveal?

I came to only one possible answer concerning the problem of understanding the Crucifixion. We have not been confused about Jesus so much as we have been confused about the nature of God. We cannot begin with Christ on the Cross or the baby about whom Mary pondered in her heart. We need to begin with the God Jesus truly knew and was trying to make known to us, perhaps especially on the Cross!

Jesus' whole life was spent revealing God in human terms that people could understand. *We cannot understand Jesus without understanding Jesus' God,* which means, God as Jesus experienced and perceived him. What Jesus did and said, he claimed, was all at God's request:

> The words that I say to you I do not speak on my own authority;
> but the Father who dwells in me does his works. (John 14:10)

Did Jesus thoroughly accept every action and word of God in Hebrew scripture as true to the God he seemed to know in such a personal way? That would have been impossible. The Hebrew Bible notes a thousand accounts of violence by God.[6] In comparison, Jesus, who could have caused an insurrection instead of dying on the cross, was one who lived and died to reconcile. Six times in the Sermon on the Mount we read: "You have heard that it was said … But I say to you … " (Matt. 5:21-42). Those are words that might be paraphrased: "Truly, you have heard and respected these teachings from the past, but there is a better way to understand them." Jesus, probably through prayer, had come to a clearer, more evolved view of what God was like.

The story I hope to tell will, here and there, refer briefly to the progression of Hebrew and Jewish faith through the centuries before Jesus. It will show how Israel's perspectives changed and how God seemed to change as well. *But did God change? Or was it* human perception of God that grew through history?

Representing a God of Love

If it was human perception of God that changed, we believers are responsible for how we have represented God to others. Perhaps we have offered only a partially true representation. Perhaps, since we are simply contingent creatures (created by a power greater than ourselves), we have sometimes been in error, even greatly in error. How do we know? Could it be that we now should speak and write in defense of *Jesus'* God, who was often quite different from God as perceived in ancient sacred story and theology? This question applies not only to Judaism, but to all religions with extensive history.

We have filled our lives and minds with so many theological conjectures and practices through the centuries that what is left, to some extent, has become a barrier between us and the God of unlimited, unconditional love. Yet most Christians today will tell others that it is God's love that has drawn them to God. They will say experiencing God's grace is more important than anything else. To most of us, that is far more important than any ritual or any theology.

But if God's love is so important to us, why do we feel righteous about retribution and "deserved punishment?" Why do we allow unenlightened measures of prosecution in our societies? It is in society, government and law, as well as through the Church, that we live out our faith. Many judge it unwise for the church to have an alliance by law with the state. But it is impossible for anyone, believer or not, to act without reference to their highest allegiance, whether it be themselves or others, or God. The way we treat each other is integral to faith, and faith without that concern would be insipid. If God is responsible for the way the world works, *it will be through us and not by imposition.*

Naked Before God

When times of darkness come in my life, it is easy to feel half dead. But, when I begin to revive and I am spiritually healthy, I experience a God who is *alive* – mightily alive in spite of all the negatives we know. I have a glimpse, and sometimes a profound experience, of the Way, the Truth, and the Life. Then I realize once again that we are all on a journey toward greater comprehension and deeper relationship. As the unknown author of *The Cloud of Unknowing* wrote, I realize that we are called to be naked before God.[7]

Many see that advice as meaning to surrender all images and ideas about God, hence the "unknowing." It also may indicate surrendering our attachments to created things – hence the "cloud of forgetting"[8] or letting go. I agree with those interpretations found in *The Cloud*. But for me, there is also the request to be completely honest. Without that, our relationship with the Holy is built on falsehood, trying to keep God from reaching our real selves, a fruitless attempt. God always addresses our real selves, but if we present a substitute for ourselves, if we present a mask, a persona, we get in our own way. We will be unaware that God's life in us is deeper than our own self-knowledge.

But the author of *The Cloud* is speaking of *naked intent*. He urges his readers to yield to God in prayer so completely that nothing but God matters at that time. We do not care about personal gain or release from suffering. We "desire only God and [God] alone." God is loved only for God's own sake. Focus, awareness, and love are centered on the One.[9]

In all of life, we are surrounded by the Holy: the energy and presence of the Spirit. We are offered guidance through using what I call Receptive Prayer: a resting of the psyche while receiving the Spirit's presence and, sometimes, its guidance, motivation, and insight.[10]

I do not know how it is possible to experience a God who is *alive* without prayer. Belief will never substitute for it. Nor can we substitute the faith of parents or anyone we respect or revere. In that sense, we are responsible to God and ourselves first. We are responsible for our own prayer. Using a prayer written by someone else can be wonderful. But it also may be less than honest, less appropriate, or less expressive of who we really are at that moment.

Squeezing God into Theological Boxes

Perhaps we have been grossly unfair, trying to squeeze God into a theology that may wrap God up in neat little packages of ideas. We have attempted to define unlimited deity in limited human words, which are all we have. Those who are angry at God or the Church or with theology, as well as those who teach theology, can find this concept useful: theology cannot be perfect. This is especially true since theology is a human attempt to explain what can never be fully understood, let alone, analyzed. Yet everyone has a theology.

The theology of some is that there is no God at all. They have plenty of reasons to support that view. Others may believe that there probably is a God, but if so, that God does not matter much to us and we don't matter much to God. Then there are those for whom God is the beginning and the end of all life. For them, it is God who gives worth to everything and everyone. *God, who is Spirit, is in our love for others and is in our respect for ourselves and our world.*

Those who have taught about God over the centuries have created a picture of God in the minds of us who have followed. We think we know a great deal *about* God and therefore make assumptions. But it is more important to *know* God. We can have a personal relationship. Who can imagine Jesus teaching about God without the intense life of prayer that was his connection to God? Through prayer he would have opened himself to the mind and heart of God. According to the Gospel of John, Jesus, who knew his Abba well, said that knowing God is *eternal life* (John 17:3). Do we fully realize what that means? For me, heaven is the consciousness of the presence of God, eternally.

When we are greatly influenced by another or we are in love with a wonderful human being who loves us in return, to be in that person's presence is to be our better selves. A life of prayer, of sensing the Spirit, is the same. To feel and reciprocate the love and faithfulness of God is to know eternal life on earth. Heaven touches time when we are aware of the nearness of the Holy and the Eternal just where we are, with no preoccupation about ourselves.

God's Image: God-Given Ability to Relate to God

I believe that we can relate to God, because we are made "in God's image" (Gen. 1:27). That can't mean we look like God, although some theologians actually have thought just that. Colossians 1:15 refers to Jesus as "the image of the invisible God," making it sound exclusive to him. But neither understanding should mean that the Holy Spirit cannot speak to or through human beings, including women. Nor should the fact that Judeo-Christian scriptures speak of God as male mean that a woman cannot be a pastor or priest. Why would physical organs have anything to do with being anointed by the Holy Spirit? Do such organs affect our receptivity to the Spirit of God? Both sexes, that is, all people, were created to be "temples of the Holy Spirit," according to Paul (I Cor. 3:16-17).

A favored term for Spirit in Hebrew writing was *ruach*, a female noun. And when Spirit seemed to be replaced by Wisdom or *hokmah* in later Hebrew writing, that term, too, was feminine. But the Hellenistic Hebrew philosopher Philo Judaeus (c.13 BCE – 40 or 50 CE) was most influential in the early days of Christianity, and he was partial to the Greek term *logos*, "the Word." A great deal of his writing focused on that term. He intentionally moved his discourse from *hokmah* to *logos*, contending that "Wisdom's name is feminine, but her nature is masculine." Such an approach had to intensify thoughts of God as exclusively male.[11] That, in turn, naturally influenced religious leadership, restricting it to men.

The Creation story in Genesis 1 tells us that both male and female were made in God's image. Furthermore, the Priestly storyteller, inspired by God – whom he called Elohim – told of a god or group of gods (before monotheism) possessing multiple male and female characteristics. This god or group was therefore conceived of as containing the "fullness" of deity. Genesis 1:26 can be translated: "Then Elohim said: 'Let us make [human beings] in *our* own image.'" If God's being included both sexual aspects, it would be fitting for such a God to create the divine image as integral to both male and female. It also would allow for God to have been conceived of, not only as androgynous (combining both sexes), but also as transcending androgyny. A truly fascinating question can be posed here: *What would have happened to religion and to history if the perception of one God as more than androgynous had caught hold and won? Is it beginning to happen now?*[12, 13]

But again, what does the "divine image" mean? Cuthbert A. Simpson wrote that it means spiritual power – the power of thought, communication, and self-transcendence.[14] My understanding has focused on relationship to God. Must not God's Image in us mean that we have been created similar enough to God so that we can *relate* to God? We love God because we can't help it; God loved us first, and we can experience that love! Psalm 139 testifies that, while we are thinking, God knows our thoughts. We go to God for guidance, and sometimes we are sure we have received it. We are given strength and inspired dreams and a calling. So we sing and work to make God's dream come true "on earth as it is in heaven." This kind of closeness is what past mystics have called "*cor ad cor,*" that is: from one heart to another, from God's heart to ours, and from our hearts to God's. Any kind of connection to God or consciousness of the Holy is prayer, and the wordless kind is best because then we don't do all the talking. We can live consciously in the presence of the Spirit[15] until it is as real and as faithful as our breathing.

Prayer as Receiving the Spirit
This is the heart of what I call Receptive Prayer, the many possible forms of meditating, focusing, listening to God and receiving the Holy Presence, its inspiration, and its guidance with an open heart. I have counted at least twenty-one forms of prayer that I have used and studied, and about which I have written extensively.[16] Although Receptive Prayer begins with a simple focus, it can become deep contemplation in which there is no thought, but only the experience of the presence of God. A person can simply sit quietly, gratefully knowing that they are in the presence of the Holy. Others may choose to breathe in the nourishing air that surrounds them as they simultaneously, with an open heart, welcome the Holy Spirit into body, mind, and being. Exhaling, they let go of pain and of disturbances and garbage in their lives. Finally, they come to the point of breathing out what they are breathing in: the love and life of God. For many, this is the easiest and most effective way to begin conscious Receptive Prayer.

One other form, useful especially when I am overly excited or disturbed, is *lectio divina*, a prayerful, receptive, perceptive reading of the scriptures. It may well begin or end with new questions. It may end with analytical thought or inspired directions for a course of action or the writing of poetic prose such as you will find here in the Prologue. Another means has been even simpler. In that experience, I offer myself and my work to God. Then I simply listen, think, and work in the Presence of God.[17]

Such receptivity in prayer may also come by focusing on something such as a few repeated words or a phrase, often from scripture. Many

Christians now call this Affirmative or Centering Prayer. Hindus and Buddhists know it as using a mantra. Muslim Sufis, in particular, see it as a form of *dhikr* or *zikr*. Others may focus on a cross, the heart of a beautiful flower, a stained glass window, wordless music, the ocean or the sky, while mentally entering into the beauty there – simply looking, simply hearing, being surrounded and filled. Receptive Prayer has taught me more than anything else in my life.

But we do not receive from God only in silence. We can receive while we are acting, speaking, singing, dancing, and praying aloud. "We do not know how to pray as we ought, but the Spirit within us prays," (Rom. 8:26) and sometimes it leads us to new thoughts or new words when we are praying aloud or writing in a journal. Icon painters respond stroke by stroke and singers in every vibration of sound. Inspired pastors may sometimes change their sermons. You may be aware of being led while talking to a neighbor in distress or attending a committee meeting. Such are examples of what I call Active Receptive Prayer. There is, as well, the approach I use in writing, mentioned above. All are discussed in two of my earlier books, one of which has already been noted. The other is referenced below.[18]

The Importance of Questions
A child of three has the ability to ask "Why?" incessantly. With maturity, some of us lose that curiosity. It is a true loss. We may no longer possess the stimulus and motivation that lead us deeper into life. If we retain the deep and incessant desire for inquiry, we may continue asking deeper and ever more profound questions until we die. In spite of all the tribulations of age, questions can keep us alive.

Questions are an important aspect of this book. So are their answers. There are more inquiries in the beginning than at the end. Forming questions of your own before reading the thoughts of the author will help you to be aware of what *you* think at this point. With this approach, your reading can become a conversation with the author. Furthermore, if you are enriched by what you read and by your own new conclusions, those new understandings can become part of your true self. None of us can live fully with someone else's answers or another person's faith.

The Creed We Really Live

Often, in my classes, I ask my students to write their own creeds, to think about, discover, and write in their own contemporary language what they believe ultimately matters. They are to write the convictions they try to live by, although none of us ever does that perfectly. Our ideals are always ahead of our actions and need to be. Knowing this helps a great deal when we are disappointed with ourselves.

Many may discover that, at heart, we believe most strongly in the importance of ourselves and our own wants and desires. We may see that our needs and cravings threaten important relationships and disturb our peace. Everyone alive instinctively begins life with attention on the self, but only some honestly face that common deep-seated focus. Yet, sometimes, there comes an awareness of awe and a sense of God's unselfish, forgiving, and uplifting love. For many, that gift is more sensed than thought. It is nameless and beyond us, but it touches us deeply – inside.

Some of you now reading these pages might like to write your own creeds. If so, you will probably discover that you have taken some things for granted that you want to consider further. Honestly and freely look at what *you* think, with no one guiding or judging you. I am sure you will get closer to what you believe most deeply. You will discover that real faith can only be your own.

You may perceive that you are not accustomed to asking yourself deep questions and need to learn how to express – in words – matters you rarely discuss. This is the time to bring into your private mental space the questions you have avoided for fear of what others would think and those you have avoided for fear of where they might lead you. When you are finished with the book, I suggest you write another creed without referring to the first until you are done. One caution is important and should be stated as strongly as possible: Please do not use any creed you know as a pattern. Your creed should begin at *your own beginning point* and should not be influenced by any other. Words of the fourth century are unlikely to be what you would naturally use.

As you write you will be asking: "What really matters to me? What do I cling to? What is my foundation? Whom and what do I trust? How are the love of God, of my family and the world related? What do my beliefs have to do with the way I live my life? The creeds we write today may change, even change radically in the future. We may be surprised.

Growth in God sometimes appears to be in a crescendo, but it is always interrupted by challenges that can only be used as goads if faith is to survive. Selfishness and sin are synonyms. They are both inside and outside us. We will be strengthened when we are aware that what we know now is not all there is to discover. There will always be More beyond. To know that the More is deeper than what we previously have understood may be what sustains us in dry or painful times.

The Inspiration for This Book

Throughout these pages, most of the important insights shared have come to me as a gift. To begin with, I did not read thirty or forty books in order to write my own. The treasure that I most want to share is made up of understandings that have come through the frame of mind I call Receptive Prayer while thinking of what I have previously been taught, and while reading scripture and listening to people. That meant attempting to remain open, to learn in silent receptivity and sometimes, to be given fresh interpretations of what I thought I knew. It also has come in conversation with authors while reading their challenging and enriching insights.

I am grateful that a number of discerning authors are now writing on some aspect of the subject that is presented here. Some of their work is outstanding. There are sections of the book where a few are quoted, but I have selected some favorite quotations, which appear in a section of their own before the indexes. I hope they will affirm for you much of what is here, increasingly clarifying, deepening, and enhancing the subject we are focusing on: *true grace, which requires nothing but the love of the Giver and the grateful receptivity of the receiver.* This freely-given, freely-received grace of God must be far more adequately addressed beyond ancient, early Christian, and medieval thoughts and terminology.

You will note that major points will sometimes be repeated. This is intentional, to help the reader remember, and also to demonstrate that the concept applies in more than one situation. You will note that a verse from II Corinthians 5:19 (NTP-IV), which captures the essence of this book and serves as the epigraph, is scattered throughout. I have chosen not to quote one of the words exactly as it appears in that version: where the NPT-IV version says "God was, in Christ, reconciling the world unto Godself," I have chosen to use "God" rather than "Godself." Please also note the use of BCE (Before the Common Era) and CE (Common Era), terms now adopted in most scholarly work rather than BC (Before Christ) or AD (Anno Domini – the Year of our Lord – the year in which Christ was born).

From today on, will you consider being more sensitive to life, to both beauty and need in people and places you usually do not really see? Will you write these perceptions down in an online log or in a bound spiritual journal so that you may fasten them in your mind? Then, notice, if you will, in those hair-breadth spaces that float in and out of consciousness, what holiness is and how we seem to be living – not below it or beside it, but inside it, as in the atmosphere of God.

Read with questions. Soak up what helps. Respond to me in the margins of your book. Or call on me for lectures or a retreat!

Grace Adolphsen Brame
Wilmington, Delaware
grace@gracebrame.com
www.gracebrame.com

PROLOGUE

Jesus' Perception of God, Himself, and Us

How did Jesus perceive God?

"The Father is greater than I"
are his words.[19]
Jesus prayed to God, trusted God,
and loved his Father.
He conceived of his own life,
his words and actions,
as his way to reveal
what the transcendent God is like
in human terms.[20]

going beyond normal limits

So thoroughly did he do this, that
he *embodied* the Way, the Truth, and the Life
on earth, in words and actions we could comprehend.[21]

express in concrete form

Then he called for us to see what he perceived,
to understand and follow,
to receive and embody God's love as well,
to hug and hold and heal by grace.

"No one comes to the Father but by me,"
are the words that John reports.
By me? Does he mean by "embodying that which I am?"[22]
by "attempting to do God's will and work as is my task?"
He even promised that we, his future earthly body,
charged to continue his mission,
would do greater things than he had done.[23]

representing in bodily form

That would have been impossible
had he not given his disciples and his first followers
a fresh infilling of the Holy Spirit.
It was the Spirit in and through them,
that gave them power.

Luke wrote Jesus' words in his first chapter of Acts:
"And you shall receive power
when the Holy Spirit has come upon you …
and you shall be my witnesses to the ends of the earth."[24]
This is the gripping revelation
that so many of us have missed.
This is what we refuse to accept.
Barring a remnant of the lovers of God,
we are asleep. We live life unconscious
of all that we could do and be
for the Lord we think we love.

Yet, on the eve of his death,
Jesus said to his followers,
"You have not chosen me,
but I have chosen you,
that you should go and bring forth fruit
and that your fruit should remain."[25]

Since then, those words are said
to every single person on the earth
who can hear and can respond.
Each one of us is called to be a *christ*,
chosen and appointed to do God's work
and to speak God's life-giving grace
in our own unique way.[26]

It is humbling. It is glorious.
To those who have comprehended it
for the first time,
it is almost unbelievable.

When will we wake up?
When will we become conscious?
When will we admit we are *afraid*
of the divine potential in us?

Every prophet has been afraid,
and yet they did what they were called to do.[27]
Both they and we have been told that
no true call is given
without the gifts needed to fulfill it.
We have been assured
that both the gifts and the call
are irrevocable.[28]

Without telling anyone,
Without any announcement,
When will we begin
to live our "Yes?"

God was, in Christ, reconciling the world unto God, not counting the people's trespasses against them, and entrusting the message of reconciliation to us.

> II Corinthians 5:19

Chapter 1

THE CROSS: PAYMENT OR GIFT?
Asking Essential Questions First

Was the Cross a payment *to God* for human sin so that we might receive eternal life instead of everlasting punishment? Or can it be seen as a life-giving gift *from God* – meant to reveal unlimited, unconditional, and healing love for us – in time and for eternity?

These questions are crucial. What we think of God and, therefore, how we relate to God, hangs on them.

Furthermore, our understanding of Jesus, his relationship to his Father, and his mission on earth, are based on what kind of God Jesus knew, loved intimately, and disclosed to us.

For Jesus, God was his Father, his strength, and inspiration. Through their continuous connection in prayer, Jesus came to know that his mission was to reveal what his Father was like. The Cross must have been part of that understanding, for it was he who chose to walk toward it, toward Jerusalem, the "city of peace," where so many of the Prophets had been killed.

For many Christians, Jesus' Father has been our God as well: a God of love, wisdom, goodness, and constant faithfulness; a God who inspires and encourages; a God who challenges and calls; a God who has been experienced as ultimate, transcendent, and incomprehensible, but is so immediate and immanent as to live in and through us as Spirit!

Yet, for many, those treasured beliefs, even when based on personal experience, have been challenged repeatedly by critical, agonizing questions. They are questions that have to be asked in order to find truth we can understand and then express in our own words. It also has to be our truth and not another's. The questions continue.

Would God have punished all humankind eternally without the crucifixion of Jesus? If so, what a waste of a good creation! On the other hand, perhaps God, through Christ, used the Cross to say: "I will do anything to show you how much you mean to me."

For most Christians, God is, first and last, a God of love and life. It is difficult to believe that, in the Crucifixion, God was first, a God of justice, and only afterward, a God of grace. It is painful to think that payment – by the death of Jesus – was of primary importance and the gift only secondary. We can't help but think that grace – *God's unconditional and undeserved love* – could have been given without Jesus' payment in our stead.

In addition to all of the inspiring stories, wise teaching, and tender words of ancient scripture, we have strained to understand perceptions of God as wrathful, jealous, undependable, inconsistent, and even unfaithful. Early biblical accounts list one thousand acts of vengeance and violence by Yahweh.[29] Some have been compelled to ask: "Was the Cross more of the same?"

If God's intention was to forgive us, why would Jesus' death be necessary? That horrendous torture could not have been essential to God's willingness to forgive.

Could God not simply have said: "I love you. I forgive you"? Certainly Jesus did not have to die so that God would say those words! But he did die, and God did speak through his death. Perhaps that message is just what God *was* saying through Jesus on the Cross.

For Jesus, it could have seemed necessary to *show* us the truth, to help us to *experience* it. When God's love, forgiveness, and claim seem invisible, we may not even believe that they exist. But if we see and experience such grace, we very well might receive what we could not otherwise believe: God's love and life are given us, poured out on us, in front of us. All of that is revealed and made real – there, on that Cross.

The Tradition of Sacrifice

For centuries, Hebrews embraced a tradition of sacrifice. According to Hebrew scripture, before Jesus' life and crucifixion, God forgave Israel countless times for various transgressions such as greed, envy, murder, and worshipping false gods. Often, but not always, sacrifice was involved in forgiveness. It was carried out according to specific commands, believed to have been given by God, many of which can be read in the first sixteen chapters of Leviticus. But as time went on, God seemed to ask only for repentance: no sacrificial ritual (Isa. 55:6-7). Although once perceived to have been ordained by God, by the time of the Later Prophets, much sacrifice was strongly condemned by God and sacred Law.

A newer, softer, more loving approach is sometimes seen in parts of Isaiah. There, through one great passage of scripture, God asked Israel only for an open, receptive heart, a heart that would feed on God's love. Its words ring out:

> Ho, everyone who thirsts! Come to the waters. And you who have no money [who cannot pay, who have nothing to give in return], come! Buy wine and milk without money and *without price*. (Isa. 55:1) (emphasis added)

God says: "Allow me to love you! Please don't try to pay me! You are thirsty. Let me give you drink. Let me offer you, freely, what I know you need."

Then, just before Jesus' ministry began, John the Baptist offered baptism in the Jordan River for the repentance of sin (Matt. 3:11). Sacred ceremonies, including those of repentance, spoke for people and to them. They marked dramatic changes in the direction of individual lives and really became rites of passage. Thereafter, those involved were expected to think and act as though they had been transformed. Some of the reforms were costly, as were conversions from long held habits. But they were meant to replace hindrances to a healthy spiritual life.

Salvation for A Price
Did God send Jesus to pay for our sins? John 3:16-17 says: "For God so loved the world" that God sent Jesus to save it. But those words do not explain what salvation is, nor do they indicate anything about how salvation would be accomplished. Perhaps God had other means of saving humankind, means other than punishment and other than *salvation for a price*. Surprisingly, the idea of payment by Jesus, important as it has been in the Christian church, is not familiar to the Gospel writers. In all of the Gospels, there is only one sentence suggesting payment. It is found in both Mark and Matthew. There, Jesus is quoted as having said: "The Son of Man ... came to give his life as a ransom for many" (Mark 10:45; Matt. 20:28).

In Jesus' time, one use of a ransom was to make a payment in order to free a slave. In the Pauline writings that preceded the origin of the gospels, Paul stated that "in the flesh" he was a "slave to the law of sin" (Rom. 7:25). The quotation about the life of Jesus paid as ransom has been interpreted as a way to free people from slavery to sin. But the reality is, it has not worked. Jesus did not free us from sin. It is still here. It exists in abundance. Modern day believers are inclined to see the ransom as freedom from *punishment* for sin: in other words, forgiveness. Ransom was punishment for the one who paid. Instead of us, Jesus paid. We were forgiven. That is what most of us have been taught.

But Jesus' intent pointed strongly in another direction. Jesus considered his whole life to be God's gift to others. His mission was to give himself completely for the one he called his Father, thus revealing God in earthly ways that people could see, hear, touch, and understand. *Could it be that Jesus died by crucifixion in order to emphatically and empirically complete his message in a historically unforgettable way?* The consequences of the Crucifixion are innumerable in human history. Because of who Jesus was, how he died, and the experience that he now lives, the world will never forget his message or the life he lived.

It seems to me that the Spirit in Jesus was crying out from the Cross: "I will go as far as possible for you! See me! Hear me! My life is my message! I have shared the joys and the depths of life with you. Now I share the valley of the shadow with you. It is all for a purpose: to break down walls, to reconcile, to forgive, to show you how deeply you are loved. Through me, my Father is saying: 'I claim you for my own. Live in me, and I promise: I will live in you'" (cf. John 15:4, 5).

Jesus timed his crucifixion to occur when Jerusalem was bulging with people who lived outside the city and who may or may not have heard whispers of a Messiah. But they would see the fullness of God's love in him, would hear his prayer for forgiveness of those who murdered him, would suffer with him, and would never forget! Jesus had always given away his life. The Cross was his final gift. He had lived a completely human life. Now he would die one of the worst of human deaths. He would have participated as fully as possible in what it means to be human. But, at the same time, he was as radically open to his Father as any human could be. He must have perceived the Cross as the only way he could fully "give life, and … give it abundantly" (John 10:10).

If that was Jesus' purpose, could it not have been attempted without the Cross? Perhaps. *Would the world have noticed?* I doubt it. Had Jesus already tried by everything he said and did? Yes. But the death and resurrection of Christ were what brought Christianity into world civilizations as a major way of relating to the divine. Was it all worth it? Incomparably. Was God's message through Christ fully comprehended then? Surely not. Is it now? That is for all of us to answer.

Punishment or Payment?
One wonders if punishment is godly or human. If it is godly, as early Hebrew scripture contends, it could be intended to deter abuse, set limits, and teach self-discipline. Otherwise it would have been purposely intended to harm, inflict pain, or even destroy. Punishment is rarely rehabilitating. People naturally want to strike back in anger at anyone who harms them, causing greater violence. But, throughout history, some measure of destruction often has been the intent of those who think themselves righteous or *just*. It is difficult to face or to understand that we are part of that response.

The motive and use of punishment turns out to be significant. *Is it really possible to pay for sin?* Can the felon in our prison system really pay for crime committed? Can family or friends pay for it? Can Jesus pay for the self-centered desires in *our* hearts and the consequences of *our* sin affecting the lives of others? Can Jesus pay for our self-destructive attitudes and actions? All these suggestions seem utterly impossible to me.

If it is impossible to find a way to compensate for sin, then why punish? If the consequence of unforgiven sin is eternal life in hell, it would seem of no use to God, and the God I am familiar with is neither vengeful nor wasteful.

There have been many who might have "missed the mark" (one definition for sin) but who have found the threat of hell a deterrent and, therefore, a protection for those whom they might have harmed. Furthermore, in a world of practical consequences, fear – especially fear of hell, God's eternal prison – can be extremely useful for those who would like to make this a law-abiding world. But it is common knowledge that psychological manipulation of people through the use of fear has turned many away from Christianity. It has angered those who have been the targets of such manipulation. Often, their anger has been toward God rather than toward the responsible human speaker. That anger has created a monstrous barrier to receptivity to the Spirit of Love. There must be another way!

Paying the Devil
During the first eleven centuries after Christ, a number of explanations for the Cross were offered. The most long-lasting and shocking one was that *Christ died to pay the Devil.* Why? Well, the Devil was considered to be "the Prince of this world," as Jesus called him (John 12:31). There were those who presumed that he had taken over as ruler of the earth when Eve and Adam disobeyed God. It seems people believed that to pay the Devil a *ransom* would release humankind from both the Devil and sin. If that were true, it would make more sense to think of paying ransom to the Devil than to God.

In traditional Hebrew practice, ransom was paid to regain property not rightfully obtained as well as to free a slave. At one point, it was paid by each individual at census time as a type of spiritual insurance against illness (Exod. 30:11-16). Captives once held in Babylon considered themselves ransomed and "redeemed" and given their freedom. And in several places in Hebrew scripture, ransom is known as "the price of [one's] life," paid so that a person would "never see the pit," known as Sheol (Ps. 49:7-9). That concept is closest to the one most related to the theology many Christians still hold today: ransom is paid to a criminal to obtain the freedom of some imprisoned person who is valued. It was easy for early theologians to think in these terms. Who would not want to be free from the Devil? Who would not desire freedom from temptation and sin?

One might wonder if the Devil, like Eve's serpent, is a metaphor for our own self-centered inner nature. It seems that, ever since human beings could choose values, we have projected our weaknesses and destructive words and deeds *outward,* just as we have done when saying: "The Devil made me do it!" We personify evil and name it Satan. We objectify it. We say it is outside us when it is an inner possibility, waiting for our "Yes" or "No." The early Church put evil outside itself also.

Theologically, the Church has tried to *pay off* the consequences of evil with the death of Jesus. But this is a solution exterior to the real problem of deep-seated self concern. We should, instead, confess that human self-centeredness and greed were so extreme (and still are) that Jesus could hope to awaken and transform us only by a radical teaching tool: his life – forfeited on the Cross and glorified in his resurrection.

For slightly more than a thousand years – more than half of Christian history – the Church continued to stand by some theology of the crucifixion as a way of dealing with the devil. In the sixth century, Pope Gregory the Great told a story that compared Jesus' death to bait with which to "catch" the devil (see Chapter 7). Theologians made joking references to it. Even the great reformer Martin Luther told the story. It was a contrived idea that had no meaningful results. Unbelievably, it lasted even past the proclamation of Reformation theology.

The Influence of Anselm of Canterbury (1033–1109)
Finally there came a challenge to the theory of payment to the Devil. A new theology taught that Jesus was paying God for human sin because, by sinning, we had offended God's honor. That was seen as a powerful and acceptable reason, even though it is not found in scripture. Paul's writings had said that Christ *died* for our sins, not that he *paid God* for them by dying.

Thus three theological points were new. Jesus was paying God, not the Devil. The payment was for human sin. This erased the blight on the Creator's reputation. The idea's were those of Anselm, an Italian monk appointed Archbishop of Canterbury in 1093. Theologians had not considered a theory such as his before.

A churchman and scholar with great authority, Anselm possessed considerable influence. His theology of reparation and salvation quickly gained a powerful foothold and has been taught across the world ever since. It has impregnated our thought, our liturgies, our hymns, and our prayers. And it has been given such credence that one might think it was direct, divine inspiration, popularly canonized as though it were scripture.

Anselm first destroyed the old theology of paying the devil. His new understanding was loving and freeing in comparison. Human beings would not be held hostage to Satan, evil personified. Believing that humans carried a heavy burden of guilt, Anselm was, by his theory, relieving that burden. Had the Church continued to say that the Crucifixion paid the devil, the Church, as an institution, could hardly exist today. For some, it would mean that there is a rival god. Others would simply consider it absurd.

The new concept was much like that of providing bail for a felon. It was "bail," however, that would be effective for eternity. Only once in all history would payment need to be made (Heb. 10:14), even though people kept on sinning. Human beings who felt guilty and wanted to be thought of as righteous accepted wholeheartedly. It is easier to pay for something and be done with it than it is to trust, to depend upon God's grace. It is easier to have someone else pay the bill than it is to live a lifetime receiving the love of God, responding to it, and sharing it responsibly. In fact, such a theology seemed not yet to have entered people's consciousness.

Unfortunately, Anselm's theory of reparation and salvation overshadowed and even superseded what was to become the church's treasured theology of grace: the unmerited love of God, freely given, as the expression of selfless love and genuine appreciation for the inherent worth of those to whom it is offered. God's very being is thought of as grace.

Anselm's theology of recompense to God is called the forensic approach, used in arguing in court. Although the concept was lawful, it was not grace-filled. It centers on human sin and guilt, creating a debt that must be paid to God. Jesus, as the son of God, was considered to be the only one pure enough to pay such an overwhelming obligation. Furthermore, such a debt could be paid only in blood, in the ancient way. Jesus' life must be forfeited. According to Anselm, payment or redemption through Christ's irreplaceable life was deemed necessary in order for God's grace to be given.

The theory that Jesus had to die to pay for our sin became highly favored, and it survived to become the only theology most Christians, and even the whole of the world, would be taught for centuries. This book was written to say that *Anselm missed the most important point of all: the grace of God, which precedes any theology of law. The Cross was not a payment, but a gift.*

Nevertheless, as Anselm and the Church have taught it, God would not forgive without the Crucifixion. But the old idea of the necessity of a victim who must bleed to death to satisfy God is abhorrent. What can God do with blood? According to a Hebrew psalm, God does not "drink the blood of goats" (Ps. 50:13). And the New Testament book of Hebrews (10: 4) adamantly states: "It is impossible that the blood of bulls and goats should take away sins."

Is Anselm's view our image of God? To me it is shameful. It insults God! It insists that God requires *payment for grace, payment for forgiveness. If so, they are not gifts.* Surely we cannot think that God was unable to forgive without insisting Jesus die! God had been forgiving long before Jesus appeared, and God continued to offer grace in the words and healings of the Son (cf. Luke 5:12-26).

The gift of grace had been important to Augustine (354-430), whose theology is considered foundational to the Christian church. He wrote about grace seriously in his early life and thereafter.[30] It seems to me, he spoke increasingly and extensively about original sin, heavenly predestination only for the elect, and the inability of the human will to do anything good. He claimed that the human will has no inclination to holiness and is not capable of cooperating with the work of the Holy Spirit in human hearts, a view defined as *monergism*.[31]

From my point of view, this theology is one of the most destructive in Christianity. It has degraded and brought contempt upon the simple love of God in many a heart. It says that the human will cannot love God unless God empowers it to do so. Why was it not clear to Augustine that godly empowerment is by the Holy Spirit which is forced on no one? It can only be received by a will supple to the love of God and a heart with the capacity to receive it.[32]

A thousand years later, when speaking of salvation, Luther proclaimed strongly: "grace alone!" But Luther was Augustinian, and the concept of God's love as receivable grace was not acknowledged by him. As a result, any understanding of grace as freely given to a receptive heart was weakened. It was soon crowded out by Anselm's theology of salvation, which pays no attention to the effect of the Crucifixion on the human heart and mind and dwells only on the interpretation of Christ's offering as an objective necessity for salvation. But no one has seemed to notice. Payment, not grace, still comes first, especially in much of the liturgy, song and prayer in today's Church.

Catholic theology, while revering Augustine, has, nevertheless, spoken of *potentia obedientialis*, the innate power to obey God, which to me, means the power to respond and to receive. Faith cannot be commanded. Faith is not possible without a *given, responsive* will. The incentive to write my book *Faith, the Yes of the Heart* is based on this point of view. And my book *Receptive Prayer* has this as the fundamental assumption.

An old hymn states Anselm's theology succinctly. "There is A Green Hill Far Away" contains the words: "There was no other good enough to pay the price of sin. He only could unlock the door of heaven and let us in."[33]

Anselm's theory is a reconstruction of the priestly teaching of sacrifice, increased to the greatest measure possible. Yet nowhere in the gospels does Jesus say or imply that God wishes sacrifice as payment. He never says: "You will have to wait for God's forgiveness until someone dies to pay for your sin." He makes no mention of recompense. He preaches about forgiveness: that we forgive others as God forgives us – completely. His teaching of the Lord's Prayer (Luke 11:1-4) indicates that, as we pray, we are forgiven in measure as we forgive.

This prayer, offered by millions daily, makes clear that the grace of God's forgiveness cannot get through to us if we have erected an interior barrier. If we refuse to forgive ourselves or others as unworthy of being loved, our unyielding attitude will bar God's gifts. Jesus has taught us to offer our humble request to be forgiven, but also asks that we offer others what we pray God will give to us. He opens our hearts to follow forgiveness by living lives of mercy. But he does not dwell on paying God.

The Catholic theologian, John Dwyer, has commented upon the Anselmian satisfaction/reparation theory as dominant since the Council of Trent (1545-1563) at the beginning of the Catholic Counter-Reformation. Dwyer mentions the absence of any real foundation for Anselm's theory in Paul's writings. While referring to Paul Tillich's theology, he states his own view saying:

> *The Anselmian theory is arguably the most harmful ever to surface in the theological tradition.* It has transformed God

into a strange being whose demand for justice must be satisfied before he can, or will, show his mercy.[34] ... A "god" who must be placated and who demands repayment in pain and suffering ... is not real and never was, and "believing" in such a god has nothing to do with Christian faith....[35] Tillich's rejection of such a god may well represent his most enduring contribution to theology and to the Church.[36] (emphasis added)

Why Have We Retained Anselm's Theory?

Why, after listening to Anselm's argument, did the Church adopt it so thoroughly? Although numbers of theologians today disagree with Anselm, this question still does not seem to be adequately addressed. But let us begin to try.

Perhaps a potent reason for retaining Anselm's theory (and it is just theory) is his concept of the necessity of justice. Over and over, I have heard it explained that God's love must be balanced by God's justice. Otherwise, there is fear of seeing God as weak and sentimental. The problem is that human beings want to interpret justice as the privilege of righteous anger, punishment, and revenge, rather than considering any form of rehabilitation and restoration as the godly form of justice. As long as we can think of God as justly destructive and threatening, we can allow ourselves to be that way as well. Besides, such a human attitude is far easier to comprehend than is unlimited and unconditional love.

All this is not to make sin inconsequential. It has never disappeared, and its effects can be agonizing and monstrous. But I doubt that God's judgment is our enemy. Sin always destroys something. Sin always has its own enduring consequences, which are not administered by God either now or in the future. I believe that those consequences are met not only in life but, eventually, within our souls, when we finally have to face ourselves.

As far as I know, until later in Anselm's lifetime, no well-known, better alternative theology was presented. Anselm wrote about his theory more than once. His most famous treatise, however, written while in exile, was entitled *Cur Deus Homo*.[37] Written without any punctuation marks, it can mean either "Why God Became A Human Being" or "Why Did God Become A Human Being?"[38]

In spite of being exiled by the Pope for disobedience, Anselm was, in his own time, respected for his teaching. He is known today for his ontological "proof" of God and remembered for his statement: "Theology is faith seeking understanding."

In spite of his intense interest in salvation, Anselm "did not think many people" would enter heaven. The American theologian, Roger Haight, states that according to Anselm, "one would, practically speaking, have to be a monk to be saved."[39]

He also was a fatalist. Like many of the ancient Hebrews, Anselm wrote of the Almighty: "What [God] wills must occur, *and what [God] does not will cannot occur.*"[40] That would lay all the wars and rapes of history at God's door.

The Theology of Grace – Inconsistently Applied

In comparison with Anselm's view, we are presenting here another theology of the Cross, one that focuses on grace first. This is an approach that the Church – in this, the most important case of all – has missed. The Church believes it has always spoken of grace first. The term it has used is *prevenient grace*: "grace that comes before" anything else. But in using Anselm's thought to explain the Crucifixion, Christian theology became inconsistent. *If Anselm was correct, grace does not come first; it cannot be prevenient.* In his scheme, grace is second: the payment of Jesus' blood sacrifice precedes the gift of grace. It is as if God had said: "Pay me first. Then, I will offer you salvation. Only after Jesus sheds his blood will I forgive you."

For some of us, *grace first* puts into words something we have long sensed: God is love. Therefore, love (grace) precedes everything else. There are those of us who believe that Jesus' life and death spoke to us saying: "I will do all I can to show you that you are loved, forgiven, freed, included, and made whole. This is salvation. Receive my gift and use it for me. Be my instrument to share what I offer."

> Although "Jesus died for us," as Christians have said for two thousand years, his reason was not to pay for human sin, but to make God's love visible and experienced in an unforgettable way.
>
> God was present through Jesus, revealing eternal love – even in the depths of human experience: hate, pain, and death – with blessing in the present and hope for the future.

Dwyer, again speaking for Tillich, writes: "Real love always expresses itself in sharing the concrete destiny of another, and in Jesus, God has participated without reserve in the human condition."[41]

Throughout the life of a Christian, the Church's liturgy, hymns, and prayers teach people what to believe. They teach even without sermons or confirmation classes. "What we pray is what we believe" was the medieval way of putting it, expressed in Latin as *"Lex orandi, lex credendi."* Literally the sentence is translated as "The law of prayer [is] the law of belief." It means that worshippers have repeated the same beliefs so often in their worship services, that to use those same words is the only way most Christians can explain their faith. We have learned while we worshipped because we have sung, read, heard, and prayed one particular theology every time we have gone to church. What we have sung and said is Anselm's explanation of why Jesus died on the Cross.[42]

In an earlier writing entitled *A Meditation on Human Redemption*, Anselm contends: "To sin is to dishonor God.... In order to be restored to that end for which he was created," the human being must rescue God's honor, that is, must "satisfy God" by offering "something of his own which is not owed, something which exceeds everything that is not of God." It was Jesus who "paid the sum for others who did not have what they were indebted to pay."[43]

But surely *Jesus did not die to restore God's honor*. God is God and does not have to resort to weak ego-centricity to defend godly honor. If a strong, almighty God is focused only on love and giving life, there is no place for or possibility of self-concern. What God seems to deeply care about is self-giving, not self-defense. Furthermore, in the mind of the God of Love, what could be reparation for a bruised reputation?

Those devoted to God offer gifts, ostensibly to God, but for the sake of serving God by serving others. Yet, because God does not need or use earthly things, the only gifts God desires are the human heart and a life given to share what I would call God's Great Intention.

I believe God's Great Intention is first, the awakening of all humankind to God, who loves us in spite of any hindrance. Then, second, it is for us to live, loving as Jesus loved – inspired and empowered by the very Spirit that was in him. God's Great Intention, I believe, is what we are describing here as the alternative vision of the meaning of the Cross: Jesus died to make God's love visible and experienced by humanity.

Touching Upon Abelard and Others
In an ensuing chapter, we will take note of the French theologian, Peter Abelard (1079–1142). He was born only forty-five years after the famous Anselm, and he had a far different theory, which, I believe, should have been taken seriously by the Church. Essentially he argued that Jesus died to effectively show the life-giving, saving love of God. He believed, as do I, that love is so inspiring to those who can see it, that their lives are empowered and dramatically changed.

Abelard is always mentioned in regard to the theology of salvation. But then he is passed by without much discussion, as though his thinking was not worthy of attention. In Abelard's earlier years, Anselm – considered by some to have been the greatest theologian between Augustine and the influential scholastic philosopher Thomas Aquinas – (1225-1274) must have been a strong and overpowering presence. Yet Abelard's strength is shown in that he dared to question Anselm's theory.

He also dared to secretly marry Heloise, a nun whom he had tutored and with whom he was deeply in love. Yet both of them continued to live by their vows, except for that of celibacy. When her uncle, Fulbert, the canon of the Cathedral of Paris, discovered the deception, he had Abelard emasculated by hirelings. Thereafter, both Abelard and Heloise lived within their vocations until the end of their lives. How news of their relationship affected the response to his theology apparently was not recorded.

Furthermore, Aquinas was born less than a century after Abelard. Although he adopted and adapted Anselm's thinking, Aquinas omitted some Anselmian theory he considered overly juridical and offensive. However, he supported his own edited version. The respect given Aquinas has been unparalleled, except for that shown to Augustine, upon whose work he built his own theological system. Aquinas became known as "the Angel of Catholic theology," and his thought has been unquestioned by many.

Today, named as "the pre-eminent philosopher and theologian of the twelfth century ... [t]he teacher of his generation, Abelard is also famous as a poet and a musician ... arguably the greatest logician of the Middle Ages and ... the first great nominalist philosopher."[44] But his doctrines were declared heretical by the Council of Soissons in 1121, and much of his writing was condemned by the Council of Sens in 1140.

Abelard had much to say regarding the theology of the Cross. His work should be read for itself and in his own words rather than in a short summary about him. It is a critical error to forget him. *The Church would be very different today if it had followed Abelard instead of Anselm in regard to the meaning of the Crucifixion.* In Chapter 6 we will discuss why.

There are other theologies of the Cross that should be known and briefly evaluated. From my point of view, a number of contemporary writers are the most insightful. They will be quoted in a section at the end of the book.

But perhaps more important than anything a person reads is his or her own response to the texts. Should not intelligent people who love God seek to find their own theology, one that is genuine and makes sense to them? Everyone is a theologian to some extent, including the atheist. Those outside professional ranks are said to be "first order" theologians, and professionals are considered to be "second order." Both are assumed to root their theological thinking in the experience of prayer.[45] All of us have the privilege and responsibility to base our lives and values on knowing what we believe.

Professional theologian or not, it would be inspiring to us all to dwell on the perspective of the Eastern Orthodox Church. The Eastern church holds that a true theologian is not just a scholarly thinker, but one in whom the Word (logos) of God (theos) truly lives.[46]

It Is God Who Saves – Through Christ – By Love

It was God's love in Jesus that made him the Christ. Many, experiencing it, are overwhelmingly grateful. We see Christ having given everything to express God's love, which saves us. *It is God who saves - through Christ.* The Cross was surely meant to clarify our relationship to God. It also shows us what can happen when human beings utterly give themselves to reveal the love of God. What would the world be like if Jesus had never lived or had not wholeheartedly received and lived by God's anointing Spirit? And what would the world be like if many of us today took his example seriously as the inspiration for our own lives?

Anselm's theology confuses our relationship with God. He has described God to be like a demanding human monarch. That monarch lives by the laws of human justice rather than by the grace or the wisdom of unconditional love. Anselm has put God into a vise of "righteousness" instead of acknowledging him as unlimited grace. Righteousness and grace are simply not the same. Righteousness is a measurement of the law. Grace has no law but love. Love is reciprocal *giving and receiving*.

Rehabilitative, restorative justice is a form of grace meant to empower transformation of the spirit. Such a process historically has been known as sanctification. Restoration cannot happen without a vision, and the vision is given by God through people and prayer, experiences of acceptance by God and others, empathy for those in pain, and the nourishment of goodness and beauty. Grace undergirds new choices, disciplines, and letting go of unhealthy attachments and destructive habits. Grace offers inspiration, excitement, and hope.

No one can make such transformation happen. Sanctification is God's gift, the Spirit drawing us to itself. But we can desire to know and love God, be open to the Presence, and receive and cooperate with the Spirit. Often, quite unaware, we are privileged to play a part in offering this grace to others.

If Jesus provides for us a revelation of what his Father is like, it is important to notice he did not reveal a God demanding retributive, punishing, destructive justice, but rather One seeking to restore souls to fullness of being. Justice, which is more than anger and punishment, learns from grace and implements it. Justice is a necessary way to limit those among us who might hurt each other. It is not a way to "pay our bills" to God. I have never received an invoice from God. Perhaps that is because God is not in the accounting business.

Jesus at the Center
Our ways of worship have put Jesus at the center of the Christian creeds, liturgy, and life. The word for this primary emphasis on Jesus is *Christocentrism*,[47] placing Christ at the center instead of the God whom he lived to reveal and serve. Nothing in Jesus' life pointed to himself. That was the horrendous lie his detractors told (John 19:7). Jesus himself is quoted very differently. "Why do you call me good? No one is good but God alone," he cried with fervor. In other words: "Please pay attention to my intention!" (Mark 10:18). Jesus' intention was to point to God whom Jesus knew as Father.

But the Church sings and teaches about the Cross as though it is principally establishing a relationship with Jesus *instead* of God. It should be establishing a relationship *with God through Jesus*. Why has this happened? Because we began our journey of faith as children. To teach children about God, we teach about Jesus. It seems so much easier. It makes more sense to a child, we think. We can talk about human beings in a human way. How do we talk about God?

There is a story told about a little girl who had always prayed to Jesus. She was beginning to learn the Lord's Prayer, but was having some problems. "What's the matter, darling?" her mother asked. The little girl replied with fervor: "I want a God with a skin face!"

How understandable that is! Some of us make the transition from skin face and flesh and blood friend to a loving Spirit easily. Perhaps it is because we have had strong experiences of the presence of the Holy Spirit. Others of us, worshipping regularly with cross and altar before us, seem never, even in adulthood, to go any deeper or to make any transference to Jesus' God, to whom Jesus, himself, prayed. *Jesus' God is our God too.*

Both the Apostles' and the Nicene creeds as well as the liturgy's "Gloria in Excelsis" place Jesus at the center with God and the Holy Spirit as parentheses. Jesus is the greatest object of praise, placing Christ at the center, instead of the God he lived to reveal and serve. Jesus' mission, however, was to be a window through which anyone who looked could see God clearly. It would break his heart for the glory due to God alone to be given him instead. Jesus did not come to replace God, to be an idol. He was completely dependent upon God. Otherwise he would not have known what to do or say. His prayer was a constant receptively, continuingly connecting him to his Father. That was his need, his strength, and his glory.

There is another reason for Christocentrism. Christ was seen, heard, touched, and experienced in an historical, human way. The impression was indelible. To put things in perspective, we simply need to remember his own declaration, repeated in some form in the Gospel of John nineteen times! The quotation noted in the Introduction bears repeating: "The words that I speak to you I do not speak on my own, but *the Father who dwells within me does his works*" (John 14:10).

The Cross is a gift of life, and life is impossible without love. Like being in love and promised to someone whom we trust, the Cross speaks to the deepest part of our being. It says we matter, in spite of all our inadequacies. We are loved even when we have been unloving, even destructive of another's life or hope. Even if we need to be forgiven seventy times seven, the Cross insists we *can* begin again; we can live! The Cross claims we are forgiven and freed to be all that we can be. The strange, sad thing is that we may not forgive ourselves. When that happens, I know of only one possible solution. Although focusing on our own guilt may keep us from receiving forgiveness, if we can sense and receive God's forgiveness we may be able to use it as our own.

The Cross reconciles us to God, the Spirit of Life and Love; it reconciles us to others; and, if we will allow it, it even reconciles us to our fractured selves and wipes away self-hate. It gives us the hope and strength needed to be different. If God can forgive and love us like Jesus did on the Cross, we are able to forgive others and even ourselves! We become new creatures by the love we have seen on the Cross, a love that has lifted us and given us the strength of hope and faith (see Chapter 5).

Could God not have given us all these gifts without a cross? Yes, they have always been offered, but never so clearly as through Jesus. An offering is an offering until it becomes the *gift* intended. It is not fully a gift until it is received. But so often we do not recognize God's gifts. To receive them is to confirm our relationship with God, to commit to serving this One whom we love, to depend upon each other, to trust. Receiving welcomes and is grateful for the Lover's gifts. It strengthens the *innate Image of God between us*, which is the everyday potential to relate and respond to God. By simply living in awareness, we are connected to God. That must be what "prayer without ceasing" is (see Introduction).[48]

Did Original Sin Necessitate the Cross?
There are many theologians who teach that the sin of the first earthly human beings, at the beginning of time, made Jesus' death on the Cross mandatory. We have noted that Augustine coined the term "original sin,"[49] to describe what happened. Aquinas, copying Augustine, also wrote that the taint of sin was passed on through the male sperm perpetually![50] Those men are probably the two most powerful Christian theologians preceding the twentieth century. Unfortunately, many theologians who followed them have believed that the image of God was so deeply marred in human beings, that, to restore it, there was no other way than the Cross.

To begin with, the myth of the original sin intends to expose something extremely important. Let's look at it in the following way.

The Bible tells of the first woman choosing her own will over God's and tempting the first man to do the same. What is such a story but an acknowledgement that sin against God and others derives from self-centeredness, from the desire that "*my will* be done"? As touched on above, Eve's serpent may well have been her own desire, inside her and not outside, speaking her own language, which no natural serpent could have managed! That inner serpent told her she could be "like God." Then she would not need God, or be required to obey God. She could be her own "ultimate concern."[51]

Few of us are willing to admit that, when we yield to abject self-centeredness, we make ourselves God.[52] That is, our first allegiance is to ourselves. We may not even realize it. Our wants, our desires, are more important than anything or anyone else, including God. We take God's place. The mystical heart of all religions maintains this. Mysticism clearly says God calls us on a journey that moves away from natural narcissism, that is, from self-centeredness to selflessness, to loving others with God's love. It is only when we turn in the opposite direction, look outside ourselves to appreciate others and the world, and begin to detach from what we see as our own needs that we begin to experience the fullness of life.

Sin is not just "missing the mark." It is destruction of the good and a self-centeredness that leads to brokenness within ourselves and between us and others, us and God. There is only one thing more real than sin in this world, and that is God's love in and through us.

The Image – Our Capacity for God
As most Christians believe in their heads, but may not experience, the process of salvation has nothing to do with any attempt by us to be righteous or good or beneficent in order to be saved. We are simply the recipients of God's love. We are offered the abiding presence of God which, itself, means unconditional love, now and always. *To open to it, to allow it to give us life, and to live with that awareness is salvation.* The ability to receive God's gifts and thus to be in relationship with God, others, and ourselves, is part of the Image of God inherent in our being.

But if there is original sin, it could not have destroyed something so innate as the God-given image! Theologians have argued interminably about this. Yet it is obvious that, in spite of our history of sin, we can still pray, still listen for God's voice, still be guided, strengthened, and inspired by God, and still love others through God's Spirit. That must be because the image is still there. The image inside us cannot be a *thing*, but rather a *capacity*. That capacity to relate to God has not been destroyed and is inherent to our salvation.[53] As Henry F. French recently wrote: "That capacity is our salvation."[54] It is true. How can we be saved, that is, made whole and healed over and over again, unless God and we can communicate with each other, unless we can sometimes experience God's living presence? Tillich writes: "Man can have communion with God only because he is made in his image."[55] Because of the image, we may actually know each other in the deepest and most intimate of ways. Our response to such love and closeness to God is faith.

Faith begins when we open our hearts to the wistful love of God. Faith lives as response-ability and grateful giving. The love that causes faith can gradually erase our self-centered desires. That is sanctification: growing towards God, drawn by God's love.

God is not only creator, but healer, fixing what has gone wrong when, working with God, we allow it. People first loved Jesus because he healed them. His name means "he who saves," and healer is literally another word for savior. His own given life heals ours, and therefore saves. Salvation, itself, literally means "healing and wholeness." Therefore, salvation is the history of who God really is.

For those who open themselves to receive God's healing love, these words from Isaiah are treasured:

> O Israel, you will not be forgotten by me.
> I have swept away your transgressions like a cloud,
> and your sins like a mist;
> return to me, for I have redeemed you. (Isa. 44:21-22)

A similarly cherished passage is found in the pages of Jeremiah:

> I will put my law within them, and I will write it upon their hearts;
> and I will be their God, and they shall be my people....
> They shall all know me, from the least of them to the greatest,
> says the Lord: for I will forgive their iniquity,
> and I will remember their sin no more. (Jer. 31:33, 34)

If God once said those words to humankind, was any payment necessary after that? God forgave human beings before Jesus appeared on earth, and God continued to do so through Jesus' life, death, and resurrection. No one needed to wait for Jesus' last expiring breath.

At no time in the Gospels do we see Jesus asking for payment in order to forgive. It is beyond our imagination. But he did forgive, and consequently, God was able to heal, to save through him.

No one needs to pay in order to be forgiven. God's love already includes forgiveness and goes far beyond. That love heals us from the inside out and stretches through all eternity. The whole world is faithfully held within God's nourishing Being, which is forever pregnant with God's unbounded, life-giving love.

Chapter 2

METAPHOR AND MYTH
Pointers Toward Truth

Metaphor and myth are pointers toward the truth, but they can never be its cage. They put us in touch with the inexpressible so that we can experience it and know it, but they can never imprison all of its life or meaning.

A spiritual life is full of metaphors. Each symbol is a metaphor, a means of referring to something not expressible in ordinary language, often something greater than itself. Ceremonies are metaphors. They are valuable in themselves, but their meaning exceeds the deeds done and the words said. Art is a metaphor and so are words. They put us in touch with the life behind the symbol so that we can experience it. But they never can embody or contain all there is of that which they express. A picture of my mother can so move me that I feel close to her. Yet the picture does not compare with her full presence. Just so, the love of God is greater than any words or actions that say that it is real.

Metaphor: Stumbling Block or Stepping Stone
What is a stepping stone for me may be a stumbling block for another. But it is also true, that what has been a stumbling block can become a stepping stone. When one's "ah-ha" moments come, the difference between one perception and another is in one's understanding.

A person exclaims: "That man is a lion!" Another whispers: "That woman is a goddess!" Are they really? Or are those descriptions metaphors? A metaphor says that one thing *is* another. A simile describes one thing as being *like* another. An analogy, much used in Jesus' parables, points out similarities saying "It is as if…" or "It is like…" – imagining a story much like a myth that has an important message, but not necessarily one based on a historic happening. The Bible uses all of these figures of speech.

One of the potentially exciting discoveries ahead is to learn more about the Semitic mind and its constant, daily use of metaphors. We cannot always know when something is to be taken as literal truth rather than understood metaphorically or symbolically. In scripture, an analogy or a metaphor is a valuable stepping stone if we understand its meaning. If we do not, it can become the stumbling block that inhibits comprehension.

In our own society, someone may exclaim: "I'm scared to death!" but no one will take that person seriously and call an ambulance. Another may cry: "I'm in a jam!" But in the Middle East, it would be more appropriate to complain: "I'm in a fish!" Middle Eastern people have always used such figures of speech as well as metaphors to bring stories alive, to add imagination and deeper feeling to a story or situation. Christians elsewhere do too, saying and singing with great enthusiasm: "Our God is a Rock!" or "A mighty fortress is our God!" To us it is obvious that God is strong, faithful, and dependable when we are weak. God will shield us. God will not change. But God is neither a rock nor a building!

When we look at religions in and far beyond the Semitic areas, we discover that all of them use metaphor through art and architecture, music and poetry. Islam, for instance, has no portraiture of either the Prophet or of God, for to them, they would be "graven images." But Islam does have ninety-nine metaphorical names for God, and a name in Islam and Judaism, is supposed to reveal the essence of the god or person to whom it belongs. All of Allah's names – each an attribute of the divine – are descriptive adjectives. "Why are there ninety-nine?" someone might ask. The answer would be: "Because we can never fully describe God. If we listed one hundred, it would appear that we comprehend all that God is."

The same is true for Hinduism, which claims to have three thousand gods. But God and "gods" are different conceptions to them. The clearer truth is that Hinduism counts innumerable ways of seeing and describing one God, Brahman. God's Self (the one Brahman) is really experienced as hidden in darkness, thus following the truth of the Judeo-Christian tradition that "No one has ever seen God" (John 1:18). Some dark-skinned southern Indians have said the darkness of the divine is represented in the temple by a black figure.

The Hindu will say that one or many of Brahman's attributes can be noted, experienced, or artistically represented in daily life. Most

Christians call these representations "idols." My own definition of an idol is anything that assumes God's place or stands between us and God. That is up to the perception of the worshipper. A picture, an icon, or statue of Jesus, Mary, or a saint probably helps a Catholic to worship. Such representations would distract a Quaker. For Hindus who can see beyond the artistic representation and experience what it means is to participate in *darshan*, or spiritual seeing. It is a sensitivity that sees into and beyond the exterior and the apparent to the Reality which has inspired it.

Metaphors and figures of speech are used to reveal great truths that need to be vicariously experienced, not just explained. In a culture replete with them, such expressions were once understood in their context. However, for us, untranslated and taken literally, they can become an unyielding cage for truth.

Our creeds are full of metaphors, and, oftentimes, so are our hymns. Unaware that we may be misunderstanding, we may read and sing them literally, almost setting our perception in stone. How fascinating a study group might be, meeting to look into the use of metaphors in scripture and creeds, studying their symbols and their etymology, their roots, the origins of the terms we have used for so long. There is a very long list of figurative terms including the throne of God, heaven, the right and left hands of God, the Son of God, Satan, light, darkness, the substance of God and the forgetfulness of God.

The word *heaven* is not heaven itself. The word is a symbol or designation for something we have never seen, but have only imagined. Even if, intellectually, we see it as a new life existing beyond death, we never can have a concept that is complete. Heaven appears to be the final stopping point because we cannot see beyond death.

But there may be another way to look at it. People preparing for death can think of the word *heaven* as a metaphor for a continued path of life that may never stop. For many of them, it is life as a *constant consciousness of the presence of God*. John 14:2 hints of such a possibility: "In my Father's house are many rooms." My own strong supposition is that those rooms are not sitting rooms but starting points to move out in different directions into the new life lived in that wonderful and expanding consciousness. I see the path as one leading on and on past the experience of physical death. It leads further on in service and deeper into the More, the unending richness that is God.

The writers of all scripture wrote stories that often went beyond fact to express meaning for themselves and to unlock the mind of God for their readers. Their goal seemed to be to discern God's will and God's commands as far as they could comprehend them. But they had to use human language to make their points clear. They spoke of God as anthropomorphic, that is, as being in the form of a human being. That was helpful, as a bridge concept, as a metaphor. There were times in my youth when I found the concept of God as my Father extremely helpful. But such language can be harmful when, by using it, we seem to confine God to human attitudes or limitations. Authors of scripture had to speak to their own culture and to people caught up in inherited practices and systems of belief. But even during the time the psalms were being written, one poet wrote for God: "You thought that I was one just like yourself, but now I rebuke you, and lay the charge before you" (Ps. 50:21).

What many call "God's Word" was written in spite of normal human limitations. II Corinthians 4:7 indicates how Paul saw God's glory shining through such efforts.

> But we have this treasure in clay jars, so that it may be made clear that this extraordinary power belongs to God and does not come from us.

Henry French recently queried: "Is scripture God speaking to humans or is it humans speaking to each other in an attempt to interpret and communicate their experiences of God to each other? Or, is it in some way, both?"[56] Either way, people throughout history have considered themselves touched by God through what is believed to be a divine message, often told through metaphor and myth.

According to early Christians, there was more to come as God was revealed by the Spirit through those who followed Jesus. God had not yet said everything! In fact, many of us perceive that the Spirit is speaking now: interpreting, strengthening, guiding, revealing God and godly inspiration. No scripture can reveal all that God is. Nor can the whole world of nature. Nor a lifetime of prayer. Nor exhaustive study. God is always More, and More never can be contained or curtailed.

Struggling with Stories, Especially Myth
Today an increasing number of people are coming to realize that the Bible has many kinds of writing in it. Parts of the Bible are teaching stories about the history of the children of Israel. Some parts are prayer or poetry or law. Other sections are written as parable or as myth and are not intended to be taken as literally true.

Myth, used for the two Creation narratives, for instance, attempts to respond to the great mysteries of the universe. Its object is not to state facts. In the case of Creation, its greatest contribution is to affirm the presence of God in the beginning and in every situation thereafter. It is especially useful in responding to our inner intimations of that which seems to be real but which we cannot ascertain or comprehend.

Myth deals with the deepest of all questions like "Why is everything the way it is?" "Where does everything come from?" "What are good and evil, and what makes them good or evil? " "What is the meaning of relationships?" "What is the purpose of being alive?"

These are not questions the scientific method is ever likely to answer. There was not even a concept of scientific method when the first myths were written. But there was an intimation that there is meaning behind all life and purpose for all lives, meaning that can be intuited and spiritually sensed. Therefore writers have attempted to put us in touch with a Reality that is deeper than anything we can affect. We cannot cause it, manipulate it, or destroy it. The stories are composed by inspired imagination which, like other forms of art, like music or architecture, enable us to be in contact with what we cannot explain in words or diagrams or numbers.

The skeptical, popular conception of a myth is to define it as an untruth or a lie. Yet it is just the opposite. The facts may be fanciful, but the objective is to point to the deepest truth the author knows. No one can pin down Original Reality, which most of us, using personal terms, call God.[57] But we can be in touch with it. Myth provides a way to pay attention to something far beyond our ability to explain, and even aids us in relating to it. It is a story about something deeply and lastingly real, which we will never comprehend, but which we value, we experience, and therefore personally *know*.[58]

The Bible is not intended to be primarily a book of history and certainly not one of science, but a book of faith. That means that the writers' perceptions of God and God's will, thoughts, and actions would have been recorded as they perceived them to have been revealed. Over the centuries, millions of people have read scripture because they have believed that there really is Ultimate Goodness, Endless Love, perhaps Incomprehensible Forgiveness, and Creativity that never seems to stop. It is understandable that people had to find some way beyond the ordinary to express it.

In every culture there is something supremely valued that is more Real than explanation. Explanation exists only because of that which existed *before* an explanation of it had to be given. When a person teaches theology or Bible, they are always challenged to retain that awareness. Theological explanation can become so all-important that the presence of the Original Reality begins to disappear. Then, it misses the perspective of true mysticism, which is the present awareness and experience of what can never be explained, but is the very source of life.

There is something we experience that is not an opinion or a considered possibility. It cannot be confined within the limits of what can be analyzed and repeatedly reproduced such as scientific proof demands. Belief based on it has become not just a thought or an observation, but an experience of Being itself – a life and a consciousness to which we personally relate. That strong abiding relationship in each other – living in God and God in us – is called *faith* (John 15:4, 5). It can be very strong. It can captivate us completely. When it does, as Luther said, "one stakes one's life" upon it.[59]

Some people just naturally seem to understand what stories from the Bible mean. But there are those who can make little sense of scripture. Others cannot believe in miracles or tales about wise men and shepherds, but they can comprehend and accept them if they see them as metaphors. They can interpret them as saying that Jesus came for both the poor and the humble, as well as for the wise and the learned, the powerful and the wealthy. And those same individuals may recognize how the advent of Jesus has *transformed* the lives of many, great and small, and made them into *new creatures* who uplifted the world around them.

Asking Hard Questions

Another major challenge is confusion about which questions we must ask. We cannot feel secure without asking them. Some of them are hard questions. We fear that they will give others the impression that we doubt God. Yet, in reality, we doubt our understanding, or we are perceptive enough to realize that what we read in scripture seems not to make sense according to logic or recorded history. We must find another way to deal with it.

One example is that a particular description of God seems to be the opposite of faithful love or patient goodness. Or the wisdom shared seems inauthentic or not the same as what had been said elsewhere in scripture. We ask: "Is the same writer still communicating, or have others added their perceptions to the work without signing their names?"

For instance, Psalm 139 is my favorite psalm. I have asked for it to be read at my memorial service. But I have left definite, strong instructions that the last few verses not be included. The spirit in verses 19 to 24 is of self-centered superiority, and those verses are an example of something that most likely was written by a different poet. They are not of the same spirit. Since ancient manuscripts have, more than once, been pieced together, it is entirely possible that the final verses were not only from another source but possibly from another time.

Scholars want to read and analyze the psalms. We are reminded that they are expressions of human feelings, and that, when we use them, we are in solidarity with our spiritual ancestors. But those songs of the Israelites also are used in worship services – not as a historical report, but as personal prayer. Since people come to church to worship, it seems destructive to have them pray a text that Jesus would have respected as history, but surely never would have used as his own sincere prayer. Either the worshippers will not notice what they are reading, which makes the reading useless; they will feel confused or guilty; or they will refrain from speaking lines that Jesus, himself, never would have spoken as his own sentiment. Tradition is not more important than truth. It is vitally important that what we sing and say in worship is genuine and not a copy of insensitive thought and practice of the past.

Jesus doubtless read all of the Psalms, probably many times. He was a great and powerful soul, but also seemingly an unaffected person of modest demeanor except when he was compelled to strip away falsehood and presumptive exteriors. We may have winced when we first read of him calling certain Pharisees "whitewashed tombs" (Matt. 23:27). But we would not recognize him if he were expressing his own feelings by quoting passages of hate or self-righteousness.

There are passages in the Psalms that reek of superiority and claim that worshipping the right god has given the worshippers an advantageous position. How can any Christian pray a prayer of superiority over others while remembering the humility of Jesus when Pilate asked him who he was? How can Christians pray to a Lord of love when the text asks God to dash the brains of the enemies' children against a rock? (See Ps.137:9).

A friend said recently that not all who call themselves Christian are, in fact, Christian. That statement has merit. Christians are those who have been so deeply influenced by Jesus that they are known by a name derived from the title given to Jesus: the Christ. And Christ stated his purpose very simply and clearly: "I have come to give life!" That means that our goal is to feel, think, and act in a life-giving manner. It is to lift up the world, help all people to see the value of each person, as Jesus did, and encourage others to build up, not tear down, true community.

At times, an author of a book in the Bible seems deeply inspired by the Holy Spirit. Then we are inspired as well. But at other times, that same writer reveals some fallible human attitude: perhaps a prejudice against women; a sense of superiority over people thought to be sinful because they were sick; or hatred against a member of another race, another tribe, or a group constituting a sexual minority. Some of this attitude can be attributed to ingrained cultural attitudes that the writer still has not recognized in himself, but that interrupt divine inspiration. The presence of people from outside the tribe of Israel was threatening to the small but expanding community that felt weak beside others who were stronger and "different." Are we to pay equal attention to such diverse writings? How do we know what parts of scripture are those we should follow?

Our guide for evaluating scripture and the Christian life is that simple statement noted above: "I have come to *give life abundantly.*"

A nation may consider itself the only one treasured or "chosen" because, at some special time, it seemed to be the only one to perceive how much it was loved, or knew that it was chosen for a mission, or had been given a special task. But all people on earth have been so loved and so called. The Hebrews are the first people I know of to perceive that they were deeply loved and to accept the affirmation and responsibility of being chosen to serve God. Those who have realized this are privileged, but not superior. To be chosen is to be given a magnificent task, but perhaps a very normal position. In the end, all great honors become responsibilities.

Sometimes we feel confused because it seems that there might be more to a biblical story than is told in its pages – something useful that is missing. It is difficult to say that aloud if some respected authority previously taught us that all God ever wanted to say has already been written in the sacred pages of the Bible. For this very reason, the canon (the approved content) of the Bible has been closed. But an honest intellectual question need not be judged as dangerous heresy. Furthermore, it can lead, as it always has for scholars, to much buried treasure.

Fear of Losing God

Who has not been unwilling to ask the hard questions about scripture and history and God? Are we afraid we will not be answered, or will be disappointed or more confused? Will others think us naïve? Or do those challenges not really matter, since we already have made up our minds? Or are we too lazy to think and to care?

Perhaps, if we cannot accept a story on a literal, historical, factual level, there will be nothing left in which we can believe. Perhaps, we are afraid, as I once was as a seminary student, that I might *lose God* if I interpreted familiar scripture in a new way. After a whole semester of confusion and true spiritual agony, I gradually realized that some things in scripture were not meant to be literally true.

Then I began to realize how wise Jesus was. Had he spoken like a philosopher all the time, his own people would not have understood him. They might have felt so separated from his perspective that they would have distrusted him. So he told stories that people could remember far better than abstract statements.

Moreover, we *experience and remember* stories. We can *live* them in the imagination. An abstract theological statement will never be remembered as well as a story one can see and hear and actually experience in the mind. The stories become pegs upon which our minds can hang further information as we accumulate knowledge and experience.

Much later I realized that Jesus *lived* his story. He preached and taught, but he did more. He lived what he believed and said.

I am no longer afraid to ask hard questions. In fact, I *must* ask them!

The Caring, Questioning Mind
For months, while in that first semester at Union Theological Seminary, I was in a quandary. It was agonizing. I was so ashamed of doubting my heretofore strong faith I did not even confide in my advisor.[60] I began to think of the writers of scripture, so different from each other, each with their own perspective and perceptions, with chosen points to communicate, writing at different times, and with different audiences to influence. We have allowed all of them to tell similar stories in our sacred scripture, but we also have accepted that they were told from the individual perspectives of the authors. In the case of differences or even contradictions, the reader may be less likely to ask: "Who was correct?" than to note that the story was told from the writer's point of view. We accept each story as an expression of the author's faith as well as an account of his historical knowledge. Even if all of the gospel writers had been present in identical situations, their personal experiences and interpretations probably would not have been exactly the same. Much later, they would have described conversations and events very differently, perhaps even forgetting what another remembered, or noticing what another did not perceive. Reading their accounts, of course readers would have questions.

Often, I thought of Hebrew scripture with two different Creation stories written a hundred years apart, each with a very different picture of and a unique name for God. Why two? Could either possibly be factual since no person had yet been created, and there was no means to record when light was separated from darkness? Are not both necessary to give a fuller, more complete, picture of God?

There is God – almighty and transcendent – commanding Creation to BE. Then there is the second story (although written first), in which God is immanent on the earth, with a personal, tender touch, sculpting the first one of us, from the inside out, then breathing into that first person. Because of that breath, that soul became alive!

The story says, God breathed into that first human God's own Spirit, the Spirit that is life. In a profound sense, that very Spirit was breathed into all of us who followed. It is as if to say: God, who is Spirit, gives of God's own life. We human beings are alive by the life, the spirit, of God!

"Why are there two accounts, each quite different from the other? Why is God so dissimilar in the two?" When I first posed these questions to Villanova University freshmen, the answer was: "So you can take your pick!" I was both amused and horrified! But when I suggested that without both accounts an understanding of God would be incomplete, they listened. Then we thought of how Judeo-Christian theology describes God. God is experienced as *both* transcendent and immanent, powerful and gentle, commanding but careful to pay exquisite attention to the formation of the first human body. They nodded in assent. I later realized that I had unwittingly taught them one definition of mysticism: the transcendent encloses and permeates the immanent.

The experience of the transcendent in and permeating the immanent is termed "the unity of opposites." It can refer to paradox, or to the completion of one thing by its opposite, or to the experience of one reality within another. One example might be the negative or detached way of life as compared to the affirmative, positive, and attached way. Detachment is a life of letting go of something or someone in order to live closer to God. When undistracted, some individuals believe they can do God's work more fully and effectively. The affirmative, positive way is to live attached to the world in love, working for the welfare of others, meeting some of the same challenges, and sharing their joy and pain. Most spiritually committed people would choose to combine the two as the coincidence of opposites suggests. They balance and complete each other.[61]

Learning about the relationship of opposites was an important lesson for the class. We reasoned that perhaps opposites need each other in order to be perceived. Darkness cannot be defined or perceived except in comparison to light. We considered that one opposite may be necessary to fill the other's need. We asked how much of what we thought was due to our perception and the only culture we knew. We learned that to ask "Why?" is a critically important question in all growth, and surely that holds true when reading scripture. Therefore, in every class, we asked "Why?" over and over.

Together, my students and I thought of the four Gospel writers, of the way they wrote and their reason for writing. We noticed Mark, the youngest and the first, breathlessly telling the story of Jesus. Then came Matthew, who so deeply desired to show all Jews that Jesus was theirs and cherished the same tradition. Afterwards came Luke. Some think he was a compassionate physician who knew the tender hearts of people. He seems to have written to reach the unnoticed and the excluded in society: the downtrodden, the ordinary, and the poor. Unlike Matthew, he spoke of shepherds, not wise men, when he told the story of Jesus' birth. Finally, there was John, with the perception of an eagle, the last to write. But this time the story was about the meaning of the extraordinary life of Jesus and our call to live as he did, doing the work and speaking the words of God. His gospel is the one that most strongly emphasizes that call to us.

Thus, four different Gospels were written; three of them were to be a summary of the life of Jesus. Each author told the story with his own explanations. Each reflected his own relationship to the friend they all loved and to God, whom Jesus called his Father. All of them told of the most extraordinary life they had ever known. Yet they related it differently, as various siblings might write of their parents and their childhood, and of people and events that affected them so differently. Even their facts varied. But they each were effective in telling the wonderful story in their own way with their own perceptions.

It took a while for me to realize that God would not vanish if my rational understandings changed. Nor would my deep, loving relationship with God be hindered. I could not deny the God who had loved me, called me, healed me, and inspired me all my life. Those things were real. Furthermore, my brain was not my heart. I needed both. Nor were all my original conclusions perfect.

I realized that my love and relationship were the foundation of my faith and that my reason was given me to help me comprehend and attribute value where it belonged. I could ask any question. I could change my human, uncomprehending mind. And my understandings could continue to grow without ever losing God. God would hold me, surround me and fill me. Even if I lost God, God would not lose me.

Now I strongly believe that inevitable, hard questions matter greatly. In order to grow in God, we need to ask them. They can be the door to deeper faith after we have cleared away the sometimes confusing wrappings of custom, tradition, and incomplete instruction. No teacher, no authority, schooled and wise, knows everything, and neither they nor we should expect them to. Hard questions are sometimes asked that they cannot answer. Those questions should not be construed as doubting God. Our God is too small if we think that the Spirit is worried about our questions. In fact, it is possible to see "questions ... as the deepest expressions of trust."[62]

If God created brains, should they not be used as far as limited human thought can go? Our questions show we care about what we have been taught. They are part of learning more. There is no scholarship and there is no wisdom that is not built on caring questions.

Does God Change? People's Perceptions Do.

When we finally are secure enough to ask the hard questions, we may discover that a major answer to them all is that people's perceptions of God changed with time and circumstances. That means, had their perceptions been more like those of Jesus, we might not have had many of our queries.

Yet, as we read the Bible, it *seems* that God *does* change, at least according to the way the authors saw things. But if that is true, how do we know what to expect from God? If God changes, how can we trust God?

Long after Creation, the biblical story continues. It begins to speak of Yahweh as a god of war and as a great ruler who commissions priests and commands twice-daily blood sacrifices. Yahweh institutes temple worship and laws, it seems, for everything.

Time passes. Life changes. So do some of the ways that people think of God. God sends prophets, then later, even greater ones. Through them God scorns and derides blood sacrifice and commands that it be stopped! Isaiah 1:11-20 quotes a passionate God: "I have had enough of burnt offerings. I do not delight in the blood of bulls. Your appointed festivals my soul hates. Seek justice, rescue the oppressed, defend the orphan, plead for the widow." More of God's numerous derisive comments about sacrifice are documented in chapters 6 and 7 especially.

All these recorded perceptions have influenced followers' beliefs. It is impossible to collapse history into one moment, to say that each act and each command of God, as described in scripture, reveals the same intent. It is also impossible to put all understandings of God found in the Bible into one. Nor can all types of human relationships with God be classified as the same. Throughout scripture, there has been much evolution in understanding, practice, and even in law. The differences are all part of a process.

We want so much to see God, but we cannot – except as Jesus perceived his Father. Seeing God through Jesus, we recognize much of the same message that the Prophets said God had given them. But it also will be obvious that earlier writings on authority and sacrifice, holy war and ancient law, are very different from Jesus' inspired convictions about forgiveness, inclusion, and compassion.

Almost a thousand years had passed from the writing of the first story of Creation until the birth of Jesus. A comparison of priests' and prophets' ways, of law and prophecy, of blood sacrifice and mercy, demanded attention by Jesus, and it does from us as well.

I cannot help but tell you how I came to perceive what I now pass on to others.

During my first semester at Union Theological Seminary, I took my first course in the Bible with Mary Ely Lyman, a wise and sensitive woman. In class one day, I asked intensely: "How can anyone know who God really is when the descriptions of God in the Old Testament change over and over? God closes people's ears and then opens them, allows cities to burn and then "saves" them. Here we are reading the Prophets, and God is described so differently as compared with more ancient texts that it doesn't make sense!"

That wonderful woman calmly replied: "Look at all these sacred revelations as the perceptions of the writers. It was *they* who each perceived God in their own way." From then on, I not only read scripture, but I noticed when it was written, who had written it, why they seemed compelled to do so, and who the audience was. The approach, of course, is form criticism, a marvelous way to understand each writing in more depth.

The impatient desire to ask questions need not threaten anyone. Questions are absolutely necessary to make understanding our very own. I would hope that we are always learning and growing, for God is in the process with us. Later, we will know far better what we believe and will recognize how perception can be the instrument of revelation and the foundation of belief. *We believe what we perceive.* Seeing is believing for most of us.

Belief Arises from Perception

Seeing is believing? I have lived almost all of my adult days in a community of scientists. They have spent their professional lives believing what they perceive. Many of them base their value systems on facts, on things that can be proven, not just by logic, but by repeatable experiments. Only now, with the New Physics and other continuously emerging scientific approaches, is past insistence on objectivity being effectively challenged. Beginning with people like Fritjof Capra, philosophers and scientists have been saying that there is no such thing as complete objectivity in science.[63] No one can be completely separated from the object being studied. Even the choice of experiment or the manner in which it is run, or one's assumptions as to the final results, affect what eventually happens. Our perceptions are affected by both our conscious and unconscious selves. All things are related. Perception can never be completely unaffected by our acquired knowledge, our belief system, our expectations, or our choices.

All symbols, including words, numbers, art, and even scientific descriptions, *refer* to what they describe. They cannot embody or contain all that it is.

We can study objectively about God and the relationship between God and human beings, but that does not mean we know God personally or intimately. And even that personal knowing is far from the next stage of embodying the Truth, the Life, and the Love that Christians have witnessed in Christ and, in measure, in his devoted followers.

There are really three stages of relationship with God, and they do not always come in the following order. One stage is to learn about God and what our authorities say about the divine. We can even become authorities, ourselves. Another is to experience the truth, the presence of the Spirit of Life: to realize we are inside it and it is inside us, to relate to it, and to know subjectively that it is real. The last is to embody the Spirit, even slightly or momentarily, and then to give it away. The aspects of love, for instance, are these: to hear, learn, and know about love; then to be in love; and finally, to be love, to embody it.

Jesus lived in and through all of these stages. He was taught by parents and rabbis. In a life of conscious, continuous connection (prayer) with God, a relationship like father and son developed. Based on that, he established deep, loving relationships with people and brought forth profound healing in them, expressed his own compelling mission, and thus fulfilled his own life's purpose. Surely, from our perspective, he was the embodiment of abundant love. We spoke of it in the Prologue.

What is embodiment? In spiritual terms, It is living a life that expresses the essence of a quality, whether evil or good. We see the devil as the embodiment of evil. We see Jesus or Buddha or Mother Teresa as the embodiment of goodness, compassion, and love. When we, even momentarily, are selfless, it is possible to embody that which is greater than our ordinary selves.

The Perception of Truth and Meaning
Truth is a different matter than literal, historical, empirical, provable, repeatable facts. We all perceive what we think truth is, as does every religion in the world. Truth deals with something other than facts alone, although some facts are necessary because religion is constructed in time and space, and it concerns people and events. Truth deals with meaning within history and beyond it. It is discovered, say our spiritual giants, in the experience of God.

What, then, is the difference between temporal fact and timeless meaning? Between an objective fact that appears to be true, and truth as essence and significance?

I believe that truth is deeper than observable fact because it deals with essence and meaning. We find fact experimentally. We find truth experientially. It is the experience of truth that initiates faith as a trusting relationship. We think about these experiences and evaluate, explain, and describe them. In trust, we live out our response in relationship with God and others, those we depend on to be faithful.

Mystery
Truth comes as *mystery*
which we sense, experience,
and in which we even participate.
We wonder about it, try to analyze it,
and argue about it,
but we never can prove it.

The deepest spiritual mysteries
must be everlasting.
Our questions seem to be as well.

Why do we exist?
Is there one Ultimate Reality?
Is it good … kind … and faithful?
Why do so many call it "God?"
Why are we able to love?
Why is there suffering?
Who was the one called Jesus?
Why did he allow himself to be crucified?

The book that you have begun to read does not have the ultimate answer to anything. The most important contribution it may make is that it will be a *pointer toward the truth*.

CHAPTER 3

WHO WAS JESUS' GOD?
The God Who Forgives, Heals, and Frees

When Jesus knowingly walked toward his almost certain death in Jerusalem, he had to be aware that the way he died would say a great deal about the God for whom he had lived.

The meaning of the death of Jesus does not begin with him, but with God, whom he defined as Spirit (John 4:24) and experienced as "Father." It was the Father Jesus loved, worshipped, prayed to, and followed. And it was the Father to whom Jesus so utterly gave himself in life and death and in the life beyond his death. In John's Gospel, as we noted, Jesus once explained his awe by saying simply: "The Father is greater than I" (John 14:28).

Jesus' Mission: To Reveal God

Jesus had been given a mission that would ask for his whole life and could even cause his death. That mission was to reveal God, whom he knew as his Father, in a way that a human being could reasonably expect to know God. In fact, that was probably the most outstanding – the most "miraculous – thing about him and the most helpful aspect of his life for us: he was a *fully human being* who, as scripture speaks of him, was *completely available to God*.

The great wonder of Jesus was not that he was God acting like God, but that, as a human being like you and me, he received and lived by the Spirit to such an extent that God lived on earth through him. Through him, in an incarnate way, God could be seen and heard and touched.[64]

Since Jesus' mission was to reveal his Father by the way he lived his life, he was challenged to speak for God in understandable human terms. His language was to be that of the people to whom he was born. His references were to be in line with everyday common culture. His lifetime was to be spent in thoroughly human ways, within the human limitations of time and strength, location and culture. By this means, perhaps, those whom he encountered could better understand who his Father was and what he was like. There could be no better or more comprehensible way to translate the ineffable God than we have found in Jesus.

As a human being, Jesus was completely dependent on the Spirit in him, as the Gospel of John notes repeatedly. Apparently, he focused on the person in front of him, intently listening and responding to that individual. But he was unable, at least sometimes, to speak to or to touch or to heal each member of the crowds that followed him. He healed and spoke to those he could reach, for he initially believed his particular call was limited to "the lost sheep of the House of Israel" (Matt. 15:24), not to all who were his Father's children. It appears that, later, the Syro-Phoenician woman gave him reason to think further about this.[65] Still, he restricted his travel. which was by foot, during the years of his ministry.

Yet this human Jesus was to bring the awesome, transcendent, and unspeakable Almighty into the earthly experience of human beings. Even the truest name of God, signifying God's very essence, and unknown to everyone but the High Priest, could be uttered only once a year by that priest in the Holy of Holies. To speak anyone's name, especially that of the Most High, was to touch the revered essence of the one designated. Such intimacy disrespects the Holy. Yet it was that wondrous God whom Jesus knew intimately as Father, the one in whose presence he knowingly lived and to whom he listened receptively in prayer.

Jesus' Hardest Teaching?
Jesus' task was deeply important, for his personal knowledge of God was not always the same as that of the writers of scripture who preceded him. Sometimes his approach was radically different, as was shown in his conversations with the devoted but proud and legalistic Pharisees. It was up to him to translate old ideas into new understandings. On many occasions, it was also his responsibility to go beyond a revered belief to suggest that there was another divine way and a fuller, deeper comprehension.

Many times, Jesus did not perceive God as his earliest ancestors did. In particular, he did not follow some of the meanings and practices they held about justice or forgiveness in God's eyes. What we call the Sermon on the Mount is a primary source of many of his revolutionary teachings.

On the subject of retribution we read: "You have heard it said, 'An eye for an eye and a tooth for a tooth,' but I say to you, Do not resist one who is evil. But if anyone strikes you on the right check, turn to him the other also" (Matt. 5:38-39). Jesus did not seek revenge for violence, cruelty, or insults by returning more of the same or worse. He did not cower nor would he react in the same way he had been treated. He could have, for that was the response of custom and of law. His way was to choose a path of dignified, unilateral, non-violent resistance to evil. But he goes further.

When Jesus speaks of forgiveness, he emphasizes the extent to which we are asked to go: far beyond what most of us ever do. "You have heard that it was said, 'You shall love your neighbor, and hate your enemy.' But I say to you, Love your enemies and pray for those who persecute you" (Matt. 5:43-44).

The response to Jesus' teaching on the love of enemies may be the highest point to which we are ever called. What greater love is there than the love that is offered to those who have stolen the best of what is ours: not only property, but opportunity or our good name, our self image, or our hope, and, therefore, our future? Some may have stolen the work of years and claimed it as their own. Worse yet, how does one forgive another who has lured away their spouse or, by skillful manipulation in some cultures, has stolen the allegiance of their children so that even they become their parents' traitors? Jesus told us it would happen (Matt. 10:36).

Jesus' words do not apply only to the first century CE. Today, in fifty-two countries, *the greatest persecution of Christians in the history of the world is taking place*, yet most of us are unaware.[66] Our brains do not want to accept the reality. Even if faced, the challenge to do anything about it seems too great to handle. Furthermore, other deeply important allegiances have already asked most of us to do more than we can accomplish.

Yet there are martyrs today, taking Jesus' teaching not only seriously, but literally! Reading Richard Wurmbrand's book, *Tortured for Christ*, I was touched by information everyone on earth should know.

Wurmbrand's story tells of a dedicated and imprisoned pastor living in the twentieth century under a totalitarian regime hostile to Christianity. Utterly faithful to his congregation, he would not reveal his people's identities in spite of anything that was done to him. He was beaten, tortured with red-hot irons and knives; starving rats were released into his cell; and he was forced to stand for two weeks. Finally, his fourteen-year-old son was brought into his cell to be tortured in front of him. At the point when he could stand it no longer and had become half mad, the father was about to give his tormentors the names they craved. But his son cried out: "Father, don't do me the injustice of having a traitor as a parent. Withstand! If they kill me, I will die with the words, 'Jesus and my fatherland.'" Enraged, the Communist captors beat him to death, spattering his blood over the cell walls. The enormous grace of the child had saved the entire congregation. But the father has never been the same.[67]

Yet that is not the most profound point of the book! Its pages say that throughout those fifty-two countries today, there are martyred prisoners who, instead of hating their captors, love and pray for them. There are tortured and dying prisoners who have loved their jailors into loving Christ and offering God their lives.

John Shelby Spong has written a gripping paragraph on the power of loving those who do not love us.

> A life defined by love will not seek to protect itself or to justify itself. It will be content simply to be itself and to give itself away with abandon. If denied, love embraces the denier. If betrayed, love embraces the betrayer. If forsaken, love embraces the forsaker. If tortured, love embraces the torturer. If crucified, love embraces the killers. Love never judges. Love simply announces that neither the person you are nor the deeds you have done have erected a barrier which the power of this invincible presence cannot over-come....
>
> To share love is nothing less than sharing God.... When one sees a life that loves wastefully, it is said of that person, "God was in that life."
>
> Love lifts us beyond our quests for survival. Love enables us to transcend our limits. Love frees us to give ourselves away.
>
> [One who is loved is] so deeply affirmed that he can give [love] away freely. He can submit to his outrageous fortune. He can expend his energy in the act of affirming the being of others.[68]

Did Jesus reveal a God like this? If so, would such a God worry about divine honor?

People may sometimes wonder if there is anyone on earth who has gone as far as possible to follow the teachings of Jesus. Wurmbrand's stories offer many answers.[69]

More Than Law

Jesus' respect for Jewish law and the teachings of the prophets is evident in the Sermon on the Mount. Carefully he prepares his listeners for what else he is going to say: "Think not that I have come to abolish the law and the prophets; I have come not to abolish them, but to fulfill them" (Matt. 5:17).

In Hebrew scriptures, the first five Books of the Law – the Pentateuch or Torah – have anchored ancient Hebrew and later Jewish life for centuries. It is law and sacrifice that form the very foundation of the people's existence. The importance of continuous temple sacrifice will be examined further on in these pages. Here, however, it should be noted that the movement away from that emphasis occurred not only because the Temple was destroyed, but because the consciousness of Israel gradually was transformed by the Later Prophets. Their emphasis was not upon righteousness through following priestly ritual and retributive law, but on mercy and justice for the sinful as well as for the oppressed.

Jesus seemed to be far more comfortable with the Prophets than he was with the Priests. Jesus, who appeared to know God intimately, seems to have perceived God more fully and more joyfully than those who came before him. When his early enemies tried to catch him breaking the law proclaimed by the temple priests, he responded: "Tell them something greater than the temple is here! And if you had known what this means, 'I desire mercy and not sacrifice,' you would not have condemned the guiltless" (Matt. 12:6). Jesus' comment shows that he boldly questioned the appropriateness of the use and abuse of both the law and sacrifice. There is a larger perspective than that found in temple laws. Mercy comes far ahead of being right and righteous.

Jesus' urging to go beyond Jewish law reveals the difference between his understanding and teaching compared with that of his forebears. For instance, he no doubt knew that "An eye for an eye and a tooth for a tooth" (Exod. 21:24) was already an enormous evolution in law, compared to previous punishments far worse than the original crime. Yet he was prepared to take his listeners further.

Ancient God: Ancient Law
In some cultures, even today, further progress has not occurred. "An eye for an eye" is very much the code of criminals and gangs throughout the world. It is taken seriously in many cultures in Africa and among those Muslims who consider it to be sacred Shariah, that is, law. The practice of cutting off a thief's hand, for instance, is well known and is considered a practical and appropriate punishment.

As Arnold Toynbee looked at the religions of the West, he perceived that the fanaticism and intolerance of neo-pagan faiths in the twentieth century was the product of the beliefs and practices "of all the Judaic religions: Islam, Christianity, and Judaism." He wrote: "[I]ts ultimate inspiration is one of two Christian and Jewish conceptions of God, which, as I see it, are incompatible with one another."

Toynbee continues: "Christianity and Judaism have one vision of God as being self-sacrificing love – God the merciful, the compassionate, according to the Islamic formula – and another vision of God as being a jealous God.... These two visions ... seem ... to be irreconcilable, and the presence of both visions side by side in the common tradition of Christianity and Judaism and Islam has produced in these three Judaic religions an inner contradiction, which, I should say, has never been resolved."[70]

Let me dare to say, however, that I see it resolved in Jesus. But none of these "religions of the book" (religions with revealed scriptures) have adequately perceived the God of Love whom Jesus seemed to know so intimately and understand so clearly. At the most critical point in Jesus' life, his arrest, one of his followers tried to defend him with a sword, cutting off the ear of the High Priest's slave. Jesus is said to have reproved the disciple, then to have touched the man's ear and healed him, saying: "All who take the sword will perish by the sword" (Matt. 26:52). The Gospel of John quotes Jesus as saying: "Am I not to drink the cup which the Father has given me?" (John 18:11). Is it likely that a jealous and vengeful god was revealed by the Prince of Peace, a pacifist son? Or did the unconditional love, steadfast protection, and freely offered grace revealed by this son reflect the true nature of an imperfectly perceived god? This is one of the major points of this book.

Since the God of ancient Israel was thought of as having human characteristics (which seems never to have been doubted), it is understandable but shocking to read stories in sacred Hebrew scripture that reveal Yahweh as a merciless and terrible force against Israel's enemies. During the earliest years of recorded Hebrew history, Yahweh was the Israelite god of war. One may easily forget that before monotheism became firmly entrenched in Israel, it, too, had several gods, but Yahweh became supreme, at least as time went on. In those days, when Israelites described Yahweh, they probably would have said that their god was almighty, powerful, and belonged to Israel. They would not have said: "Yahweh is love."[71]

The book of Joshua recounts that when commanded by Yahweh to destroy several cities in order to found the Israelites' own land, Joshua could not have been carried out those vengeful orders more thoroughly. Not a single man was left alive.

Then, according to the biblical story, Joshua turned to Yahweh and asked what should be done with all the women and children left in five cities. Yahweh's perceived response is, to us, revolting. It was: "Slaughter all that breathes!" (Josh. 10:40).

The Swiss theologian, Raymund Schwager, writes of "Yahweh's blazing anger, ... revenge, ... and threatened annihilation." In discussing Hebrew scripture, he contends: "No other topic is as often mentioned as God's bloody works." Then he makes a deeply important statement: "A theology of Old Testament revelation that does not specifically deal with this grave and somber fact misses from the very start one of the most central questions and thus will hardly find the right perspective for a profound understanding of ... revelation."[72]

The Push of the Prophets

I am grateful that I did not live in Joshua's day. I am grateful that the God of Everlasting Love has been revealed in Jesus and that I came after him. I am grateful that I am not stuck in more of the past than I am.

Christians read Hebrew scripture emotionally on the side of the Jews. After all, we consider ancient Israelite and later Jewish history as religiously, our own. We know many, many of these stories and consider them to be part of our own religious heritage. We read Hebrew scripture expecting to be inspired. Often we are. But their stories also can be confusing and even disheartening. God's character seems to change, even erratically. What can we trust? We are limited in opportunity to study and to learn. Most of us do not have the time to study Hebrew scripture well enough to notice the evolution of knowledge about God. We may not perceive that gradually, throughout Hebrew history, views of God softened or even were replaced as time went on. The Prophets Elijah and Joshua were very different from the Later Prophets, Isaiah and Hosea. Righteousness and might began to yield to verses of comfort, empathy, and inspiring encouragement. The evolving perception of God was behind it all.

If a continual awakening of understanding were not critically important, the world would not need prophets. There would have been none in Israel if people had not needed to be goaded into seeing and doing things in a new, if not revolutionary, way. Furthermore, although the Prophets later held a position of honor in Israel, their declarations in their own day often made them so hated and despised that they were forced to flee their enemies. It is no wonder that Jesus, as he intentionally walked toward the capitol city before his death, commented that all the Prophets had been killed in Jerusalem, a city whose name, ironically, means "possession of peace" (Matt. 23:37, Luke 21:33-34). Yes, he was a prophet, and he knew it and accepted the consequences – even though he was far more.

The common public perception of a prophet is, of course, one who predicts the future. In Hebrew scripture, a prophet proclaims what will happen *if things do not change*. He predicts what will happen if people do not repent and turn to another more God-centered direction. Hebrew definition of a prophet usually was of one who would speak for God and, therefore, would have to be inspired, that is, breathed into by God.

The word, inspiration, means to inhale, to breath in physically. But it also means to receive spiritually and thus to be inspired, to be breathed into, infused, motivated by a spirit. That spirit was first conceived of as divine. *Webster's* definition says: "originally, to breathe or blow upon or into, to infuse life, etc, by breathing." To study that definition is almost like reading Genesis 2:7: "Then the Lord God formed man from the dust of the ground and breathed into his nostrils the breath of life; and the man became a living being." God breathes out God's own life into those inspired. Their response is inherent: they receive; they inhale. Thus a Prophet is infused by the divine Spirit. Only by receiving it can a Prophet speak.

But there is more. To be a prophet is to *perceive*, to *understand*, to teach – and to warn. To be a prophet is to stretch the minds and hearts of others. To be a prophet of God is to goad people into stretching, expanding, trusting that there is always more of God to be known. Prophets were learning even as they taught. Their own understanding and growth was often painful. They must have cried out sometimes: "Who are you, Yahweh?"

Resisting Growth

Some individuals honor those they consider prophets. There are others who ward off any prophet, teacher, or helper who comes near by saying: "That's the way I am!" as though the status quo is always defensible. They refuse to be influenced. Defending the person they have been so far, they negate the person they could become. The problem only compounds when they insist that others have not changed either. If their perception of God has not evolved since early adolescence, they also may not have grown. Without knowing it, they may be trapped in what was "right" (and limited) a long time ago.

Recently, I had to have my car fixed. Sitting in the owners' lounge with a woman I didn't know, we got into a deep conversation. She was a simple person, but her thoughts were profound. The subject turned to fear of change. She immediately applied it to her church and an intractable situation. "Why are they so afraid to alter their attitudes?" I asked. Her answer came immediately: "Because they have to be right! If they change their way of thinking and acting, they think they will be admitting that they were wrong before! Their pride won't let them admit that they were never perfect! They would rather be stuck where they are!"

All of us resist growth sometimes.[73] Growth rarely seems to happen without sacrifice and, often, without suffering. The result is that we may sabotage our own future, avoiding our own potential and making little, if any, contribution to the world around us. We may even forget to dream, to hope, and to plan. Life, once seen as an awesome gift from God, can become meaningless because we are afraid to grow. Change means we will find ourselves in a new place where we have never been. Will we be adequate? Will we have the security we have now? Will we know ourselves and be comfortable with who we are? Yet who would want a chick to fail in getting out of its shell? And who would want a rose to end its life without ever being in bloom?

Walking ahead into the future is to walk where God already is. But what we see and fear may be far more obvious than God is sometimes.

If the Spirit dreams of a different, more wholesome future for the world, there are those of us who do not wish to be aware, because we will have to bear the consequences of letting go of what we have. Some people, who are already highly regarded, fear change, thinking that they have too much to lose, New ideas, new leaders, and stronger passions question the past and point toward a new future. The status quo is often defended as though it were perfection. It may even become regarded as holy. That surely has happened in the Church and in the Synagogue. Those who challenge others to change and to grow in understanding and practice, may be regarded with suspicion, ignored, or may even be considered the enemies of God, as Jesus clearly warned. They may even be killed (John 16:2).

No wonder there were those in high positions religiously, socially, and politically who were threatened by the prophet from Galilee. He knew God very differently than did some of his accusers

When we dare to question our own theology, we do not need to feel that God is suspiciously looking over our shoulder. God is aware of our immaturity. "Be ye perfect" as the old banners read, literally means: "Grow up!" Perhaps that is what we are here to do. God does not expect that anyone will arrive at all truth in this life. We are not loved for our "perfection" or maturity. But growth is God's idea. It is inherent and necessary in anything that is alive.

Spirituality is a never-ending journey. We arrive at new insights only to be led on to others. We feel our weakness before we find new strength. Sometimes the challenges are frightening, sometimes wearing, often exciting and hopeful. Life in the Spirit takes courage: usually more and more. There are times when God seems to disappear. At other times, we feel engulfed in holy Life and there is only joy.

As the Nicene Creed attests, the Holy Spirit "spoke by the Prophets." It was the Prophets who were willing to think new thoughts and to go where no one had gone before. It is still true. They give us courage. Sometimes, but not always, they give us clearer perceptions of God.

Reassessing Perceptions of God
Is God, as Luther's younger colleague, Phillipp Melancthon (1497–1560) contended, an all-powerful judge whose decisions absolutely control time and eternity and us? Is God an accountant who adds up divine grades for all our thoughts, actions, and even our intents? Does the Creator scorn our imperfections, which are bound to be present if we have free will?

Is God a god of wrath, of everlasting, unremorseful punishment and eternal destruction? Is God inconsistent and, therefore, not to be trusted? Does the One "whose mercy endures forever," who will "never forsake" us and will be with us "until the end," ever give up on us and simply turn away as Hebrew scripture claims?

Is God like humans? Does God think like we do, operate by "tit for tat," hold a grudge, or give favors for the best sacrifices? Is God so small and self-centered as to worry about reputation?

We have all heard some of these views. Some of us have been taught them. Some of us have "given up on God" because of them. Others never have been comfortable with religion because of judgmental attitudes that accompany such teachings.

If such attitudes have formed our perception of God, we can not even begin to realize that there is a God whose grace and mercy come before, not after, justice. God's grace tells justice how to restore rather than only to punish, discipline, or limit the weak for the good of all. Grace is not just sweet and loving. Grace confronts us. It asks if it is ever right for us to destroy. The erratic God portrayed above is not the one whom Jesus described as the God who forgives and begins again and again to help us heal and become whole.

The descriptions above are far from knowing One who can give life to dead bones and dried-up spirits, who can transform us completely, and even sanctify us (to make us like God's self). The all-powerful judge does not appear to be the creator-parent God who mourns any missing child and who waits everlastingly until we turn around, realize what we have missed, and run home as fast as we can!

Am I saying that there are many gods? By no means! I am saying that scripture contains numerous *perceptions* of God. Many of those perceptions would not fit Jesus' description of the Father to whom he prayed consistently. If there is any God at all, there can be only one, for to be God is to be supreme, singular, and unrivaled.

The Old Testament God of Deuteronomy 32:39 proclaimed: "I kill and I make alive. I wound and I heal." But Jesus' God was not warlike or wrathful, oppressive or frightening. Except for the story of the sheep and goats in Matthew 25, Jesus' God is not a heavenly accountant, consumed with recording human errors. His God would not cause calamity in order to save the earth. Nor would Jesus' Father have broken bones in order to heal them, although ancient Hebrew scripture claims "He" did this and more. Jesus' God would not send evil, suffering, or temptation in order to create the need for a Savior.

Jesus' Father did not rule or command from afar. His God was immanent – always present and available – as well as transcendent to all creation. God was faithful, not here one day and gone the next, not pouting or feeling unappreciated, not brooding on being dishonored by "his people." Jesus obviously did not know a needy, insulted, or jealous God. Jesus' God needed nothing, but desired our love. His God was concerned about the earth, the world, and the many generations of the children of God.

Human Pictures of God
There is a reason we have been confused about the identity of God. For thousands of years, human beings have perceived the Almighty not only as loving, gracious, generous, and encouraging, but also as petty, demanding, exacting, wrathful, and often unfaithful.

One of our problems is that we are inside our own skins. That means we live with all sorts of human limitations. We have no other recourse than to describe God by using human language in human context. What other kind of language and what other context do we have?

But the result is that we have put God inside skin as well! We have made God anthropomorphic, literally meaning "in the form of a human." We have yielded to speaking of the transcendent God as we speak of an awesome human ruler with human foibles. We refer to God as having human form, gender, and attributes, both good and bad. Like the more ancient forms of Hebrew scripture, even today we describe God as tender and angry; petulant but forgiving. Considered as a whole, scripture presents God as both fickle and faithful! At times, God abandons Israel in disgust, but then returns. Yet Psalm 136 exults repeatedly, "His mercy endures forever."

Genesis 1:27 says that, at Creation, God made human beings in the divine image. But we have powerfully reversed that metaphor! We speak of God as in *our* image because we have not learned to think of God as Spirit, the life-giving Spirit of Love. God as Spirit is a deeply important concept that a number of giants in the field of spirituality have mourned as missing. We shall look seriously at this concept in the next chapter.

God Beyond Definitions
In the three thousand years of Judeo-Christian life, there have been numerous thinkers who, whether writing scripture or commenting upon it, have emphasized that God can never be put into a box of words or concepts. Among those who are said to have produced "proofs of God" (which are logical suppositions, but certainly not proofs) is the scholastic philosopher, Anselm, of whom we have already spoken. In addition to writing the theology espousing payment to God for our sins, he authored some much-respected theology. Of course, his "proof of God" was no more proof than those of any of the other religious philosophers of his time. But his idea is important. He contended that God is that which is beyond any possible conception. In other words, if we attempt to think about what God might be, Anselm says we will fail. It is impossible. We only know that God is more than we can imagine or describe.[74]

There is also Pseudo-Dionysius, now thought to be a fifth century Syrian monk, who wrote the famous *Mystical Theology*, five chapters of which describe all that God could not possibly be. His aim was to show that we, who are so much less than our Creator, are helpless to pin God down, to say precisely what the power is that began and continues life.[75]

Yet life *is* and we are inside it – now.

Enigmatic? Yes. Discussions such as these are only "talking about" God, attempting to make God into an object we can define.

God, by these definitions, is beyond all definition – beyond all that we can conceive or imagine, measure or describe. To that, it seems, many would assent. As you will see in the next chapter, Jesus defined God by saying in John 4:24: "God is Spirit." Spirit cannot be encaged or measured and yet, experientially, is often real and motivating. None of our perceptions and conceptions and none of our experiences of God can equal all that God is or all that God would tell us. Therefore, God can be deeply experienced, but never defined. Those who love nature and beauty or are in awe of the human brain and body often claim to be aware that manifestations of God are seemingly everywhere. The Prophet Muhammed remarked in wonder: "Wherever you turn, there is the face of God!"[76]

Inspiration, the breath of God, comes to us in flashes throughout life. Sometimes we pay attention and respond. Often we are distracted, and an insight disappears as quickly as it came. Writers of Hebrew scripture had these flashes and caught them long enough to write some down. Yet, though the insight was preserved, apparently none noticed the importance of some of the inspired words. In the book of Numbers, for instance, the writer realized that theology had limited and imprisoned God by thinking of the Divine as a human person. The author wrote: "God is not a man, that he should lie. He is not a human, that he should change his mind" (Numbers 23:19). Had the religious establishment given those words serious attention, much of later scripture would not have thought of God in human terms, as anthropomorphic.

One of the Hebrew prophets who believed he spoke for God, wrote in Isaiah 55:8: "My thoughts are not your thoughts." If that is true, then whose thoughts are we reading when we take up "the Word of the Lord?" Since God is so much more than human, those who would speak for God must put into human language, messages they believe they have been given by the Spirit in receptivity. They will always be inadequate, but they may be beautiful, inspiring, meaningful, and helpful. If they were written "in the Spirit," they may well convey something far beyond a mere, or even an exact, combination of words.

Scripture writers, artists, scientists – all of us – describe according to languages bequeathed to us: languages using combinations of words, poetry and parable, music and myth, painting and dance, numbers and symbols, in various arts and disciplines.

Since I was twelve years old, listening to a high school band concert, I have asked myself what music is. I never found an answer until this year. Yes, I knew that music was a language and that language means that we can communicate; we can connect minds or spirits. That, in itself, seems to me a miracle. But, all my life, something was missing, in spite of what now seems to be the obvious answer.

I finally realized that the power of music, even the amateur music of a high school band, was saying to me: "You are sensing more than you hear. Hearing is simply your way to know that it is there. It is not only in and through the music, but behind it. It is what you have been calling 'the More.' Behind even the most ordinary music, there may be the urge to expression of a truly magnificent music, unheard by any human ear, and sensed only in the deepest consciousness. And behind that urge is the Reality that makes all beauty possible." God lives through us, even in our most inadequate expressions. The Spirit imprints our lives even when its presence is only a whisper, difficult to discern.

Many times I have heard orchestral music within my mind that my ears could never hear. Because I am a communicator and want to share as much beauty as I can sense, it was both extraordinarily inspiring and painful. I am not skilled in writing what I hear in my head. I could not write it down to preserve it and pass on. So I asked that it be taken away. From that day onward, it was. But I shall always remember its presence, greater than anything I could picture with notes on paper, more than what I could sing with a single voice.

Those who feel they have a personal relationship with God will come to the point of realizing that the Absolute cannot be confined inside any spoken language, any theology, dogma, or creed. Nor can it be confined by any art or any story, whether historic or imagined, or even the glorious or powerful expressions of nature. All of them are *inadequate*, but they are *useful*.

Pointing to God; Not Defining God

All these experiences and expressions can point to the Great Truth which precedes, outlasts, and is behind them all. They can point to Ultimate Reality because of which we exist and because of which we are real too.

A man known as Coventry Patmore once wrote a tiny book no larger than the palm of an adult hand. Entitled *The Rod, the Root, and the Flower*, it might be completely forgotten were it not for Evelyn Underhill, who copied from its few pages these words:

> "God is the only reality, and we are real only
> so far as we are in His order, and He is in us."[77]

Paul Tillich probably would have understood and appreciated Patmore. Tillich may have offered to the theology of our time the best theological comprehension of symbols in his little book, *Dynamics of Faith*. Simply put, he would say that all sacrament is symbol and all symbols point to a deeper reality in which they participate.[78]

To read this book is to know that Tillich was not just a theologian, but had a mystical side. The thought he expresses regarding symbols is at the mystical heart of all religions, if one goes deeply enough. For instance, the Buddha (meaning "the enlightened one"), is remembered for his completely silent Flower Sermon. "Standing on a mountain, with his disciples around him, the Buddha ... held aloft a golden lotus." That was all. A follower, known as the "master Gutei, [when] asked about the meaning of Zen [Buddhism], lifted his index finger ... silently."[79]

To speak of the Great Mystery behind all things, all words and other symbols merely *point* to what is behind and beyond them. What is ineffable simply cannot be held within a cage of words or symbols used in religious practice. Yet we would not be able to manage without these things. They connect us, in a human way, with the divine and with each other. They help us to identify more clearly what we know and to express more effectively what matters.

Do We Belong?

If we live sensitively, we may perceive that there is greater wisdom, strength, creativity and love than that which we call our own. Many have concluded that somewhere there must be perfection – a perfection from which we are separated but to which we belong.

Is our perception of God similar to that of Jesus'? Or is our God the same as the God of the ancients, the one whom we understandably fear but are told we must trust in spite of our questions and our qualms? Is our God only sometimes the Holy Spirit, the *Ruach ha Qadosh*, which has been present since the world began (Gen. 1:2)? Or is our God the Spirit, given to abide with us forever?

We have already noted that God has not changed, *but human perception* has. Those ancients who felt inspired to tell the story of God could hear and see and understand only insofar as their culture and personal sensitivity empowered them. The perception of God has changed throughout history. As the saints have taught, *we grow toward God* as plants grow toward the sun.

It doesn't happen in a flash. Paul wrote in II Corinthians 3:17, 18: "Now the Lord is the Spirit … And we, who with unveiled faces, all reflect the Lord's glory, are being transformed into [God's] likeness with ever increasing glory, which comes from the Lord, who is Spirit,"

We are being taught. Human learning and growing are a continuing process. Luther, in one of his most lovely passages, contended that that process of transformation continues at least until the end of life. And he predicted more. He wrote: "This life, therefore, is not the end, but the beginning."[80]

The Methodist theologian, James Fowler, has helped an enormous number of people by discussing the possible stages of faith in the lives of those who believe in God. Integral to all he says is the believer's changing, growing perception of God.[81]

These stages of faith do not happen without temptation, challenge, and sin. In his famous phrase, "*simul justus et peccatur*, Luther spoke of being justified while we are still sinning."[82] But that does not mean there is no hope, no future, no opportunity to learn, no new thoughts, or no progress in faith. We *know* that we are not the same in our more mature years. We may be better or worse, stronger or weaker, wiser or still clinging to naïveté. Our challenge is not to let life just happen to us as it will, not just using up life, but to be immersed in life and in giving life as God intended.

Among my cherished friends is a pastor I came to know when he invited me to lead several retreats and give lectures in North Carolina. He tells a short, humorous story of a young friend who angrily shouted: "I don't believe in God and I never will!" "Oh," responded the pastor. "What is this God like that you don't believe in?" After the young man hotly presented a long list, the older man looked into his eyes and simply said: "I don't believe in that God either." It makes a difference when we consciously know what kind of God we have been perceiving.[83]

If it was Jesus' God who was revealed on the Cross, it was not a God of exacting law, but of unbelievable grace. If it was Jesus' God, it was not a God whose choice was an earthly view of justice: punishment or payment. Rather, the love of God in Jesus was the impulse to give life. It was to magnify and multiply goodness as Spirit, across the face of the earth.

If God can mourn, God must do so when the sole response before the Cross is continual shame and guilt. As a child, I sang with all my heart: "Who was the guilty? Who brought this upon thee?" The hymn continues finally to confess: "I, dear Lord Jesus. I it was denied thee. I crucified thee!"[84] Yet we claim that Jesus died, not only to forgive sin, but to take away our guilt.

Selfishness crucifies Love every day of our lives and has done so all through history. Each of us *has* crucified Love, and some of us have been crucified for it. The Cross makes us face what we have done.

But the Love and Life that pour from the Cross to this day are a greater truth without which we could not live. The Cross lays bare the darkness of self-concern in which we all participate. But its work is not accomplished until those who stand beneath it receive all that it has to give of joy and strength because we are so deeply loved. It is then that the Spirit irresistibly moves *in* us and then, *from* us, in the impulse to love others to life. Life, in all its fullness, is what God is, and giving is the essence of God's movement. Were I God, with all my being, I would yearn for my loved ones to receive all I have to give. In the receiving we intimately "know" the God who cannot be defined, but who is real, and to whom we point when we speak.

CHAPTER 4

GOD, IN JESUS, ON THE CROSS
"God Is Spirit"

According to the primary scriptural text for this book, "God was *in* Christ." But anyone might ask: How was that true? In what way was God *in* Jesus? The answer surely is: Because *God is Spirit*, and that animating spirit was the inner source of his life.

> Spirit is God's unrestricted being – not something derived from God or a product of God, not a *part* or *piece* of God, and not just rays of energy flowing out of God, which the Greeks have called *proodoi*. When God *sends* the Spirit, it is God's own self who comes in measure that we can experience and to which we are empowered to respond.
>
> Perhaps the most important theology in Christianity is pneumatology, the understanding that God is Spirit. That may also be the simplest basis for understanding who Jesus was and why and how he died on the Cross.

The sentence, "God is Spirit," came from Jesus himself, sitting in the noontime heat on the side of a well in Samaria, conversing with a woman and responding to her questions. Like some of us, she wanted to know how to be religious and appear righteous. Perhaps she secretly wanted to be acceptable, since she may have been derided for her five marriages. Yet her question came out of her own community, the only group to which she belonged, and she probably was ready to defend their point of view. So, once again, she began one of the old unsettled arguments between Samaritans and Jews. But this time, she perceived that she might get a better answer. She recognized already that Jesus was a prophet.

Her question was about religious practice. Should people worship God in the Jerusalem temple, as Jews believed, or should they worship on the mountain, as was the custom of the Samaritans? Jesus implied that neither was of paramount importance. But then he got to the essential point. What mattered, he said, was to experience that "God is Spirit." The complete biblical text reads: "God is Spirit, And those who worship him must worship in spirit and in truth" (John 4:24). My understanding of those words is that when we worship from the heart, it is because of the compelling Spirit within us, inspiring us and leading us to experience the Truth. Worship can take place anywhere if it is *in truth*, that is, if it is genuine worship. God, as living Spirit, is where we are – always. Everywhere and anywhere we are called to prayer, to keep a connection to the One who never leaves us.

Jesus lived in the Spirit and it lived in him. Its presence seemed unmistakable to Jesus. Luke 4 tells the story of the influence of the Spirit when it came time to choose the direction for his life, "he was led by the Spirit into the wilderness," where for forty days he faced the most demanding of temptations: hunger, the desire for power and position over others, and the lure of using the Spirit's gifts to exult in his own uniqueness, proving the supreme authority of God. In resisting temptation, he came to discernment of his future path. There, in the wasteland, the Spirit called him to his mission and anointed him in ordination. Thus, "filled with the power of the Spirit," he returned to his own people and, he began to share what he was being taught. From then on, it was the Spirit that spoke and healed through Jesus. And when nearing the end of his life on earth, he was convinced that the Spirit asked him to go to Jerusalem to reveal his Father's incomprehensible forgiveness, encouragement, and love.

We know the story. He was questioned, humiliated, beaten, and condemned to die by crucifixion. He endured that terrible sacrifice only by the power of the Spirit. And by its grace, he forgave those who crucified him. But, at one point, he lost consciousness of that great, lifelong animating power and cried: "My God, my God, why have you forsaken me?" (Matt. 27:46). In his extremity, he experienced all that a person could feel while enduring agonizing human pain. It broke his awareness of the Spirit. Utter abandonment was all he could feel. He knew his Father would not step in to save him in some miraculous way. Angels would not be sent to bear him up as the Devil had suggested by his taunting in the wilderness (Luke 4:11). Alone on the Cross, he was unable to sense that his Father was still with him and would never leave him. In his exhaustion, he no longer could feel or employ the power of the Spirit. He had reached the limit of human physical and emotional endurance.

Blessedly, some moments later, he returned to consciousness of the Spirit, realizing the task to which he had been called was finally finished. His sacred burden could be relinquished. Offering himself to the One he had loved and served, he prayed: "Father, into your hands I commend my spirit" (Luke 23:46).

For Jesus, his Father was the beloved, personal aspect of God. The Spirit, apparently, was Jesus' name for God as the living power inside him as well as the transcendent Creator and Sustainer of all life within which he lived. He knew the Spirit as a pervading presence, providing far more than a personal relationship because it was inclusive of all existence.

The Spirit: Inspiring
The Spirit who lived in and through Jesus has called all people across the earth to awareness of the Holy. It did not come for the first time on the day of Pentecost. It has been here all along. Genesis 1:2 in the Authorized King James Version of the Bible speaks of the Spirit "brooding upon the face of the waters." The New Revised Version says instead: "a wind from God swept over" those troubled depths. It was the Spirit that spoke chaos into cosmos (order). Then, as Chapter 3 describes Genesis 2:7, the work of the Spirit became unmistakable: the Lord breathed the Spirit into Adam, and his life began. In one seminal phrase, the Nicene Creed describes Creation as the work of the Spirit, "the Lord and giver of life."

Considering the original meaning of the word *inspiration*: to breathe upon or into (see Chapter 3), we know that it can refer to God breathing life and creativity into a human being. But, because today we frequently use the word *inspire* to mean *inhale*, it is important to understand that the term means both to breathe into *and* to inhale. It is reciprocal, and its biblical use includes both interpretations. God gives the Spirit, and the human being receives: God inspires, and the human breathes in. Both are necessary for life. This is the basis of the verse from II Timothy 3:16: "All scripture is inspired by God." Scripture is a vehicle of life-giving Spirit.

All written revelation of God is a human understanding of perceived inspiration. God's Spirit not only made the clay form of Adam into "a living soul,"[85] but it still, according to biblical thinking, keeps us alive both physically and spiritually. Unless we breathe in, that is, receive the life that God breathes into us, we cannot live.

All of us *do* breathe in until we die. Breathing is not a choice; It is automatic, built into our being. Jewish theology makes it very clear that all living bodies are kept alive, whether consciously or unconsciously, by the divine breath of life. To the Jew, the being we label "person," at the basic level of animal life (including senses, emotion, and some measure of understanding), is called a *nephesh*, "a *living soul*."[86] But the open, conscious, receiving spirit in a person[87] is more than physical life. It is willing, intentional dependence on the *ruach ha kodesh*, the Holy Spirit in Hebrew.[88] It was that spirit – acknowledged and claimed in the Nicene Creed – that: "spoke by the Prophets." The Prophets intended that the Holy Spirit enter and take over their lives and even their voices.

The Spirit: Revealing

When inspiration leads to knowledge of something new or something beyond ordinary human perception, the word *revelation* is used. Revelation literally means "to draw back a veil" so that what was formerly unknown, but actually present, can be clearly perceived. Even though Truth may have been available before, it was unrecognized. It was therefore unknown, not yet revealed. There had to be a receiver who could perceive the Truth as sent by the Spirit of God.

Revelations of which we read in scripture have been received by someone other than ourselves. Personal revelations, of course, are based on our own experience. But what is uncovered, unveiled, or discovered by us is already available and only waiting to be perceived. It is not seen, heard, or understood until a receiver is present. When the revelation occurs, deeper truth enters into us and we perceive it, or even sense that we already know it. It is not just a cognitive knowing, which is a matter of thinking. It is a new consciousness, an experience of reality at greater depth (see Chapter 10).

But when God makes Truth or Love available to us or to any human being, it can only be fully received if the person is aware of what is happening. That individual may say they "heard" or "saw" what was revealed. Regardless of the term they use to explain the experience, that word will express a state of receptivity. Receptivity is so real and so basic that theology has not yet objectively recognized its importance. It is not a state of active will, as it has been misperceived. It is an attitude of willingness. When we forget, refuse, or deny God, we put up a barrier to receiving. Our greatest problem may be to understand why a person who is open to the Holy Spirit sometimes feels alone and unguided, in some measure, as Jesus felt abandoned on the Cross. We do not know all the answers.

A revelation takes at least two: the sender and the receiver. The inspiration sent is offered. It is *revealed* only if it is received. That means that the revelation is heard or thought or intuitively known in one's own language and culture, with one's own ability to receive. In fact, Muhammed, who at first was persecuted and almost killed, was eventually successful in founding Islam by emphasizing that the Qur'an was Allah's revelation to the Arabs in particular because it was written in Arabic. The revelation then could be welcomed by Arabic minds in Arabic culture. It was *their* revelation. Once they held it to their bosom, they would not let it go. It became the basis of their identity. At the same time, Allah, meaning "the One God," became theirs as well. It was a tribal adoption, just as the Hebrews claimed Yahweh as their own.

The receiver of revelation is, in every case, a culturally conditioned, fallible human being who has the awesome responsibility of passing along that which was revealed. But not every receiver of presumed revelation is just the same as another. Nor is anyone's receptivity always constant and fresh. Revelation is very much a relationship with the divine. It cannot be objectively detached, as the scientific method *attempts* to be in its own field, because the experience of receptivity to the divine is so intimate, personal, and often visionary. Sometimes a vision is precognitive, meaning to exist before thought or definition or logical viability exists in the mind.[89]

Creating Our Own Theology of the Cross

Having conscious revelatory experiences of our own is not why most of us believe in God. But many do read, discuss, and are taught the revelations found in scripture. On such a basis, most of us accept, partially accept, or reject those teachings. All of us, including those who have spiritual experiences not shared with others, construct at least some of our own theology about revelation.

In deciding what we really believe, one of our problems is that we respond to questions too quickly. Our answers are almost automatic. We learned them long ago and have not revisited them to obtain deeper insights. Originally, we accepted those quick responses as *true* because pervasive culture or the right authority had passed them on to us. That authority may have been a parent or priest, a professor or the printed page.

But the book you are now reading asks each of us to question our deepest selves and be as honest as we can be, not imprisoned by *answers* we have already learned. It is important for us to dare to create our own theology while respecting the theology we have been taught by our families, by the church, and by the world. We are fortunate if we already have a foundation on which to begin, for that means we can make comparisons and we already have a sense of values and how to find them.

Then we need to challenge ourselves to ask if our previous understanding conforms with our present experience and suppositions. My simple criteria have long been the following.

> God, as Spirit, is unconditional love for everyone in all times and all places.
>
> God is unbounded, permeating Spirit that can be ignored or forgotten but never will vanish.

Based on these convictions, I continue to learn what I never knew. I feel free to allow my views to change as I experience the life of God in new and challenging situations.

It is important to create our own theology knowingly. Why? Because we *act on our convictions*. If the structure of our inner belief contains great empty spaces, it will not hold together well. Then, our response to faith is half-hearted. Our enthusiasm is next to non-existent. We may feel easily threatened and angry if someone tries to challenge us about the foundation of our faith. Furthermore, if we are convinced that we absolutely must accept only what others have taught us, we will have no sense of ownership and will not feel our beliefs are really "ours." Then we may respond to inherited faith with respect, but it really will not matter. It is part of the outside world that simply is accepted dispassionately. But it is not founded on our inner world where daily decisions are based on what matters most to us and what we perceive to be true. It is an uninvolved acceptance.

Questioning Ourselves – Forming Our Theology
One of the most important questions on earth is this: "Is there a Reality that existed before all other derivative realities were here? Is there a primary, fundamental energy, something ultimate that is behind everyone and everything we consider real in our world?" Then, do we sense it as life and power, or is the *real* merely an idea or a thought? If the latter is true, then, perhaps we create that which exists. Many disbelievers challenge that human beings have created God through imagination and the desperate hope for meaning in life. Therefore, they argue that human beings have created God in *their* image. But if we have experienced love that is forgiving, healing, and inspiring, we recognize that a life-giving spirit, even if undefined, must be the source, a beginning. If that is true for us, then we sense that we are not alone in the world, and there is a reason for being here.

Whatever our answer to the question of fundamental, Ultimate Reality that answer may well affect whether we think life does or does not have significance and whether, by any measure, we can live by faith. Sometimes faith is an intellectual assumption of what we consider important. In this case, it may have more to do with individual self assurance than with sensitivity toward the divine. Faith may be built on knowledge – what we think we know. Or it may be founded on relationships with treasured and wise people on whom we depend, people without whom life would have no meaning. Faith may be built on the Church rather than on God, whom it intends to represent and serve. But faith also can be conviction about and personal response to an initiating force, something far more alive than we seem to be – and everlasting.

If we believe there is no such fundamental Reality, life can be lived according to the values we put on human associations and on appreciation of such things as beauty, possessions, and some measure of power to affect and even better the world around us. But If we assume there is such a basic reality, we are challenged to inquire further: Is it good, ambivalent, or evil? Does it care about living beings? Is it life-giving and life-sustaining? Can we trust it – or love it – or live for it? What does it have to do with a personal God or with a life-giving Spirit?

Such an investigation into our own consciousness about what is real and what is important to us leads to a far more solid personal theology than one that is merely accepted because of our respect for the teaching of others.

If one concludes that there is an Ultimate Reality and then looks at the history of the Western world and the effects of Christianity upon it, that person may very well question the influence of Jesus and the Crucifixion. They will be prone to ask why there was a Cross and what it meant. For centuries, human beings have wrestled with Jesus as the Messiah, with the overwhelming pervasiveness of sin, with the inevitable suffering of love, and with atonement, ransom, redemption, salvation, transformation, and even deification (see Chapter 7). Scripture, itself, contains many points of view. It has blamed Judas, the Sanhedrin, the Romans, the mob, Jesus' bull-headedness, and God as responsible for the Crucifixion. The last named is no doubt the most important.

Furthermore, to say that "God was *in* Christ" is very different from the focus of the Nicene Creed. That creed emphasizes who Jesus was, not how he was able to do what he did. Its primary effort was to state that Christ, while having a human birth, *was* God: "true God from true God." What were the writers struggling to say in mere words? Did they understand by logic and experience what could not be expressed? Were they trying to write about something that, in the end, was impossible to explain, something that never could be put into words?

First let us speak of history, theology, councils, and the Nicene Creed. Then we will speak of essence and meaning in the words and theologies chosen for us – hundreds of years ago. All of them are related to the meaning of the Cross.

History and the Nicene Creed

A creed is a statement of beliefs. It states what people hold to be true and foundational to life. It has importance because it often becomes the basis for action, even unthinking action.

There were numerous creed-like statements of religious beliefs used when people were first baptized into the early Christian church. They evolved into one creed from the Roman side. A tradition grew that each of the twelve apostles had contributed one of the twelve phrases. Therefore it was named the Apostles' Creed and used at baptisms. From its basic structure, the Nicene Creed evolved.

Although the Nicene Creed did not become official at the Council of Nicaea in 325, its statements were ratified by later councils. In 381 there was another ecumenical or "world-wide" council of bishops in Constantinople, attempting to put Christian belief into words. Ever since, their conclusions have been professed in what we now call the Nicene Creed or the Creed of Nicaea-Constantinople.

Yet, as the years passed, there were passionate and even violent discussions in attempting to decide how Jesus was related to God. In 451, with the Council of Chalcedon, the bishops came to a conclusion and declared that there were two natures in the one person of Christ: divine and human. Although the bishops finished with a statement similar to that of their predecessors, there was a decided variance of opinion within those one hundred twenty-six years. The final agreement had been neither obvious nor immediately clear to them when the councils began, even though they prayed to be led by the Holy Spirit. Therefore it is not strange if we do not immediately understand and accept what it took the councils so long to decide. Furthermore, for us, it seems imperative not to accept that creed because it was ratified by an ecumenical council, but only because it speaks the truth for us today.

Some of us would surely respect the Orthodox insistence, not just at those councils but today as well, that the truth revealed through Jesus was not abstract truth, but personal for each believer. The American Orthodox theologian, John Meyendorf, expresses it this way:

> Truth ... is conceived by the Byzantines [the Eastern Orthodox], not as a concept ... expressed ... in words ... but

as God ... personally present.... Not Scripture, not conciliar definitions, not theology can express [God] fully; each can only point to some aspects of [God's] existence."[90]

While the first council was being held in Nicaea, a popular and liberal view dubbed "Arianism" existed. It emphasized the humanity of Christ far more than does the final version of the Nicene Creed. Arianism taught that Jesus was "greater than we but less than God."[91] For years, even people on the street, many of whom spoke Greek, excitedly argued, discussing things like *homoiousios* (a similar essence) and *homoousios* (the same essence). At the councils, disagreements became extremely heated as the bishops battled back and forth about those two concepts. Was Jesus *like* God or was he the *same as* God? *Homoousious* won the battle.[92] At the council meeting in Chalcedon in 451, it was finally decided that Jesus was not just the Son of God, as had been commonly expressed, but truly the same as God: God, the Son. This was a radical difference in language and a supremely consequential decision. From that time, councils proceeded to substantiate that point of view.

It is important to note something that people are inclined to forget. What the various councils decided did not alter who Jesus really was. Whatever they said about Jesus or God did not change either one of them. But the final decision rendered by the Councils did make clear *their* position that Jesus was the same as God in essence (in being), and the councils represented the Church. Rulers like Constantine then could point to the authority of the Church and to one binding decree. Having only one voice and one creed helped immeasurably in holding government and people together. The state has co-opted the church frequently in history and vice versa. History is full of the consequences of church-state interactions. After all, church (or religious institutions) and state have long been the two most powerful institutions in the world. *Church*, of course, is a Christian, not a generic, term for organized religion. Unfortunately, this is an understanding to which our government officials and the media have not yet come.

Although the councils finally decided that Jesus was "fully God and fully man," there is no place in the Gospels where this concept is voiced outright. Paul comes closest to it, though, in Colossians 1:19: "For in him, all the fullness of God was pleased to dwell."

It is questionable whether any human being can truly comprehend such a possibility. Most people appear to believe that Jesus looked like a man but really wasn't. To them, he is God. But that was not what the councils eventually decided. In 451, they rejected monophysitism, the belief that claimed the human nature of Jesus was totally absorbed by divine nature. And in 681, they condemned monothelitism, the position that Jesus had only one will, the will of God.

Jesus prayed to God. In his time on earth, no one prayed to him. Nor was he omnipresent across the face of the earth, as most believers would say of God. For Jesus to have claimed to be God would have been blasphemous – to him – not just to the Jews or to the Romans who were required to consider most of their Caesars divine.

So the questions, dealt with by every generation, are repeated. Simply put, they are:

> Who was the figure on the Cross? Was it God who appeared to be a man called Jesus? Was it, somehow, completely God and completely man? Or was that figure the human Jesus – in whom God, who is Spirit, dwelled – offering himself on the Cross so that people could experience the saving love of God in their own lives?

Over the hundreds of years during which the councils met after Chalcedon, the council members spent a great deal of time deciding which theologies about Jesus were heresy.[93] The view that Jesus only *appeared* to be human but was really God in a human body was called *docetism* and was condemned within the first two centuries. *Dokein*, the Greek word from which docetism derives, refers to appearance. It is interesting to note the great number of docetists who are members of the Christian church today. Yet no one calls them heretics.

Perhaps we do not dub them heretics today because we realize that no one ever will be able to definitively explain God or the workings of the Spirit in a human being. Or perhaps it is because people want Jesus to be fully God and therefore do not really believe he was a natural human being. People tell his stories, talk about him in human terms, and pray to him as they speak to a friend. There are fewer words and ways to speak of a God who is also transcendent and has never been seen, but is the source from which all is created.

One important, but probably unconscious reason for emphasizing Jesus' divinity is that, if people saw Jesus as someone like themselves, they would realize that they might be called to the same mission as he was: to reveal God in all they do and say. It is much easier to avoid responsibility and excuse ourselves from something that demands such complete dedication. It is much easier to retort: "But Jesus was *God. He* could be that way!"

The question remains: Is it possible for God *not* to be *all there is of God?* A human being is limited in many ways, but there is no way in which God can be confined. What is limited cannot be unlimited. All that is unlimited cannot be subject to boundaries of any kind. Creator and creature are two different things. A human being is contingent upon God, that is, needs God and cannot live without God. For Jesus, that was especially true. Without God, to whom he prayed and for whom he spoke and acted, he had no power or purpose on earth. Again, we remember the words of Jesus in John 14:10: "The words I say ... and the works I do are not mine, but his who sent me." (author's paraphrase)

Perhaps the deeper insight of God as *Spirit* could help to resolve such problems. The Council of Nicea and all those following did not seem to consider or comprehend this concept at all. Instead, they emphasized the theology of the Trinity.

The Trinity

By the time of Nicaea, the teaching Church had decided that God should be explained as a trinity. But explaining God as a trinity does a disservice *if it breaks God into three parts or three "people."* This kind of theology has been problematic for non-Christians for years. It is not much easier for a Christian Sunday school teacher!

In the Church, the explanation of the Trinity always seems to have been a stumbling block. I have found more people struggling with the concept of the Trinity than being helped by it. The word *Trinity* is not in the Bible. However, the Greek-speaking church saw it as a way to teach the various aspects of God's being and God's work: God is Creator and also Savior, as well as Inspirer, Comforter, and Guide. Reflecting that theology, the hymn "Holy, Holy, Holy," wonderful as it is, has thrown us off in our understanding. "God in three *persons*, blessed Trinity" needs to be understood as God in three aspects, three modes of being, three ways of touching our lives.[94] In normal, contemporary parlance, a person, in contrast to God, has a physical body and, therefore, limitations, measurements, and a place in space.

The word *person* comes from the Greek term persona meaning mask. Language is used to define, call to mind or even visualize the one perceived. Sometimes God is perceived as our Creator, sometimes as an immanent friend and human savior, and sometimes as the Spirit, both inside us and surrounding us, pervading all things. But the same God is behind each mask.

There is a parallel in the way we think of the people we know. We may define them by their roles, or we may define them by our relationship to them. My mother was "Mother" to me and "daughter" to her own mother. She was called "Dear" by my father, "KK" by her friends, and "Keturah" by her teachers. They not only had different names for her, but she served in a different role and relationship with each of them. This example, and the one above about the mask, is perhaps the simplest and most understandable explanation of the concept of the Trinity. Because we experience one God in many different ways, and because God is rich in qualities, religions have more than one name, even many names, for the Divine.

But this is our problem as well. If we think that "Spirit" is only one attribute of God or something that flows out of God like a product, we miss the point. We are inclined to sing: "Come Holy Spirit" as though God was not already here. In reality, those words can mean: "I open my mind and heart to you. I want you to take over in my life. I am yours."

One sentence about the Holy Spirit in the Nicene Creed has separated the Roman Catholic and Eastern Orthodox churches throughout most of our history, and it affects the way we think of God. The Catholic West confesses in the Creed that the Holy Spirit "proceeds from the Father and the Son," calling this phrase the *filioque*. The Orthodox East says that the Spirit proceeds from the Father through the Son. But if both churches would consider God *as* Spirit, there would not be this dividing issue between them.

Now we can see why we cannot consider the aspects of the Trinity as three different beings acting at three different times and places, each doing a separate task.

If the energy of Spirit did not pervade the universe constantly, all life would cease. Indeed the Universe, itself, would cease. It must be as Elihu, the youth, said to Job: "If [God] should take back his spirit to himself and gather to himself his breath, all flesh would perish as the grass, and man would return to dust" (Job 34:14, 15).

Elihu is convinced that without the breath of the Spirit, there would be nothing. That truth has not always been obvious to the Church. When one studies the gradual growth of the creeds, one sees, in each case, that the section on the Spirit was the last to be added. Sensitivity to the Spirit has come late to many theologians. But it is foundational and essential. God is what Spirit is, and that Spirit was the very life of Jesus.

God, as Spirit, Is Personal

God, as noted, is not an individual, limited human person such as each of us is. But God, who is far more than a person, can be deeply personal. Another human being cannot live within the sanctity of our bodies, but each of our bodies can be, and is, a temple of the Holy Spirit. Both Jesus and Paul have spoken of God as Spirit, who longs to live fully within us, recognized and responded to by us (John 14-17; I Cor 3:16-17). We can live and grow in that realization unceasingly. *Nothing can be more personal.*

In fact, the great twentieth century Catholic theologian, Karl Rahner, says that "God is present to us, not as some abstract power, but as the very core of our being."[95] For Protestants, those are stunning words. We would tend to think of ourselves as immodest and too bold if we were even to think that thought. But Rahner, like Luther in this case, is saying that God is united with us even if we do not know it. Luther tends to speak of the Spirit coming into us. Rahner says that God is *waiting inside us as Spirit*, to awaken us to godly omnipresence. There is no place devoid of the unseen presence of the Spirit.

Yet there is a tendency within human consciousness to feel that, if we wish, we can hold God at bay; we can keep God out of our minds and our lives. In some ways, that seems to be true. But we cannot block God from the deepest part of our being, deeper than waking consciousness. If the divine presence is omnipresent, it penetrates the universe and all that is, even when unseen, unfelt, unrecognized.

Evil, the Warping of Spirit's Power
That would mean God is in the sick room, at the shelter for the abused, in the prison cell – even on the battlefield. In any such place, and there, on the killing field, God, who is Spirit, will not manipulate or force anyone to do anything. But God is there, and if God feels pain, it must be agonizing. God as Spirit is in the life of "each of the least of these" (Matt. 25:40). Spirit is within every soldier on both sides of any conflict. It is God's power that gives each of them the ability to think and to move. It is God who makes all power available. Power, itself, can be considered neutral, but its use is the challenge. (Gun powder, for instance, is not, in itself, good or bad. It can be used to build a road or to blow a person to bits. Electricity can keep an iron lung functioning, but, used in an electric chair, it can annihilate a life.) God's power, operating in the world through humankind, is used in peace and in war, in saintliness and beastliness, in abuse and blessing. What makes evil so evil is that it tempts mortals to use God's power to destroy, rather than to give life, which has been God's purpose from the Beginning. Once life is given us, isn't giving life our inherent reason for existence too?

There is only one power in the world, for there is only one God. But, I see *evil as divine power, intended for good, but used against God.* If someone believes that Satan's power is equal, then he or she conceives of two comparable powers. They and I disagree. I have known evil first hand and very close. It is ghastly, devastating, and cruel. But if God alone is ultimate power as well as the force of life and the source of love, then evil is the use of God's power in the most warped and twisted way possible.[96]

There are some individuals who have an abiding sense of the Holy Presence. For them, the Spirit is always where they are. As Psalm 139:8 says in awe: "If I make my bed in Sheol (Hades), you are there." For Jews, that is an extraordinary statement, for they have made it plain that no one can even remember God, recognize, or know there is a God while one is in Sheol. But all of Psalm 139 says throughout, God is wherever we are, even if we don't know it. In I Peter 3:18-19 we read of Jesus, "put to death in the flesh, but made alive in the spirit, in which also he went and made a proclamation to the spirits in prison" (meaning Hades or Sheol). This passage from I Peter is the obvious source of the creedal affirmation: "He descended into Hell," or, in a careful, recent re-wording, "He descended to the dead." But both these passages tell us that the Spirit has no bounds. Nevertheless, it will not force itself upon us. It asks to be recognized, acknowledged, and received.

Trying to Confine the Spirit
How could the omnipotent, omnipresent Spirit have finite limitations of any sort? God is *self*-limited, said Aquinas, for our good.[97] But our language can betray us, especially visionary, metaphorical language. Because we cannot be precise, because we cannot "pin God down," we have to resort to symbolism and metaphor. Sometimes we have envisioned God on a throne. Isaiah did in his vision (Isa. 6). According to Matthew, Jesus used that metaphor in discussing the Last Judgment (Matt. 25: 31-46). Even our creeds speak of Jesus who is "seated on the right hand of God," whom most imagine as also sitting on a throne. (Interestingly, Muslims have the same image in the Qur'an's account of the Prophet's night journey to heaven, known as the *mir'aj*.)[98]

Nevertheless, how could anyone think of God, conceived of as Spirit, confined to a throne for eternity? The throne metaphor communicates that God is King, the supreme ruler, the One in charge of everything. In this case, using the image of God as Spirit is far more helpful. Spirit is Life! Life, ceaselessly full of energy, constantly moves. Spirit, "the Lord and giver of life,"[99] is the foundational energy of the world.

Immersed In and Filled By the Spirit
When I look at the night sky, I often sense the Spirit keenly. Then the words of Charles Haddon Spurgeon come: "There is no place where God is not."[100] We used to call that sense the omnipresence of God. Now we are more likely to say "the pervasive Presence." It is not difficult, when looking as far into that sky as possible, to believe that there must be More

and More beyond, and that it, too, exists because the Spirit has no bounds. It is there. And it is here too. In a profound sense, we are connected to it all because the sky exists within Spirit. We live *inside* Spirit, and Spirit lives *in* us and throughout the sky.[101]

Although we are immersed in and can be filled by Spirit, it is foolish to perceive our limited, finite being as containing all there is of the Greater. As long as we are "in the flesh," as Paul would put it, the greatness that is potential or that is actualized within us, will never be all that belongs to the Divine. Though some individuals contend that we are all "gods," none of us is God of all life, the Ultimate Reality on which creation depends. *All I am can be filled with God, but I can never be all there is of God.* All that is limited about us, all that each calls "my self" is an individual consciousness that was created to serve the greater, complete and inclusive consciousness we call Spirit or God.

All that Spirit is, never can be fully contained in any of us. It could not even have been fully contained in Jesus in his mortal form. He lived in spite of his human limitations by the power of the Spirit. He knew what he was requesting when he asked us to do as he did (John 15:16; 21:17). And he was right. Together, we have seen God accomplish miracles through human beings, as Jesus knew the Spirit would (John 14:12). At certain rarefied moments, we know God is in us, telling us what to say and what to do, in spite of our fear and our limited knowledge (Matt.10:19). When our time on earth is over, perhaps the Spirit living in another person will finish the task that we have begun. There may well be more opportunities for us in God's continuing kingdom, within the journey that shall have no end (see Chapter 9).

People of all times and places have attested to the touch of the Spirit, but have not called the Spirit by its name. Tolstoy claimed that it was the spirit (the living contact passed on) in art that could "infect" and be "caught" by others. For the Cheyenne-Arapahoe of America, the divine Spirit is believed to be passed from one person to another in the medicine circle by means of the medicine pipe. Through it, they breathe out the Great Spirit that is in them, and the person beside them breathes it in. It is a healing. Healing flows as well through the music in the voice of the flute, given life by breath.[102] To C. S. Lewis, Spirit is an "influence."[103] That would be, not an overwhelming power that forces its way into our hearts, but a wistful, wonderful vitality that wins its way by its goodness and beauty. Yet it also is the shocking dynamism of truth and the life of love. Were we to speak further of Spirit by other names, we would be delving into the richness of other religions that have their own terms for this presence of God, this energy of life, inside and around them.

The Goal of the Spirit: Healing and Reconciliation

The Spirit's goal is surely the healing that comes from reconciliation. To reconcile is to reunite, to bring into harmony, to put back together a relationship that has been broken. It is only the expression of Spirit – godly love – that can heal destructive differences whether its presence is recognized or not.

Paul's words from II Corinthians 5:19 were: "God was, in Christ, *reconciling* the world to God's self." That is a message of pure grace. We are the ones entrusted to receive and share it. Our wounded world can be transformed only by forgiveness, by wiping the slate clean as far as is possible and then beginning again in the power of the Spirit of Love to recreate. Wars will cease, governments will function well, and relationships across the world will be healed only when three things happen: we stop coveting what another has, we forgive, and we help each other. That goes for all sides. At the moment it seems that it will never happen. But we cannot let go of the possibility. It is surely the Spirit's dream in our hearts.

Reconcile is a powerful word. God, as reconciler, lifts us out of our self-centeredness, judgmentalism, superiority, and anger so that we can share the Kingdom here, as well as in eternity. When the envisioned future comes into the present, it is what theology calls "realized eschatology." What we expect at the very end of the world – the glorious reign of God – becomes real in time and in our own experience, in its own measure, yet not in full. We have tastes of it in individual lives that have been transformed and are entirely different today.

It is Spirit that revives, reconciles, and gives new life. That change comes not just from a transcendent God above us, or from a God who is "on our side." Nor can it be confined to a Spirit-inspired person teaching us or walking beside us. It was not confined to Jesus. The whole Earth lives *inside* the Spirit's presence. We live inside it. And from our beginning, it has lived in us, waiting and yearning for us to awaken. By our affirmative receptivity and God-given volition it will begin to move in power. As the Spirit moved in love through Jesus, it will begin, through us, to open the eyes of our minds and the imprisonments of our souls, healing the hurts that inflame our hate, empowering us to share the best that is in us, and giving us its own *Self* so that we can love one another. To be the tool of the Spirit is to be fully alive!

> "O Spirit of my Lord, the Christ,
> be the fire within my heart,
> the thought within my brain,
> and the words upon my lips!
> Speak to me and through me.
> Reach out from me and do your work.
> Be the life of my life
> so that all I do
> is what you do through me."[104]

Chapter 5

LIFE-GIVING LOVE ON CALVARY
Kenosis and Pouring Out Love as Life

The Cross is testimony to all that God is and always has been for all people: the Spirit that gives life and love. What happened on Calvary has been happening since the Beginning: God pouring out all that God is – this time through Jesus.

If it is true that Jesus came to reveal the nature and spirit of God in human terms, then his complete self-offering is a revelation of that very quality in God. Philippians 2:5-7 says: "Let the same mind be in you that was in Christ Jesus, who, though in the form of God … *emptied himself.*" That emptying is called *kenosis*. The writer of Philippians was trying to say Jesus was the Son of God who had given up life in heaven to come to earth.

But nature knows no such thing as a vacuum. In the natural world, there is no pure emptiness. Science tells us that what appears to be emptiness is instantaneously displaced by something. Jesus' purpose in self-emptying was his means to allow God's self-giving in a unique way in history. What else but God's love is the love we receive through Jesus? Life comes from being loved, even before we exist and all through our earthly lives. For those who have never felt such love, there is a sense of lostness, abandonment, or starvation. For them especially, to see and experience the everlasting creative force – revealed in Jesus as saving love – means everything. It comes from the overflowing, given life of God, poured out to us in countless ways throughout history.

In Donald Baillie's well-known book, *God Was In Christ*, he says:

> In modern Orthodox theology, especially among the Russians, there has developed the idea that the divine *kenosis*, self-emptying or humiliation, was not confined to the historical Passion or even to the Incarnation, but is something eternal in the life of God.[105]

That is exactly my point. Jesus' self-emptying cannot be separated from his self-giving. His life was visible evidence of what God has been doing eternally.

Those of us who have known true love and experienced it in our own lives, have lived by its constant re-creating power. There was one, called John, who may have said it best when it came to Jesus:

> That which was from the beginning, which we have heard, which we have seen with our eyes, which we have looked upon and touched with our hands ... the life was made manifest, and we saw it, and testify to it, and proclaim to you the eternal life which was with the Father and was made manifest to us. (I John 1:1-3, 13)

What Jesus offered us upon the Cross in human time was an expression of God's eternal action, that which God always has, is, and always will be doing: "reconciling."[106] It is only love that can reconcile, that is: forgive and heal – whether it is our inner selves or our response in community.

A hymn writer called it "Wondrous Love,"[107] and so it is.

"God so loved the world that God gave his only son" (John 3:16). God's work in Jesus was a gift. What was given to us was not intended, in return, to be a payment from us to God. We had things turned backwards. We had thought forgiveness and eternal life could be gained by a sacrifice. We thought obtaining salvation would demand the greatest sacrifice of all. But a gift from God is pure grace. It cannot be obtained. There is no required payment before the gift may be received.

Kierkegaard wrote, in *Works of Love*: "If one wants to make sure that love is completely unselfish, he eliminates every possibility of repayment." He was talking there about human love. How much more true that must be of the freely given love from God.[108]

God Wants To Forgive

The Hebrew people were chosen, loved, forgiven, and sustained throughout history. In the days of the Prophets there were those who believed that one had only to ask for forgiveness, and it would be given. It was.

Jesus did not ask his betrayers or those who were taking his life to repent before he cried: "Father, forgive them, for they do not know what they are doing" (Luke 23:34). He simply asked God to grant them forgiveness even before they could do anything to merit it, try to pay for it, ask for it, or even realize that they needed it. Surely it was the Spirit within Christ from whom that passionate prayer surged into his mind and out through his lips. God answered the prayer even before it was spoken. It was as Isaiah had written: "Before they call, I will answer; while they are yet speaking, I will hear" (Isa. 65:24). Those for whom Jesus prayed very probably did not even notice what he was doing, let alone, repent.

Forgiving is truly giving, and God's very nature is to give. It is both unnecessary and useless to bargain with God. We do not have to bring gifts to receive more in return. We do not have to prime the pump to get the water of the Spirit flowing. God is already there – waiting to give.

We are the only ones who stand in the way of our own forgiveness. Sometimes we refuse to receive. We can hurt so much from what we have done that we want to self-flagellate, to punish ourselves, to refuse forgiveness, to bleed inside. Then there seems to be only one answer: to offer our battered, self-offending hearts before the Cross so that Christ may teach us to forgive ourselves with his love, not our own!

It is sad that people who do not comprehend a true gift cannot comprehend a God whose whole being is gift. When we remember that "God is Spirit," we realize that Love is Spirit and "God is love." God is not a being, but Being itself, as Tillich reminds us.[109] And what is Being but Spirit – which is Life? God is Gift. Being is Gift. Life is Gift. Love unmerited is Gift. And all of it is Grace.

All that we can give in return already belongs to the One who made being possible. Many of us sing about that truth when offering ourselves, our lives, and our money at services on Sunday morning. It is not a *collection* that we *take up*, but an *offering* that is *received*. As it is taken forward to be placed upon the altar of dedication, we sing, "We give thee but thine own." What else is there to give?

I was reminded once that the altar originated as a *chopping block*, a place of ritual sacrifice. But it has been transformed and its meaning turned around. Now life is not forcibly extinguished there, but offered. To place our gifts there – offering love, life, and will – can be the high point of worship. It is our living response to the One who has given, and always will give, everything.

Jesus Died For Our Sake, Not For God's
Perhaps the most crucial question of all is; "Why would God have sent himself to earth to be a payment to himself for human sin?" It is convoluted reasoning. But if Jesus was God incarnate, as a majority of Christians believe, it was not for God's sake, but for ours that Jesus came and, in the end, steadfastly walked toward Jerusalem. There, on the Cross, his sacrifice was not a substitute for our sacrifice to God. His sacrifice was God's sacrifice for us. There, in human terms, through a human son, God gave everything again.

Some of those standing beneath the Cross on the day of crucifixion, could sense, as the blood of Jesus flowed down, that goodness and healing were pouring out of this one who did not condemn them, but did condemn sin, arrogance, self-righteousness, and self-centeredness. "Indeed God did not send the Son into the world to condemn the world, but in order that the world might be saved through him" (John 3:17). This one had come to bless, to "give life abundantly."

To be in that place on that day, to experience Jesus' crucifixion, surely had to *open the eyes* (as he longed to do) of some who had been *blind*. And through his obvious grace, there must have been some proud, angry, and hardened hearts set free from sickness of soul that had imprisoned them until that day (Luke 4:18, 19). There may even have been others who secretly, but like the Centurion, gasped: "Surely this was the Son of God!" (Matt. 27:54).

Priestly sacrificial thought truly might have been abandoned that day if human perception had allowed it! Instead, it was reinstituted to live again for at least two thousand years. Through the Prophets, God had commanded the cessation of blood sacrifice and the destruction of life as offerings. God had pled through Hosea: "I desire mercy (compassion, empathy, support), not sacrifice" (Hosea 6:6). And Jesus repeated Hosea's words. Yet that day, another sacrifice was offered. It was considered an execution then. But not long after, with the second temple destroyed in 70 AD, it was Christians, not Jews, who kept the old concepts of blood sacrifice alive through the ritual of communion, the developing liturgy, theology, and the words of hymns and prayers.

In the Gospel of Matthew, Jesus repeated those words from Hosea, twice (Matt. 9:13, 12:7). But the ideas of ransom and payment were never forsaken.[110] And efforts to be righteous or *good* often seem more important than loving one's neighbor. Yet God, as perceived by Jesus, seems not to have been caught up with laws and judgmentalism. Forgiveness, which recreates life, has never been new to the One who started it all.

Again and again, God's self-giving pours out life. Then God asks the same from us. *Sacrifice is not abolished, but transformed.* We are asked not to destroy life for God's glory, but to receive life and then, to give it away. Human outpouring to God and to others in God's name is known as *Gelassenheit*. The term is one very rarely heard, yet I can think of almost nothing more important than that grateful open-hearted self-giving of one's life, inspired by the giving spirit of God. We shall speak of it more deeply in Chapter 8.

Unfortunately, pre-prophetic thought and commands still grip us tightly. The ancient understanding that God requires a ransom for our redemption is still pervasive across the church and across the world. The contemporary United Church of Christ scholar, Peter Schmiechen, counts ten soteriologies, that is, ten theologies of salvation.[111] The twentieth century Swedish Lutheran theologian, Gustav Aulén, counted three.[112]

Law and Love

Although the compassionate message of the Later Prophets was strong and inspiring, human beings have always insisted on law, punishment, and retribution. Yet law is primarily necessary, not for the sake of expressing anger and recrimination. It is necessary because we do not love, or because we do not love wisely or within appropriate limitations. With law, we have agreements among ourselves as to what we may and may not do. When those agreements are accepted and enforced, it is possible to live together for what is conceived of as the benefit of the group. It is an important part of civilization.

Furthermore, laws are not only restrictive, but guiding. But if law is not based on unselfish concern for the good of all, it becomes "a demon and a beast," as Luther was wont to say. Law is limited. We can never legislate perfectly for everything. Nor can it always be for the good of all.

Paul tells his readers that the law is fulfilled by love (Rom. 13:8). Surely where God's love is, there is no need for law. If a law is godly, it is an expression of how to effectually act in love, to recreate if possible. Laws are given to guide those who do not naturally live by godly love.

All of these considerations become critically important when we evaluate the Cross in the light of law, sin, and ransom versus the magnificent actions of grace, forgiveness, and setting free.

Jesus was not ordained by an earthly religious institution but by the Spirit who spoke and acted through him. It is the Spirit who anoints us too. We remember: "You did not choose me, but I chose you and ordained you that you should bring forth fruit, and that your fruit should remain" (John 15: 16). These words, spoken to Jesus' Disciples, always will be spoken to those who are disciples in centuries to come.

For those who follow him, Jesus is Savior. It is Jesus' being and Jesus' life in our world that have inspired, guided, and given us life. But Jesus' blood, by itself, has not saved us anymore than "the blood of bulls or goats" saved the Israelites. It was God's love – flowing through Jesus' blood, his being and his entire life – that saved us.

To "be saved" is to be given life, now and eternally. That means we are forgiven and freed, reconciled and rehabilitated, healed, made whole, and given hope. That transformation is not a thing of the past, but ongoing. We fall. But the gift called salvation continues to be offered. And as we receive it, we are empowered to rise.

> To all who received him, who believed on his name,
> he gave power to become the children of God. (John 1:12)

Chapter 6

TWO TYPES OF SACRIFICE
Destroying Life and Giving Life

For two thousand years the church has retained an ancient theology of sacrifice that, when it was inherited, already had been held for at least a thousand years. It is found, not only in the religion of Israel, but in all major ancient religions across the globe, originating before monotheism appeared. The influence of the ancient approach to sacrifice seems inerasable from present day thought and practice. An evaluation that speaks to the general public is long overdue.[113] When Jesus' conception of his mission and purpose is compared with the rationale for the major form of ancient sacrifice – destroying live animals for favors and forgiveness – a great difference will be noted. Also, as will be seen, Jesus and the Later Prophets of Israel very much agreed about sacrifice.

Although there are numbers of types of sacrifice noted in the Priestly Code and later Levitical writings, there is one method and one purpose that holds central attention: destroying the life of another in the hope of obtaining enhanced life for one's self or one's tribe. The desire may be for forgiveness, more children, health, or victory at war. Even the sole intent to honor God ends with the hope of securing godly favor. For Israel to employ a whole class of priests, to make the temple a house of sacrifice, and to repeat sacrificial ritual twice daily shows the centrality of this form of worship.

All other motivations for sacrifice in Hebrew scripture are closer to Jesus' own purpose on the Cross. These can be placed under one other heading: giving life and giving of self to others. With this simplification, we are able to discuss two kinds of sacrifice, note how they were used in history, and see the impetus and interpretations behind them. They can be listed in two columns: as sacrifice that destroys life and as sacrifice that gives life. They also may be seen as sacrifice *to* God or *for* God.

The Two Major Types of Sacrifice

Destroying Life of Another
- Sacrifice to God
- Priestly approach
- Redemption/Payment
- Retribution/Sacred Punishment
- To gain favor now and eternally
- To praise God
- To restore God's honor/reputation
- To obtain forgiveness
- To express thanksgiving
- Usual Focus: self-gain

Giving Life to Others
- Sacrifice for God
- Prophetic approach
- Salvation/Compassion
- Restoration
- To fulfill God's Great Intention for all Creation, Jesus, and us
- To let God use us to fill others' needs
- Jesus' life and death
- To express thanksgiving/love
- Focus: reconciliation and blessing

The first column, based on ancient priestly sacrificial law, is summarized by Hebrews 9:22:

> *Under the law* almost everything is purified with blood, and without the shedding of blood there is no forgiveness of sin. (author's emphasis)

The second column summarizes Jesus' intent as noted in John 10:10. This is Jesus' perception of God's will through him:

> I have come to give life, and to give it more abundantly.

The first and most ubiquitous type of ancient sacrifice *destroyed* the life of another. The purpose was to acquire greater quality of life for one's self or for those with whom one identified: family, tribe, or nation. The sacrifice focused self-interest through destroying something good that God had created. Nevertheless, it was called a gift to God. The act of sacrifice gave up something valuable to obtain something even more precious. It was a payment or a bargain. Today, although sacrifice to God is not intended to destroy life, the concept of payment and bargain unfortunately remain.

The alternate type of sacrifice focuses on *giving life* by living for something greater than oneself. Such sacrifice may have one or all of three motivations.
- Gratitude for life, for God, for forgiveness, for healing and freedom (for gifts mentioned in Luke 4:18-19).
- Loving, joyous sacrifice to accomplish the vision of another's good.
- Sacrifice as a necessary part of an opportunity to live a worthwhile life of purpose and meaning.

> The difference between the two types of sacrifice is *getting* versus *giving* as a way of life. It is destroying versus using what God has given us. One is self-centered; the other is self-giving. The theology behind the first is payment to God. Behind the second is the theology of God's gift of grace, given to us and through us when, in the attitude of prayerful receptivity, we act and speak as instruments of God.

Types of Ancient Sacrifice

Although there are many types of sacrifice mentioned in the Hebrew Bible, several seem to stand out. A propitiatory sacrifice was meant to appease God and ask for favors and forgiveness. The votive sacrifice seemed to be a contract or bargain made with God in which the individual promised to offer a payment or gift *if* God fulfilled a certain request. Two sacrifices often associated with Jesus' crucifixion were those of satisfaction and expiation. Until Luther disagreed, even medieval theologians argued that the Crucifixion offered God satisfaction. It was thought to make amends, to satisfy a jealous God's supposed desire to be continually respected and honored (a concept that treated God like a human being with an ego). The sacrifice for expiation of sin expressed the fervent desire that sin be forgotten by God. Guilt offerings were intended to offer payment as restitution for damaging another's body, possession, or reputation. Note, however, that they were offered to God, and not to the victim!

The sacrifice of atonement originally meant "actual reconciliation with God, the re-establishment of an impaired relationship." It depended on "inward effort – above all on repentance and amendment," on actual changes in one's life.[114]

The last type of sacrifice that will be mentioned is shocking, but it is critically important to our subject. Tributary sacrifice is meant to honor God by offering the "first fruits" of one's labor, of one's fields, and of one's body.[115] Tributary sacrifice is reflected in the near-sacrifice of Isaac by his father Abraham. Some say it is exemplified in the sacrifice of Jesus, whom Christians confess as "the only Son of God." But a question arises that demands an answer: How does killing honor God who, we are told, proclaimed as a most basic rule of life: "You shall not kill" (Exod. 20:13)?

Child Sacrifice

Destructive sacrifice was a pervasive, human understanding of God's will in most, if not all, ancient religions. Long before the Ten Commandments became a part of the consciousness of the Hebrew people, there was a cult that indulged in sacrificial worship. In those ceremonies, lower gods, divine sons, sacred rulers, or *first-born children* were sacrificed to maintain or restore a right relationship with the Divine, or to give to those remaining, the power of the life-force (and even consciousness) in the victim's blood.[116] Animal blood was sprinkled on worshippers in Israel's temple sacrifices for the same reason it was drunk by Aztec priests: to transfer the power in the blood to those who came to worship.[117]

It is important to admit that child sacrifice was practiced in Israel. Even Abraham almost followed the old custom. His near sacrifice of Isaac clearly showed he was part of that tradition. Many professors of Christianity have taught that it was only the devotees of a rival god called Moloch who practiced child sacrifice. But there are numerous accounts that challenge such a declaration. Toynbee writes that "the Canaanite rite of sacrificing one's eldest son was practiced in Judah down to the seventh century before the beginning of the Christian era; and, in the Greater Canaan … in Northwest Africa … [it] was not suppressed until the beginning of the Christian era."[118]

An outstanding expert on sacrifice, E. O. James, gave slightly different dates, based on the end of the Exile of Jews to Babylon in the sixth century BCE. The Babylonian Captivity was a result of the Chaldean conquest of Jerusalem and all of Judah, resulting in forcible deportation of most of the inhabitants. Evidently, even captivity did not stop child sacrifice completely.[119] James writes:

> Long after this offering had been abandoned, ... the conviction that the god of Israel demanded the sacrifice of their first-born male offspring was so deeply laid that it was always liable to recur.... The revival of child-sacrifice at Topheth, in the valley of Hinnom near Jerusalem, about 600 BC was deplored. But it still persisted, and Ezekial lamented that, despite the efforts of Josiah and the Deuteronomic Law, the people combined the worship of Yahweh with passing their children through the fire to Moloch in the valley of Hinnom.... It was not until after the Exile when the first-born rite was replaced by a tribute, that the custom was permanently eliminated in Judaism.[120]

Early Hebrews did not have the sophisticated, well-worked-out theology of today's faith tradition. As in this passage from James, we can read of the times when Hebrews slaughtered and then burned their first-born sons (rarely first-born daughters) in sacrificial fire as a way of bargaining for the future, guaranteeing that the remaining years of family life would be blessed.[121]

Rolland E. Wolfe writes in *The Interpreters' Bible*: "Immemorial custom in the Near East required that the first-born son should be sacrificed to God in order that the Deity would give the couple more children and grant the family prosperity." But this was not just a custom. It became a law. Exodus 22:29 quotes God as saying: "The first-born of your sons you shall give to me." Thus, "people felt that all the first fruits were *required* by God, including the first fruits of their bodies."[122]

Before monotheism became the only religious understanding of the Hebrews, people in neighboring religions all seemed to borrow ideas and cultic practices from each other. Usually these adaptations were not official (although King Ahab's certainly were.)[123] But people were influenced by the practices and traditions of those who lived around and among them. In Ahab's time, "Hiel of Bethel built Jericho; he laid its foundation at the cost of Abira his firstborn, and set up its gates at the cost of his youngest son Segub, according to ... Joshua" (I Kings 16:34).[124]

Response

It seems nothing short of blasphemous to consider that the God we now refer to as Love itself could have commanded and sanctified despicable, savage ways. Then, is it not more painful to perceive Christ's sacrifice as God's action in a similar vein?

Far from believing God ever would have exacted any kind of blood sacrifice from humankind, there are those among us who have been inspired to give their love and lives for God's use, just as Jesus did. Those people live with a purpose: they are living and dying for what matters most, even while knowing that the offering of their love may involve their death. All love has a cost, but living for a great cause means so much that some, like Jesus, are willing to pay the price. The consequences may be, as Jesus predicted, that those followers will be not only misunderstood, ignored, and thrown out of the worshipping congregation, but hated and even crucified. "If they persecuted me, they will persecute you" (John 15:20).

We are naïve. We deny the possibility that such persecution could happen to us. We do not even see it when the same thing happens to others. In fact, few seem to recognize persecution when it occurs within the Church. We do not want to see or believe it. Believing in the goodness of the Church is so important to some people's security that they reject friends and members of their own families who report various types of black-balling, destructive discriminatory treatment, and sexual abuse.

Persecution frequently happens at administrative levels, without the knowledge of members of a congregation. Consequently, no one defends individuals who are ill-treated and have no recourse but to accept their lot. Often, as "good Christians," those who are persecuted forgive and do not fight. But both they and their persecutors have lost something precious and important.

Startlingly, persecution occurs for a number of the same reasons that Jesus was crucified. By being himself, expressing God's love on earth, Jesus became a threat to the self-centered and professionally aggressive. In the history of the Church, blatant silencing and censuring has occurred frequently, and it is done with an assumption of righteousness by those in power. To appear to be right is important in the decision-making of most churches. But cruel and insensitive actions or equally contemptible inaction by those who would muzzle the work of the Holy Spirit in others is not part of Christianity.

The effects of sacrificial laws and views of divine destructive "justice" have strongly persisted into our own time.[125] Many of today's outstanding theologians do not agree with the theologies of payment for salvation by the blood of Christ.

But the views of these contemporary scholars, in general, have not reached the public or the pews. Why have our people not been freed from the concept of – or belief in – a God of wrath for whom punishment comes before grace? Even today retributive, destructive justice appears to come first, and rehabilitative, restorative justice comes second. We seem unable to imagine another way!

It is lamentable that the idea of so-called divine justice has continued to insist on primacy today. This is especially true when we realize that, according to many ancient recordings of God's perceived actions, those actions were not just, and must be regarded as cruel, self-centered, and even extremely violent.

Could those actions have been projections onto God in order to gain divine sanction for human hatred and society's punishment? After all, if God's violence is considered just, perhaps ours can be too. Of course, that is "hitting back," not "turning the other cheek," isn't it?

We continue to believe that justice is served when we force people to pay for their crimes. Yet their punishment rarely solves the problem. We still have not learned that it is better to restore a life than to exact fruitless, vindictive retribution that later may incite greater violence. Our imagination is sorely lacking, for example, when we spend fortunes on incarceration with little or no attempt to access the human potential that is being wasted, to offer completion of a basic education, to deal with anger management, to help prisoners see their own inner goodness (which many have never conceived of), and to learn how to feel for others, including the victims of their crimes.

There is another possibility. Perhaps these countless stories of God's wrath were not really God's actions, but were the interpretation of the ancient idea that God *controls* the world and, therefore, everything that happens is caused by God. That is a subject to be discussed in Chapter 9, devoted to redemption and salvation.

Sacrifice to God and Sacrifice for God

Destructive sacrifice and sacrifice as payment have long been undergirded by religious and moral law. Obedience to religious law is seen as required by believers. But obedience may be a blessing or a stumbling block. Sometimes the unconscious reward of lawful obedience is a sense of being right and superior. Then spirituality becomes self-centered. One's own salvation can become the primary goal. Then life is focused on saving one's own soul through self-denial or good works.

Sacrifice as payment is an attempted manipulation to influence someone or something more powerful than ourselves: often seen as God. Even if done to truly honor the greater power, it is important to recognize that it also may be done to retain a valuable relationship for its benefits.

Much as human beings have tried for thousands of years, we cannot manipulate God either by great sacrifice or by repetitious or heartfelt prayer. Nor does God manipulate us. We are not forced to "be good," to do what God wants. Our choices influence many lives, even many unknown to us. To pray that God will intervene is to ask God to take away everyone's free will, responsibility, and response-ability.

However, the focus of giving life comes with the freedom to love, to lighten another's load, to support, and to inspire. It means using one's talents and strengths to benefit others. Anyone who gives, shares the happiness that others gain and participates in their sense of achievement. Givers find their lives have worth and meaning. Self-respect and a good self image grow because they are making a positive difference in the lives of others. But because of the old understanding of sacrifice as being a painful loss, few people think of self-giving and giving life as sacrifice.

I have known many people who loved deeply and sacrificially without any sign of looking for a benefit. They certainly did not give away their lives for the purpose of self-actualization. To me, those people were truly noble, though most of them never were given any earthly recognition. Several lived with unseen privation. But they never would have perceived their own nobility.

Giving, which is God's grace expressed through us, is simply an offering of love. By receiving God's love, it becomes our own, and we are moved to give it away. We are empowered to enhance life, or offer it, rather than to use it up, minimize, abuse, ignore, or destroy it.

Real love cannot be forced or manipulated. God will not force anyone to love even though all wars would cease, no one would break the law, and none of us would be tempted to hurt, kill, or abandon another. Love is a choice, or it cannot exist.

In the end, it is possible to confuse motivations. In living for others, it is easy not to recognize a subconscious desire for personal attainment – gaining the respect of others or enjoying an enhanced reputation. Most of us recognize that there is probably no complete altruism. We may do the right thing for the wrong reason. We may do the wrong thing for the right reason. It sometimes seems that there is scarcely anything that people do (except, perhaps, spontaneously) that cannot be attributed to some kind of self-gain or the enhancement of self-image. Yet there is almost nothing more important than to make a genuine choice regarding what we want to live for and, thereafter, give that choice all our strength and passion. The fire of the Spirit in human beings will use all human gifts and training in the desire to become the Spirit's presence in the world.

We have spoken here of sacrifice *to* God and sacrifice *for* God. Except for sacrifices of thanksgiving and awe, most sacrifice to God has been for human benefit. But sacrifice for God, can be seen as giving in God's name, trying to do what God would do in our place. Fallible as we are, this is not without its own dangers of pride and superiority, but it also is full of joy. Now, there remain just a few questions that we especially need to ask.

Jesus' Sacrifice: Payment or Gift?

Did the Cross uphold ancient priestly sacrificial law or did it primarily proclaim the Gospel by giving life to the fullest extent? Did God teach through the Prophets that all human blood sacrifice was wrong only to say that, in Jesus' case, it was right, and then plan for it to happen?

And what about us? Did the Cross lay on Jesus' followers a load of guilt or the freedom of forgiveness? Is our time of worship focused upon ourselves and our sin or upon God's unconditional love, which we drink in with all our hearts? Do we spend most of our worship time confessing what is wrong with us or receiving what Jesus made right and then going forth in power in his name?

Many of us remain glued in the grime of guilt and have not grown to gratitude. We cannot let go of the fact that sinful people, before our time, killed the Son of Love. In the Prayers of the Church, when we plead for forgiveness, repeatedly crying "Lord, have mercy!" we have missed the point of the Cross. Too many pews are filled with people who feel guilty and powerless. We have made ourselves impotent by not *receiving* God's power, given before we ask.

Of all Christian symbols, the Cross represents overwhelming mercy *already* granted – now and for all time. It conveys the message Christ intended, the gift that says: "I love you. God's power and grace support you. You are forgiven. Now get started in a new life!" The Church's language of prayer needs to change from asking to receiving. Worshippers can respond: "Lord, we trust you. You are always merciful!" Or we may simply say: "We are grateful!" In the same spirit, instead of uttering the endless plea: "Lord, hear our prayer!" the church where I served as pastor enthusiastically proclaimed: "We *know* you hear our prayer," and the parishioners loved those words.

It is possible to be grateful only when we have first been receptive. On Easter morning, Jesus entered a fear-filled room and, breathing on his disciples, said: "Receive the Holy Spirit" (John 20: 22). They did receive, and so did others on the day of Pentecost. Without such receptivity, there would be no Christian church. The church will continue and our lives will be increasingly effective when we consciously, humbly, and gratefully receive.

A Practical Example of Receptivity

Surely one of the most meaningful parts of the communion service for me has always been the quiet, devoted singing of the *Agnus Dei*. The congregation sings: "Lamb of God, you take away the sin of the world. Have mercy on us. Grant us your peace." When I recently challenged myself as to what those words mean, I realized that I meant far more than what I was singing. Jesus had not taken away the sin of the world. Another 9/11 could happen any day. The whole world could easily experience financial collapse because of greed, incipient in society.

Furthermore, how could I ask for more mercy when, as we have noted, Jesus has already gone as far as possible?

And yes, I crave peace for everyone. I know too many who are sick with fear.

Why did that wonderful, simple music with its familiar words mean so much to me? And what was it that my heart was feeling as I sang those words?

I took the question into my prayer time and wrote down the answer that came to me that day. I needed new words to speak more clearly for my heart. The words that came fit the music:

> God of Love, you offer me your Life in this food
> and fill me with peace. (Repeat)
> I open my heart. Your love heals my soul.

The Sacrifice of Giving Life

The most storied life in history, the life of Jesus, was given to restore human life, not to punish. "For God sent not his Son into the world to condemn the world, but that the world, through him, might be saved" (John 3:17). "In Christ, God was reconciling the world to himself, not counting their trespasses against them" (II Cor. 5:19).

Yet still we preach, pray, and sing about Jesus as the perfect sacrifice, whose blood paid God for otherwise unforgivable sin. The American theologian, Gerhard Forde, emphasizes that "Jesus comes to rescue us from our determination to live under the law." After all, "that is the way our world runs."[126] Could it be that we still don't comprehend the Good News, the Gospel? We have been attempting, not only to respect the sacrificial writings of Hebrew scripture, but to *follow* them, because we have not understood that Israelite theology, itself, moved on.

With the Prophets, theology evolved into something very different from the teachings and ritual practices of the Priests. With the destruction of the temples, sacrifice ceased. With the death of Jesus, the former theology of sacrifice and salvation should have been turned upside down! It should have evolved from asking for more mercy and moved toward increased giving in God's name. For some, it certainly did. Why have the rest of us not understood? Why has the Church not further attempted to change its language and its teaching? If the Church continues as it has, without passing on Christ's full message – "I will have mercy, and not sacrifice" (Matt. 9:13) – how can it represent the One who died in order to make God's message clear?

Today, thousands of years later, we are just beginning to comprehend what God said through the prophets about sacrifice. Yet, in their own time, their messages were stunningly clear. Yahweh was not abolishing all sacrifice, but was pleading that its abuse be stopped and its truest meaning understood. Jesus and the prophets insisted that rituals were empty and were an abomination, unless the whole self was offered with them. Finally, sacrifice must not destroy, ignore, or abuse life so graciously given by the Creator.

Now we know that life was not given by God to be destroyed for God. We perceive that God does not have to be lured into giving us more grace when what we need is already waiting to be received. With relief, we realize that sacrifice can be the eager and loving self-sharing of the Spirit that gives us life.

Someday, beyond the glass that now seems dark, we will see and we will know what God has been trying to reveal for a very long time. We are loved. We are claimed. We are forgiven, included, healed, freed, and given hope. The arms of the Cross reach out through all time and every circumstance to tell us so (I Cor. 13:8-13).

CHAPTER 7

SALVATION THEOLOGY THROUGH HISTORY
The Devil, God, and Us

Jesus was paying the Devil for human freedom by dying on the Cross. That was the theology of the early church as taught by the Alexandrian, Origen (185–254), and it lasted until the twelfth century. Some who followed Origen inserted their own modifications.[127] Nevertheless, they all contended that Satan had become the ruler of the world at the fall, so he was the one from whom humankind must be freed. Even though some of Origen's teachings later were considered heretical, amazingly this doctrine – perhaps the most important one of all those he taught – was retained.

Stories of Christ and the devil began to appear after that. Gregory of Nyssa (d. 395) wrote that God tricked the Devil into losing his authority. Pope Gregory the Great (d. 603) told a story repeated by Martin Luther (1483–1546) nine hundred years later. Gregory saw God as a fisherman who baited the hook with the body of Christ! When the Devil bit, Luther says, "Christ (stuck) in his gills." The Devil choked, and was "taken captive by Christ." (One can't help but ask: "Then what happened? What did Christ do with the Devil?) In between the repeated tellings of this bizarre tale, Peter the Lombard (1100–1160) made up his own. He imagined the Cross as a mousetrap, baited for the Devil with Christ's blood.[128] The trap worked, and the Devil was overcome.[129, 130]

Do such anecdotes indicate that the devil was "killed" or just impermanently injured? No one today would take those stories seriously. Perhaps their fanciful nature is a way of joking about evil and the devil. But they do us little good when our concern about pervasive, worldwide depravity is so deep. They deflect the real issue.

Important Contributions of Eastern Orthodoxy
In those early days of the Christian Church, the Eastern Orthodox played a primary role. The Fathers and Mothers of the Desert, following the hermetic example of Anthony, the first known solitary (251–356),

numbered in the thousands, living in huge monasteries that populated the Egyptian desert. Anthony, himself, left the desert twice: once to found an order of hermits who would live under a simple rule and, later, to oppose Arius and his beliefs, declared heretical, regarding the full divinity of Jesus as the Christ.[131]

With the split between the Roman Catholic Church in the West and the Orthodox Church in the East in 1054, most Orthodox spirituality and theology was dropped by the Catholic church. The Protestant church has followed suit. This is a great loss. Eastern Orthodox views often seem to contain a corrective that western Christianity would find to be a relief and a blessing. Orthodox spirituality and theology serve as a much needed and natural bridge between the religions of the East and West. Furthermore, the Eastern church does not separate nature and grace as Lutheran and Roman Catholic theology are inclined to do. In still other instances, Orthodox theology offers a deep enrichment to the Christian denominations of the West, depending more on spiritual experience than on abstract logic.

In one case in particular, the offering of Eastern Orthodoxy has, for the West, brought a stunning addition to Christian theology. That addition has everything to do with salvation, but it takes no cognizance of payment either to the devil or to God. Rather, it is a theology of spiritual experience called *theosis*, the power of God to change human nature from the inside out. Letting go of power, pleasure, position, and possessions, the life of the Holy Spirit becomes incarnate in human beings. The Spirit transforms them so that they become more Christlike, living to bless the world and awaken people to the immanent reality of God. Among Eastern Orthodox theologians, Irenaeus (d. 200) and Athanasius (d. 373) focused deeply on this experience, which might be best described by the Apostle Paul in II Corinthians 3:17-18:

> Now the Lord is the Spirit, and where the Spirit of the Lord is, there is freedom. And all of us, with unveiled faces, seeing the glory of the Lord as though reflected in a mirror, are being transformed into the same image from one degree of glory to another; for this comes from the Lord, the Spirit.

From that time until today, the concept of theosis has been treasured in Orthodox spirituality. In the West, the same understanding was strong, but often misunderstood, in the writings and sermons of the Dominican mystic, Meister (or "Master") Eckhart (1270–1327) and those who followed him. Among all those who taught theosis, we find some form of the same statement: "*God became man that man might become God.*"[132]

That startling sentence sounds like heresy when one first hears it. However, I see it as an attempt to explain what the West calls *sanctification*, which, in simplest terms, means growing closer to God and becoming more and more like Christ. We are drawn by God, who is Spirit.[133] Gradually we can let go of the mass of self-centered desires that hold us back from true love and give our lives, as Jesus did, to embody the nature of God in human terms. Luther called it: "being little christs."[134] Others would explain it as participation in the life of the Spirit. For the Orthodox, theosis is the greatest of all gifts to human beings before passing into eternal life.

In the late twentieth century, the understanding of theosis became a major emphasis of Finnish Lutheran theology, due to previous conversations between Lutheran and Orthodox theologians in Finland. These conversations have led many American Lutheran scholars to agree that Luther wrote affirmatively about theosis. My perception differs. Luther spoke a great deal about *union* with God (*henosis*). Theosis (deification) is a much stronger term. It is very likely to be misunderstood (as it was in the case of Meister Eckhart),[135] and therefore, misused.

Today, respect for Finnish Lutheran research into Eastern Orthodoxy has helped immeasurably in understanding spirituality. Western systematic theology has long lacked the dimension of spirituality taken for granted in Eastern Orthodox institutions. Theology in the West is more objective, and frequently prides itself on being so. Systematic theology deals with the theological understanding of God, Christ, the Holy Spirit, the Church, worship, and morality, each subject building on the previous one. Western seminaries today would find it useful to integrate all systematic theology courses with a correct and healthy understanding of spirituality from a scholarly and practiced point of view. Such an approach is essential because *spirituality – the experience of God – is the heart of religion, not theology, which describes it.*

Theological description of theosis speaks of the experience as a growing subjective response to the saving love of God through the Holy Spirit. Theosis deals with what can happen inside people, on soul level. On the other hand, Anselm's writings on the meaning of Jesus' death were focused on an objective theological explanation of why the Cross was necessary, how it saved God's honor, and saved human beings from eternal damnation. Anselm was teaching about something that happened, not only *for* us, but was offered *to* us. Unlike the view of theosis, his soteriology was not concerned with the interior spiritual lives of those who came to know God through Jesus. That is not true for the theologian who followed him: Peter Abelard.

Peter Abelard: Another View
Radically different from Anselm, Peter Abelard (1079–1142) was born while Anselm was alive. Abelard "sought to prove the impossibility of [answering the need for] satisfaction" of God's injured honor. Instead, he claimed, the crucifixion was God's love made visible, arousing the human heart to respond.[136] That is the very point of this book.

The theologian, Eugene Fairweather, has stated it clearly:

> In opposition to the Anselmian model, Abelard reasons that since human beings were incapable of paying an infinite debt to God, the purpose of the incarnation must not be the payment of anything to anyone. Rather, he understands the incarnation to be the ultimate revelation of God's love for humanity.... In the Abelardian view, reconciliation between God and human beings – that is, atonement[137] – is brought about by love, the love of God that Jesus the Christ perfectly embodies. This love is so potent that when human beings encounter it, we are actually inspired to emulate it, to love God as Jesus loved God, and to love one another as Jesus loves us. The event of atonement, then, is an event of creative love: God created the universe out of love; God became incarnate in Jesus out of love; and in and through the incarnation, God elicits from human beings a responsive love.[138]

It is regrettable that, until now, so few have even heard of Abelard's theology. It is nothing short of dismissive and misleading that so many theologians have repeatedly called it "the moral view" as though it was simply an incentive to follow another law. Much of Abelard's other work was on ethics, but I do not see ethics as part of his exposition of the theology of the Cross. His understanding was probably the most inspired interpretation of the Crucifixion given by any of the major theologians in the Middle Ages. Among the scholars I have investigated who wrote before the twentieth century, Abelard is the only one who focused on the Cross as causing a compelling human response to overwhelming divine love.

Over time, those who followed Abelard seemed to forget about him and to focus back on the work of Anselm, both agreeing and disagreeing with each other on particulars of Anselm's work, but nevertheless, propounding the essence of what he had to say. His theory was cemented into the theology of the Roman and Protestant arms of the Church for nine hundred years. Even Martin Luther was not able to change that. In the last fifty years, a number of outstanding theologians have attempted to point out that Anselm has been misleading. (See the quotation section at the end of the book.) But they have not been effectively heard.

Gustav Aulén, Martin Luther, and His Followers

Closer to our own time, in the twentieth century, the Swedish Bishop, Gustav Aulén, wrote in his book, *Christus Victor*, about three major theologies of salvation throughout Christian history. He discussed the work of both Anselm and Abelard and then turned to Luther. Aulén claims that, to Luther, *Christ's sacrifice was not propitiatory. It did not appease God.* God's love and grace were too certain. Luther's opinion here is in agreement with Abelard. According to Aulén, Protestant Orthodoxy's legalistic view has stood in contrast to what Aulén considers to be Luther's "*fundamental thought*, that Law is in one aspect a tyrant and an enemy from whose power Christ came to set men free." In the present day Church, this understanding, says Aulén, "is altogether *lost*."[139] (author's emphasis) It is law, of course – the forensic view – that insists on payment for debt.

Aulén blames Philipp Melancthon and Lutheran Orthodoxy for their "complete incapacity" to grasp Luther's understanding of atonement. He says: "Without hesitation and without delay they reverted to the Latin (Anselmian) doctrine."[140]

Paul Tillich faults Melanchthon for forming the forensic doctrine of justification, and makes this assessment: "He compared God with a judge who releases a guilty one ... simply because he decides to do so." Then Tillich replaces Melancthon's view with his own: "[We] ... must accept that [we are] accepted [by God].... Without this, there would be no salvation, but only despair."[141]

It was Melancthon's view of God as judge that emphasized the concept of *justification*, a term long held at the heart of Lutheran theology. Today, many Christians would welcome a new, more contemporary, and more accurate word for *justification*. It cannot help but bear the connotation of "making a person just" even though it is often explained as "treating sinners as though they were innocent." But why bother with such an explanation if, following our repentance, we can accept God's love and receive forgiveness? The forensic or lawful approach, used to explain Anselm and Melanchthon, teaches that human beings are forgiven for the sake of Jesus, who substituted for them on the Cross and has taken their place in the divine court of justice. Yet if God has always wanted to forgive us, to allow us to live consciously and eternally in the divine Presence, God did not need to contrive the Crucifixion to do so. We are loved. We are accepted. In fact, we are claimed. These terms are words of grace. And grace is the essence of God.

Luther and his followers have explained that sin, death, the devil, law, divine curse, and God's wrath are overcome on the Cross by the nature of God who is Love. This is the favored view of Aulén who called it "*Christus victor.*" But how could such a comment be made? Sin, death, and the law have been appallingly present in the world since the Crucifixion! They pervaded Luther's world as well. Tillich considered Luther's concept so far "above our heads" as to have no meaning in our lives.[142] Clearly, we don't experience the effects that Luther is claiming. Thankfully, Eastern Orthodoxy clarifies and responds to Luther's view by simply saying that human beings "are no longer *captive* to death or sin."[143]

In regard to salvation theology, the Orthodox have propounded that "there is no identifiable party that demanded the sacrifice or ransom of Christ." They "renounce the principle that the sacrifice of the Son is in any way demanded by the Father." Furthermore, they regret the "distortion [of] 'substitutionary' theories of atonement:[144] the theory that Jesus substitutes for us in paying for our sins since he is pure and we are not." When Mark Heim mentions that the Orthodox "never incorporated [Anselm's] doctrine as an important feature of its theology," he adds: "One major stream of Christianity managed without such a teaching for all of its history."[145] Good Friday is important in the Eastern Church and is celebrated in a dramatic way, but the theology of Easter, if anything, is enhanced. For the Orthodox, many of whom have lived under persecution for centuries, "Christ is risen indeed!" and "death no longer has the final word."[146] An Easter eve in the Orthodox cathedral in Moscow will convince anyone that Easter is the greatest day of celebration in the Eastern Church.

Luther writes that it is God's love that has overcome sin and death. But God, who is Love, was present in the world before the Crucifixion. If it were God's love alone that has been needed, we should note that it has never been missing! The crux of the matter is that God's love often has not been recognized or perceived, let alone welcomed and received. Religious people have been too busy worshipping the Almighty, the powerful, and asking for help and forgiveness. Anselm was so caught up in the forensics of justice, it is no wonder he never appeared to dwell on Jesus' compelling, overwhelming message of love. In fact, people didn't seem to be much aware of a God of love either in Jesus' time or in Anselm's. And God's love is not nearly as important in any ancient scripture as it is in the story of Jesus.

When Luther comments that God, who is Love, overcomes sin and death, his words need to be understood in a personal, not a universal, context. It has always been true that, when the Spirit of holy love is welcomed into any human heart, that heart is won and responds. Then Luther's comment makes sense. Evil is defeated in that heart, at that time, even if not in the world.

Luther writes further: "Insofar as Christ rules in the hearts of the faithful, there is found no more sin, death, and curse."[147] He is making clear that when Christ rules our souls, the power of God as Spirit is alive within us. It overwhelms the destructive power of darkness – sin, death, and curse. Salvation is not just a gift to us through a historical happening: salvation occurs inside us! (Again the understanding of Abelard and the

Orthodox appears.) This inner salvation is a sense of God's claim upon us that changes us: our attitudes, our trust, our goals, our lives. Destructive sacrifice will surely never bring that about. The message of scripture is then clear. The heart's door can be opened only through grace received by us. We are "saved by grace through faith" (Eph. 2:8).

The Church has been careless about using this complete sentence. Without *both* grace and faith there is no fullness of life in God. Yet we are told that we are healed or saved by faith as Mark 5:35 seems to indicate, saying: "Your faith has made you well." But Jesus used those words after God had already offered healing through him. His answer meant: "Your receptivity has made you well." We are also likely to err in the opposite direction, saying: "It is all up to God" as could be indicated in Philippians 4:6: "Do not worry about anything." or Jesus' reference to the lilies of the field in Luke 12: 29-30: "Do not keep striving ... and worrying. For ... your Father knows [what] you need." Neither statement says what the quote from Ephesians says. Without God, nothing is possible. Without our receptivity to God's grace, we are powerless. We are to receive the gift. Otherwise, why should God give it? Let's put it this way: no one can get a suntan without being in the sun. The sun is a gift; standing in its rays is a response, a choice.

There is caution in Luther's statement about God's inner presence: "Insofar as Christ rules in the hearts of the faithful." His first word is "insofar." He is not saying that a person can attain a perfect state that lasts forever, as many spiritual manuals (especially medieval writings) seem to imply. Life in the Spirit moves and changes. It is fluid and dynamic and not to be taken for granted. Christ's gracious rule within us is fostered by our continual openness and recommitment. It is only grace that gives us the ability to respond with self-discipline, depending on God when life is demanding, overwhelming, and we are tired or in pain.

In most lives, there are "dark nights of the soul" when we find ourselves in an arid spiritual desert as did the Prodigal.[148] It is the deepest of spiritual privations. The sensation is that we are utterly alone with no guidance and no power. Only later may we realize that there was One sustaining our living, continuous relationship and waiting for our return to the consciousness of nourishing grace. Luther writes that our union with God is kept because of God's faithfulness.[149]

The twentieth century Swedish-American theologian, Edgar M. Carlson, wrote mid-century about Swedish interpreters of Luther. They quoted Luther as saying: "As a guide for conduct, the law is good," for it expresses God's will, "but as a way of salvation, it is a tyrant."[150] Of course, if law were a way of salvation, good works must be done to fulfill the law and please God. That supposition is anathema to Luther.[151]

Aulén perceived that the book of Hebrews, the Fathers of the Church, and Luther held the "classic view" of the Crucifixion, emphasizing Paul's teaching of Christ's reconciliation of the world to God (as presented in II Corinthians 5:19–20). For Luther, God was both "making the sacrifice and receiving it."[152]

Aulén remonstrates that the twentieth century Swiss theologian Emil Brunner (d.1966), coming four hundred years after Luther, taught that law was "the essential basis of man's relation to God."[153] Between Luther and Brunner came the Enlightenment theologians whose conviction was wholly different. They said that "it was intolerable that God should be thought of as needing to be propitiated through a satisfaction offered to Him." For them, Jesus' death was the ultimate act of reconciliation. Furthermore, "as far as God was concerned, no atonement [meaning *payment* in this case] was needed."

However, sometimes the sermons, liturgies, and hymns of the Tridium (from Good Friday to Easter morning) especially, attest to another negative and confusing emphasis. The *Exultet* of the Easter Vigil of liturgical churches says: "Father, to ransom a slave, you gave away your Son. O happy fault, O necessary sin of Adam, which gained for us so great a Redeemer!"[154, 155] Wouldn't Adam and Eve be surprised to know that their "original sin" turned out to be necessary in order to bring Jesus to earth? Wouldn't they be amazed to hear their terrible error was really a "happy fault"? And what would Augustine think, since he named and fostered the theology of original sin?

Put theology to music and it locks into our consciousness without our thinking about it. Until we clearly replace Anselm's thought with a more insightful understanding of sacrifice – until that change becomes more prominent in our hymns, prayers, sermons, and especially our liturgies – we will miss the magnitude of God's love and the inspiration of its gift of freedom.

Believers have generally accepted the theologies of their authorities. But they have sometimes been distracted from basic questions about the Crucifixion and have focused on "Who killed Jesus?" or "How much did Jesus suffer?" Jesus' followers, and today's media, often have turned the Crucifixion into a matter of accusation and blame, when, for Jesus, it was just the opposite! Such a response silences his message, voiced to his torturers and murderers in the very midst of his agony: "Father, forgive them, for they do not know what they are doing" (Luke 23:34). To blame all following generations of Jews for killing Jesus is to completely disregard this prayer of Jesus and the inherent message of the Crucifixion. After all, it is likely that only Romans and Jews were present that day. To whom else would Jesus have spoken? If Jesus forgave, then and there, why are Jews (but not Italians) still persecuted today?[156]

That unconquerable and unconditional love of Christ on the Cross was meant not only to be witnessed, but to be received, then and forevermore (John 1:12). Jesus' action was more than a sight and more than a statement. It was an invitation, a call to respond down through the centuries, a call to receive forgiveness and grace and to love passionately – just as Jesus did (John 13:34).

Every religion in the world has been deeply involved in sacrifice, but the motivation and understanding of sacrifice has most certainly varied from a self-centered spirituality ("What's in it for me?") to a self-giving in love and gratitude ("Love so amazing, so divine, demands my soul, my life, my all.").[157]

Never-ending Questions About Sacrifice

Must life be destroyed to show our love for God? How can we destroy life in the name of the one who gave it? Might we, instead, *use* life for God, rather than destroy it on an altar, in imprisonment, in a "holy" war, or in some ascetic practice?

Might one type of sacrifice be more appropriate than another? Will individuals be closer to God by taking vows of poverty, chastity, and obedience? Have kamikaze and terrorists with bombs strapped to their bodies really gone straight to heaven as they believed? Can anyone follow the repentant thief on the Cross, with nothing but an open, eager heart?

Will Sacrifice Insure Salvation?

Why do people sacrifice? Is it done out of a sense of duty or because it is expected? Is it to prove one's devotion? Is it to cleanse the soul, or to be "good enough" for God, or to live up to one's own self-image? Is it, to gain a reward, or to appear saintly or superior, even if it is never admitted, especially to ourselves?

Is sacrifice simply a natural occurrence for those we love and care for? Is it an expected and accepted part of everyday life, being married, raising children, following a profession, or allowing God to speak and work through us in any circumstance?

Do we sacrifice because we feel another's pain: because no one should live sick and poor, unnoticed and defenseless, misunderstood or perniciously maligned, and alone? Is it because we can envision another life for them, and we passionately want to make it come true?

To answer these questions, we may need to disagree with respected and beloved authority figures and even with our family and friends. We may also disagree with our former selves. We may have to find a wisdom we have not known. But we can learn and love and disagree, all at the same time.

All of Jesus' Life As Sacrifice

What, then, do we perceive in Jesus? All of Jesus' days seem to have been filled with the second kind of sacrifice, a willing gift, outpoured to offer life far beyond that which we now know (Phil. 2:7).

Chapter 8

FROM ANCIENT BLOOD SACRIFICE TO GIVING THE SELF

Propitiation to Gelassenheit

A major effort of this book has been to provide the scope needed to comprehend the flow or evolution of sacrificial practice in Judeo-Christian history and then to relate it to the death of Christ.

According to the earliest records of the Ancient Near East, even gods allowed themselves to be ritually sacrificed. We read of the people of Canaan who worshipped the vegetation-god, Mot, who died to "give Man sustenance, the material bread of life." Those formerly migrant people, new to farming, observed how a single seed multiplied when sown. They had no science of agriculture, but they could conceive that if the gods gave life, then perhaps the sacrificed life of a god might offer the greatest nourishment to their fields. In this very early story, we encounter the phrase, "the bread of life," which Christians use to speak of divine life offered through the material bread of communion. The Christian concept is not far from eating grain produced abundantly because of a god's nourishing, sacrificial death.

Ancient stories are told of a son of god who was sacrificed as well. He was the son of the god Danel, divine offspring of the ancient El.[158] It was El whose name evolved into Elohim, and it was Elohim who was known as God by the author of the first chapter of Genesis and other *priestly* passages in the Torah.[159] Near the climax of the Crucifixion, it was El or Eli upon whom Jesus is said to have called in his cry of abandonment: "Eli, Eli, lama sabachthani?" (Matt. 27:46). "My God, my God, why have you forsaken me?" is the usual translation.

In the eleventh century BCE, Israel's first prophet, Samuel, was born. Since he was not the first-born of his father (who had two wives), he escaped the custom of child sacrifice. But Samuel was the first-born of his mother Hannah, who had waited and wept for years because she was childless. After his birth, she delayed expressing her deep gratitude to God until he was weaned. Then, with her husband's consent, she took

Samuel to the house of the Lord at Shiloh saying: "I have lent him to the Lord. As long as he lives, he is lent to the Lord" (I Sam. 1:28). Some children so offered eventually were "passed through the fire," as the Semites said, but not Samuel. Hannah's intention was honored. Samuel's life was offered to be used *by* God, not destroyed *for* God.

Abraham and Isaac

In Hebrew scripture, the account of Abraham's near-sacrifice of his son Isaac has become what the writer Judah Goldin calls "the very nerve center of Judaism and Christianity" ("and Islam," others would rightly add).[160] For centuries, the story has been the centerpiece of critical discussion of child sacrifice for Jews, Christians, and Muslims.

In brief, the story in Genesis 22, is that Abraham believed he had been told by God to sacrifice his "only" son by binding him upon an altar they were to build together. He was to kill the boy with a knife and then burn his body. But as Abraham raised the knife, an angel called to him from heaven, telling him he must not do the deed and should substitute a ram entangled by its horns in a nearby thicket.

The Qur'an mentions the account briefly but does not provide the details found in Genesis 22.[161] Yet both Islam and Judaism have more than made up for unrecorded details. Writers of Jewish *midrash* and Muslim *tafsîr* (theological commentary usually in story form) have all imagined what happened: the torment that must have been in Abraham's soul; the first and final questions from the innocent Isaac; how far the father went in beginning to sacrifice his son; what Sarah, Abraham's wife, may have suspected; and how she met the news of what had almost happened. One *tafsîr* has Abraham testing his wife, telling her that he did slaughter their son. Sarah, unable to bear the news, instantly dies in agony.[162]

Why would God command such an action and then stop it? Had Abraham not heard correctly? Was it an awful test? Numerous commentaries suggest that God's plan was to test Abraham, and Muslims emphasize that point of view. Many accept it, but there is certainly room to question such a supposition. If God knows human hearts, God does not need any further information. For Abraham, however, it was the ultimate opportunity to surrender to God's will, to completely commit himself to God.

In the *tafarsîr*,[163] Abraham asks Isaac if he is willing to surrender to the sacrifice, and Isaac tells his father that he must follow the will of God. One story says that Abraham cannot bear to accomplish the deed, so Isaac suggests that he blindfold himself. That done, the father plunges downward with the knife. But, tearing off the blindfold, he discovers the carcass of a goat beneath his hand and his son, standing beside it, smiling. Thus both father and son submitted to what they believed was the will of God.[164]

The heart of Islamic response to the Divine will is to surrender. Together, the concepts of surrender and peace form the definition of the word "Islam." And the position of a Muslim in prayer is intended to be one of surrender and submission even as the body is folded in submission in the womb. In comparison, a Christian cannot help but remember the words of Christ praying in the Garden of Gethsemane: "My Father, if it is possible, let this cup pass from me; yet not what I want, but what you want" (Matt. 26:39).

Of course, even though Genesis 22 refers to Isaac as the "only" son three times, we know that designation was not correct. Ishmael, the son of Sarah's maid, Hagar, was Abraham's first-born. And it was he who became the father of the Arabs. Abraham, eighty-six at Ishmael's birth, was one hundred when Isaac was born of Sarah. But when, because of Sarah's jealousy, Ishmael and Hagar were sent into the wilderness, Isaac certainly became the preferred son, the primary child, and doubtless, even more beloved.

The story often has been used as a prefiguring and a comparison to the death of Jesus. But as such, it is greatly inadequate from my point of view. John 3:16-17 says "God so loved the world that he sent his only son into the world … so that the world might be saved." Jesus has been known as God's only son, but Isaac was not Abraham's only son. Furthermore, Isaac's death would not have offered life to the whole world as the death of Jesus is believed to have done.

As reward for his obedience, Abraham was told by God that he was worthy to become the father of a great people, in numbers as vast as there were stars in the sky and sands upon the seashore (Gen. 22:16, 17). Evidently, the trial had been a question of obedience to God, not one of common sense or responsible human love. If the revered words were more than an accounting of history, one might wonder how much these important points were emphasized at the cost of factual details.

We now know that Hebrew scripture makes it plain that God's stern command through the Prophets later in history was to stop child sacrifice. Had God's mind changed? Or had the Israelites, formerly incapable of being different from every culture they knew, found it impossible to conceive of a merciful God such as the Later Prophets introduced to them? Were they simply not ready for a God of love?

We also know that God's perceived commands were not always followed. However, the concept of redemption eventually evolved to mean a bloodless payment. In excavations in the Middle East, the deeper layers at sites for sacrifice contain the bones of children. But the more recent, higher levels contain the bones of lambs that were substituted. Because a lamb was sacrificed twice daily in the temple, and because lamb is the primary food at the Passover meal, we can understand the symbolism of the first Jewish Christians in referring to Jesus as "the Lamb of God."

Today, it seems apparent that the story of Abraham may have at least three purposes:

- God is teaching: "You shall have no other loves before me. Nothing should separate us: no person, no desire, no future hope, no commitment, not even your cherished child."
- The ritual of child sacrifice that became law provided the ultimate opportunity to surrender to the will of God.
- Abraham, who wanted so desperately to do God's will, was stopped from the slaughter of his precious son and heir.

Many scholars have agreed that this must be a teaching story intended to stop child sacrifice in ancient Israel. That would mean it was more than history; it was a myth containing historical characters. Yet ancient people actually followed the practice of sacrificing first-born sons for many years after Abraham's day. For some early Jewish Christians, it would have been natural to compare the death of "God's only begotten son" to those former days of child sacrifice and to forget how strongly the practice had been condemned by Yahweh through the Prophets.

The agony of such a practice is expressed through the prophet Micah. Today we can read the haunting words of a devoted mother torn to pieces by the ancient understanding of the will of God. She cries:

> With what shall I come before the Lord. Shall I give my
> first-born for my transgression, the fruit of my body for
> the sin of my soul? (Micah 6:7)

What ghastly practices humans are capable of when they are convinced of an idea the community considers "holy!" What torture it was for that mother who, unlike Hannah, had not been allowed to find another way to give her child to God. We have every right to ask if it was done to honor God, or for fear of God, or fear that one's tribe would make a non-compliant member an outcast.

By the time of Jesus' birth, another prescribed ritual had replaced immolation of the first-born son. As poor people, Mary and Joseph were able to fulfill their duty to God by offering a pair of doves in gratitude for the birth of Jesus.

Except for Hannah's gift of Samuel, all of the sacrifices described above bear a quality of bargaining. The Latin term is *do ut des*. It means: "I'll give to you if you give to me," and it addresses God. No wonder some sacrifices were so extravagant, with hundreds, even thousands of animals slain! *Do ut des* was simply tit-for-tat, a divine back-scratching, polishing the apple.[165]

How strange to try to convince God of our love and our goodness. God is supposed to know our hearts even better than we know ourselves. But most of the time we don't seem to remember or comprehend that truth. We act as though God will bless us according to our devotion or for the quality or quantity of our gifts. Unfortunately, Anselm and we are still stuck in the story of Cain and Abel, who were said to offer unequal sacrifices. God was said to consider Cain's sacrifice not as good as Abel's (Gen. 4:4). That viewpoint, extended in regard to Jesus, becomes: God will bless us, forgive us, heal us, love and claim us forever because Christ, the only perfect and most costly gift, was given for our sake. Such a viewpoint makes salvation a bargain with God and makes the quality and cost of the gift the most important aspect of sacrifice instead of the loving, given will.

In Luther's time, both peasants and nobility paid the Church to obtain favors from God, particularly for a more speedy exit from purgatory to heaven for themselves and their loved ones. In return they were granted *indulgences,* supposedly God-given dispensations by which God indulged those who paid according to how much money they had given. Although Luther surely knew the funds were sent to Rome to build St. Peter's Basilica, his great anger against selling indulgences was largely based on his concept of grace: heaven is God's gift. It is not paid for with money or good works.

Today, most of the Christian Church finds the practice of paying for indulgences abhorrent. Yet the stunning and disturbing reality is this: If, as Anselm contends, the Cross was Jesus' means of paying our way to heaven, it was simply *the greatest indulgence payment the world has ever seen.*

Positive Sacrifice

The other point of view regarding the meaning of sacrifice was expressed by the remarkable English writer and retreat leader Evelyn Underhill. In her book, *Worship*, she wrote: "Sacrifice is a positive act. Its essence is something given; not something given up. It is a freewill offering, the self-giving of the creature to its God."[166]

This is a profound understanding. Micah, Amos, Hosea and some of the psalms spoke of sacrifice that way long ago. But we have largely overlooked their words. Some of those canonized as saints have missed the point completely, as their exaggerated asceticism and the ruin of their bodies have shown. Yet Underhill's keen insight about the significance of sacrifice is simple and clear. Her interpretation applied to the meaning of the death of Jesus is at the very heart of the difference between the two theologies we have been comparing. "Something given up" is a theology of literal redemption (payment), but "something given" is the response of grateful love to salvation as God's gift.

There are those of us who passionately desire to give everything to God. But the great challenge is to know how to do it. Which type of sacrifice will we offer? The words of Mark 8:34-37 (NTP-IV) have been an exceedingly strong challenge to later generations. Mark quotes Jesus as saying:

> If any want to become my followers, let them deny themselves and take up their cross and follow me. For those who want to save their life will lose it, and those who lose their life for my sake, and for the

sake of the gospel, will save it. For what will it profit them to gain the whole world and forfeit their life? Indeed, what can they give in return for their life?

It is important to read the words about self-denial with less emphasis upon denial and more upon the self. In saying "Let them deny them*selves*," Jesus surely was pleading, not for self-deprivation and self-destruction, but for the forsaking of small-minded *self-centeredness*, and He was asking us to give all we are and to consecrate all we have to God's use, but not to destroy ourselves or our possessions

With Jesus' challenge before us, we make our own decisions Some may choose the vowed life of priests and nuns, the dedicated life of true parents, or the loving life of one who wants to be a blessing to the world. Yet sometimes, lacking discernment or full self-knowledge, people may neglect family, health, and responsibility, believing their actions prove devotion to God. But what kind of god needs proof? Who, other than ourselves, is more responsible for our families or our own health?

Some choose asceticism. Often it is understood as sacrificial self-denial. But true asceticism is literally "training" (*ascesis*), living a healthful, disciplined lifestyle such as an athlete must do. It does not mean to spurn the world or to ignore the nourishment of human love or necessary food. As Jesus clearly showed us, the passion for God is intimately attached to the passion for humanity and the earth, rather than a denial of either.

Blind to deeper, unperceived motives, however, a person may choose a vocation that seems *spiritual*, one that appears to serve God. Yet the choice can be made without realizing that unconsciously it has been done to gain prestige and power or even to convince ourselves that we are *good* and *worthy*.

The misreading of "Let them deny themselves" has been an enormous factor in misunderstanding sacrifice. There have been dedicated people who have destroyed their bodies. And some, alone in the desert, have gone mad. St. Francis is said to have confessed, as he was dying, that perhaps he had gone too far in self-denial, sleeping upon the ground where the rats were often his companions. He had done it in great devotion, not realizing it might not be necessary or wise.[167]

To deny ourselves blessings and comforts God created for our use can come close to self-idolatry. We are willing to do almost anything to become good. That seems to me to be self-worship. But it is a worship of which we are unaware, and it can be confused with or mixed with genuine love of God. The appearance of righteousness can come from self-denial, but genuine goodness simply happens as a result of loving – the Spirit acting within us. The selves we try so hard to deny are the *only gifts* we can truly give to God or to anyone else.

God's Kenosis Mirrored in Gelassenheit

In *The Mystery of Sacrifice*, Underhill spoke of positive sacrifice not only as giving but also as *self*-offering. Quoting Augustine, she said: "It is you who lie upon the altar," meaning that we are called to give ourselves when we give our offerings.[168] Hebrew Scripture mentions this self-offering in several ways: as the sacrifice of thanksgiving; as the offering of a broken or contrite heart (that is, a repentant, humbled heart); and as a joyous free-will offering (not prescribed by religious law).

Such sacrifice has nothing to do with spiritual tit-for-tat. It is an offering of love, freely given. There is no coercion, no payoff. There is just a responsive heart. Instead of asking God for future favors, these offerings are a living acknowledgment of the life and love that God already has given. The anxiety of "being good enough," of always obeying the appropriate rules and measuring up to honored but exterior standards, is simply removed. A new kind of freedom becomes possible.

We are reminded of the meaning of the old, almost forgotten term, *Gelassenheit*: a giving of one's whole self to do the will of the Spirit who lives within us and wants to burst its bonds. It proclaims "Yes" to a God whom we can trust forever. *Gelassenheit* is the human response to God's kenosis in Jesus, understood here not just as Jesus' self-emptying, but as God's simultaneous self-giving through him. In the inspired human response, love and life are poured out for God and the world. Thus God's Spirit in Jesus, in letting go and giving, is mirrored in human letting go and self-giving. It is a long way from propitiation.

One excellent example of *Gelassenheit* is described in Philippians 3:4-14. Following the classic description of kenosis in the previous chapter, Paul proclaims his own dramatic and life-changing response.

Formerly a proud Pharisee, he lists the accomplishments for which he had previously given his life. Then he relinquishes all of them. This man, who claimed that "according to righteousness under the law" he had been "blameless," forthrightly says that all of his former earthly and spiritual attainments were rubbish, deserving to be dumped. "Leaving *everything* behind" was his only intention and his inestimable privilege when he chose to follow God's call in Christ. Jesus' kenosis became the inspiration for Paul to leave everything. Jesus' self-giving fired Paul's soul to do the same.

Thus far, in observing the evolution of sacrifice, a great deal of ground has been covered. Beginning with propitiation – sacrifice to pay for sin – we have moved to God's kenosis through Christ for the sake of the world's healing. Now we have come to the fervent human desire to pour out, in response, what God has given us: a fullness of self-giving we have called *Gelassenheit*.

In Matthew (9:13; 12:6-7) challengers asked Jesus why his disciples did not keep the law by making sacrifices. Attempting to teach the transformation of traditional practices, Jesus responded by saying: "Something greater than the temple is here," that is, something greater than the laws and practices of the temple and the priests. Then, speaking boldly for God, he pointedly added these words from Hosea 6:6: "I desire steadfast love and not sacrifice, the knowledge of God [a relationship with God] rather than burnt offering."

With even stronger emotion, Amos heatedly declared for God:

> I hate, I despise your festivals, and the offerings of ... your fatted
> animals, I will not look upon. But let justice roll down like waters,
> and righteousness like everflowing streams." (5:21, 24)

Isaiah spoke just as accusingly and cuttingly:

> What to me is the multitude of your sacrifices? ...
> Bringing offerings is futile ...
> Your hands are full of blood! (1:11, 13, 15).

But later, in Isaiah 43:25, God assures us: "I, I am He who blots out your transgressions for my own sake and I will not remember your sins." This tender God is addressed in the words of a worshipper in Psalm 40:6, 8: "Sacrifice and offering you do not desire, but you have given me an open ear ... I delight to do your will.... Your law is within my heart."[169] Paul, when writing Romans, realized that there is something more to sacrifice than payment and pleads that we offer all we are to be God's vessels:

> I appeal to you, therefore, ... to present your bodies as a
> living sacrifice, holy and acceptable to God. (Rom. 12:1)

Luther's comments sum up what we have said about positive sacrifice.

> The true sacrifice to God is not something outside us or
> belonging to us nor something temporal or for the moment,
> but it is we ourselves, forever.... As Proverbs 23:26 says:
> "My son, give me your heart."[171]

Moreover, Luther writes: "All Christians are priests.... The sacrifices they offer are their own selves."[172]

CHAPTER 9

REDEMPTION VERSUS SALVATION
To Purchase or to Heal

The Unconscious Effect of the Root Meaning of Words

All words have a root meaning from which they are derived. Over time some have veered toward a related but rather different sense. Others have evolved into words that seem to have no similarity and may even be defined as being opposite. In other cases, one word may morph into another until the two become synonyms.

The two words, *redemption* and *salvation*, in our time, are often used as synonyms. We are inclined to use them interchangeably. But, at root, they are very different.

Redemption – Payment for Freedom and Forgiveness

The original meaning of redemption has lingered in Christian theology without leaving its fingerprints.

Redemption means the act of buying back or ransoming. In ancient Israel, it frequently referred to paying for the freedom of a slave. It was a legal transaction, a requirement. Freedom was not possible without it.[173]

The meaning of redemption evolved. It came to mean paying God in order to wipe away human sin.[174] Propitiatory sacrifices were offered for that purpose. Redemption became one concept behind the legal idea of justice. As a society we now believe that people should "pay" for their crimes, and we have enacted laws to ensure that they do so. It is natural to surmise that the original meaning has influenced our present understanding of justice.

Salvation – Good or Bad

The word salvation has different roots than does redemption. "The concept can trace its lineage to the Sanskrit word sarvah [uninjured, intact, whole].... The root, *sar*, became *sal* in the Latin languages."[175] The Latin *salvus* means to be healed, to be made whole. Only in the thirteenth century did the word salvation (not the concept) become associated with the notion of the soul being *saved* from sin or from the loss of God. And by mid-thirteenth century, usage included being saved (rescued) from captivity, from physical danger, from a threat to one's well being, or from an enemy from which one must escape.[176]

Perhaps the best definition of salvation is *healing*. Tillich had this understanding and wrote about it in regard to the healing of relationships with God, others, and even one's own fractured self.[177] Such a healing surely would intimate forgiveness and freedom and would involve inclusion and reconciliation. Thus, the book's central scripture passage expresses what Paul meant when he said: "God was, in Christ, reconciling the world to God.

Salvation has nothing to do with legality or justice or payment so that we can be "popped into heaven," as Evelyn Underhill wrote.[178] God's salvation is pure gift, a gift whose only requirements are to be received and shared. God continuously *offers* grace, but God cannot *give* grace if it is ignored or rejected. "In returning and rest you shall be saved; in quietness and trust shall be your strength," wrote Isaiah (30:33).

Without receptivity to God, we can be completely unaware of grace. We need to ask ourselves how God is to answer our many prayer requests if we do not stop talking, get quiet, and simply "be" with God: allowing ourselves to be in the holy Presence and receiving, without strain, the love that heals. It is possible to build a habit of openness by setting aside daily sacred times to allow ourselves to grow into that consciousness increasingly.

In Hebrew and Jewish history,[179] however, the concept of salvation had to do with historical happenings. For the Jews (and for many Christians up until today), whatever happened, good or bad, was caused by Yahweh. If it was good, it was called salvation. (Today, most people would say such good fortune is "providence," proving that God is sovereign.) When events were considered bad, God's wrath was said to be teaching the Israelites a lesson. Sometimes things occurred that could not be explained. Yahweh was said to have caused them all. Defeat *of* one's enemies or *by* those enemies was by the "hand" of God. The human psyche, then as now, despaired of an answer for crises that could not be explained. But for the Hebrews, there was a reason for everything, and the reason was the will of God!

The rationale of God as arbiter brought about a judgmental ethos in Israel. As pointed out in the book of Job, when good things happened, people were considered righteous. When evil was apparent, the victims were twice victimized. First came the original harmful experience. Then came the assessment of society: the ones struck down had, presumably, brought it all upon themselves. Judgment was assumed by those who thought they could interpret the will of God.

All such reasoning was a way of putting responsibility on God and perceiving God as the almighty judge of people and the ruler of nature. No one considered natural law because there was no science of such things. If there were an earthquake or a great flood, it was considered punishment by God for human evil, and scripture said so. Deuteronomy 32:39 proclaims for God: "I kill and I make alive. I wound and I heal." God was variously praised or blamed for everything: for wars, the burning of cities, and even broken bones. In legal documents, we still erroneously call some of these "acts of God."

God in Control?
What does it mean to say: "God is in control"? Is it a way to assuage the conscience, to deny the truth, or to express desperate hope? Do people think that saying those words is believing them, that believing them is having faith, and, with faith, everything will be all right?

When the soul is in agony over loss, regret for wrong doing, or other trials, there is a strange security in making God responsible, believing God is in charge. We tell ourselves there must be some larger picture we do not see but is visible to God, even created by God – some grand design that will give all pain a larger purpose than can be perceived.

If we insist, though, that God is in control, we are saying that God *manipulates* the world and that we have no free will. The question, then, arises: If God controls the world, why doesn't God make everyone perfect and turn earth into heaven? Of course, earthly life with God in control would mean no one could choose to love or to trust. Without choice, love and trust do not exist. No one would choose to follow the Ten

Commandments. There would no longer be a need for them. No one would have to care about others and their needs. There would be no sick, poor, excluded, or unfortunate people. Such control would mean that the natural law of this miraculous world – created by God "in the Beginning" – a law upon which the whole universe depends, would be suspended.

When we take the easy way out and say that God is in charge of the world, we are, then, abdicating God-given freedom of choice. In times of tragedy, we can blame God. We either can be sorry for ourselves as God's victims and accept what we sadly perceive as God's will, or we can lash out at God in anger, giving vent to our feelings. Both attitudes effectively close the door to the only thing that really could help: depending upon the presence and love of God, accepting God's caring through others, focusing on what is good and possible for us to do, and, remembering that we are still alive.

It is important to remember, too, that we are not the only ones with desires, drives, and wills. We affect each other deeply, even by hidden thoughts that seep out in attitudes toward others. The effect of our words and actions can be like arrows, which lodge in the heart and in the memories of those around us – for good or for ill – sometimes, as the Commandment states, "unto the third and fourth generation" (Exod. 20:5).

As sure as taking a step and trusting that the ground will be beneath our feet, God, as Spirit, is a source of power on which even unbelievers can constantly depend. God, as Spirit, is the ultimate source from which we learn understanding, patience, endurance, and trust, often as they come through others.

Like a devoted parent or an inspiring teacher, the joy of the Spirit evidently is not to control us, but to fire us with purpose, creativity, strength, and *self*-control. It is the Spirit who, instead of manipulating us to fulfill God's Great Intention, will empower us to make choices and take responsibility for what we say and do as we go about making our everyday business God's business on this earth.

Eventually, beyond history, beyond all that we can conceive, I do believe that all will be as God wills, but only because sentient life will have understood the wisdom of God's way at last and will desire nothing more than to conform to the divine plan. In that far-reaching sense, surely, God is sovereign.

Our world has far to go to become God's kingdom – a mirror of heaven. If and when that day comes, God will continue, not to *rule* but to *guide* by the Spirit, as has always been God's way. Immediately before his crucifixion, Jesus made it clear that God does not control the world. He quietly stated: "My kingdom is not of this world" (John 18:36). It appears that God, as known through Jesus, has never been concerned with power *over people*, but is focused on power *for all created life*.

Salvation – Its Changing Meanings
Salvation, seen as the pleasant side of judgment, was interpreted by Israel as *God for us*, later a major statement in Christian salvation theology. From the Israelite point of view, even Creation had to do with salvation because God had defeated chaos to establish the world. It was said that before Creation, part of the Earth had rested upon the huge back of the monstrous, proud primordial dragon Rahab, submerged in great waters. Yahweh was praised for slaughtering and cutting Rahab into pieces, thus freeing the Earth. Although not in the biblical Creation stories, we read of Rahab in Job, in the Psalms, and in Isaiah. In poetry, the name of the mythological creature came to be used to refer to Israel's enemies whom Yahweh had vanquished.

Renewed or recreated life, whenever it occurred, was salvation, and it brought deep rejoicing. In the exodus from Egypt, in crossing the Red Sea, in finally reaching the Land of Promise, and in returning from long captivity in Babylon, Israel exulted. As foretold by a prophet: "the ransomed of the Lord" did return, "and come with singing to Zion" (Isa. 51:11).

But again and again, Israel's hopes were dashed. They hoped for a human savior, one who would lead them to victory over those who had defeated them. Although to be sent by God, that leader was not to be confused with God. Isaiah spoke for God saying clearly: "I, I am Yahweh, and besides me there is no savior" (Isa. 43:11).

Another type of salvation came to people's consciousness when it became clear that Yahweh's will often was ignored. Because God had given free will to rebellious and self-centered people, Yahweh and goodness were not at all consistently victorious. When the monstrosity of evil became increasingly obvious and God did not force divine will upon the world, the realization developed that life in this world was not all there ever would be. There must be more, both beyond and hereafter, living eternal life. In that existence, God's final victory would be known!

Consequently, the hope of eschatological salvation (salvation at the end of time) was born. Then, it was envisioned, God and God's people finally would be victorious on a redeemed Earth, which would become God's kingdom. Or perhaps it would be realized in the kingdom of Heaven, in a transformed life following the insensitive existence in which humanity had been so unconsciously immersed.[180]

Saved from What?

A friend of mine, who believes in little that he cannot perceive, said to me one day: "Why write about salvation? What do I need to be saved from?"

I think we are saved (healed) *for* something: to know God intimately,[181] to love God, and to make life an instrument of God's love. If we are saved *from* anything, it is from meaningless and self-centered lives.

Atonement – Payment or Reconciliation?

Atonement is another term that is basic to the concept of renewing the human relationship with God. Although not the focus of this chapter, a few important understandings about the term must be stated.

Perhaps the best synonym for the original meaning of atonement is *reconciliation*. It is identical to Tillich's interpretation of salvation, meaning healing, as described above. To reconcile is to reunite those who have become estranged and separated. Atonement originally meant to bring the estranged together into "at-one-ment." But, through time, it came to mean the process of removing hindrances, rather than the desired result itself. In Hebrew scripture, money, incense, prayer, or blood sacrifice were all thought to be means of making amends, said to be atoning for transgressions. Such actions were meant to change God's attitude toward those who had sinned. But originally, the end desired was to be *at one* with God.[182]

From Estrangement to Belonging

Twenty years ago, when I was asked to teach a general course simply called "Religion," I came to a more sensitive understanding about salvation. It was given to me by Michael Barnes, who wrote the text, *In the Presence of Mystery*. According to him, salvation is more than having God on our side, or being saved by the blood of Jesus, or in going to heaven when we die. Barnes argues that salvation occurs constantly in our midst, that it is the work of God in everyday life. He shows that belonging to God and belonging to a sacred community are important forms of salvation here and now. He also points to the gift of identity, of having "a true and worthy selfhood," no longer estranged from one's own being,[183] a common theme with Tillich.

Salvation can be found whenever healing is taking place, whenever forgiveness is given, true freedom is supported, and the unacknowledged and disenfranchised are included – wherever there is wholeness.

Repentance: Changing Direction to Change a Life
"Repentance does not mean taking a giant leap. It means standing in the same spot, but turning to face a new direction. Then you start moving!" That was my introduction to a systematic theology session I gave on repentance in my early teaching years.

The Hebrew term *teshuvah* or *shuv* means a turning away from past imprisonments of mind and body. It is a letting go of all that gets in the way of kindness to others and self-offering to God. There cannot be a better detachment statement than that of Paul in Philippians 3:7-17: "I count everything [worldly position and power] as loss because of the surpassing worth of knowing Christ Jesus my Lord. For his sake I have suffered the loss of all things and count them as refuse ... forgetting what lies behind and straining forward to what lies ahead, I press on toward the goal for the prize of the upward call of God in Christ Jesus." Those words alone say: "Let go and move on!"

In the sixth century, after Isaiah had been written, the rabbis taught that repentance alone was required for salvation. For them, repentance was far more than feeling guilt or shame because of wrongdoing or ill-treatment of other human beings. It went beyond penance, or even doing some favor to make restitution. It included saying: "I am sincerely sorry," but it meant far more. It meant to *change one's life*.

Without scripture pointing it out specifically, we realize that God never forces salvation. Through our God-given response-ability we are able to *receive* the gift of love and healing, which Isaiah insists God offers universally. Early Isaiah offers a vision known as the Peaceable Kingdom, proclaiming: "The earth shall be full of the knowledge of the Lord as the waters cover the sea" (Isa. 11:9). A later passage from Isaiah adds: "I will give you as a light to the nations, that my salvation may reach to the end of the earth" (Isa. 49:6b). Finally, Isaiah 66:18-20, 23 predicts: "I am coming to gather all nations and tongues.... I will send survivors to the nations, ... [a]nd they shall bring all your brethren from all the nations as an offering to the Lord.... All flesh shall come to worship before me." That is salvation right here on this earth.

Centuries later, Jesus' parable of the Prodigal Son continues to teach that God's saving love is withheld from no one, that God will wait until anyone is ready for transformation and re-creation. All people should know they are loved because, to God, everyone matters and all are worthwhile. There is, however, a consequence to such belief. As God's ambassadors, the saved are expected to save.

Both redemption and salvation can refer to being freed. Redemption, in Israel, often referred to lawful liberty, a liberty that was bought and paid for. Today, the term salvation is coming into an expanded meaning of healing, wholeness, and freedom from inner imprisonments of the spirit. Salvation happens not only to us and for us but *in* us, and it happens *through* us when God uses us to pass on saving grace.

Both redemption and salvation can intimate a loving closeness with God, a lack of the painful separation caused by sin, selfishness, and human limitations. But shades of the original understanding of redemption are still embedded in the human psyche. That truth is illustrated in the parable of the Prodigal Son (Luke 15:11-32). In that story, a callow youth took his inheritance and simply walked away from his family and his responsibilities. The older brother thought that his own devotion, faithfulness, and hard work should have elicited his father's gratitude and generosity. He believed that he had earned his inheritance, just as we might presume to *earn* redemption.

But earning was not – and is not – the issue. The prodigal, who had squandered all his property, was not bought back or paid for by himself or anyone else. When, through the gift of the Spirit, he "came to himself" (that is, he understood who he really was and who he was meant to be), he turned around, returned home, and was simply embraced. "That was not redemption, but pure salvation!" an insightful friend said to me. How right he was. That is the transformative message Jesus taught and lived.[184]

When Jesus reads from the scroll of Isaiah (61:1-3) as Luke records it (4:18-19), he affirms: "The Spirit of the Lord is upon me, because he has anointed me to bring good news to the poor, ... to proclaim release to the captives and recovery of sight to the blind, to let the oppressed go free." Those words are about present salvation, salvation in his lifetime. They are about healing, wholeness, and freedom.

The Word Redemption Rehabilitated

Many of us who read the Hebrew Scriptures are touched by the word redemption. As the days of the Prophets come, bringing changes in the practices of sacrifice and sacrificial law, the interpretation of the word redemption morphs into the meaning of salvation. The Later Prophets, especially, bring the message that God's people are loved, claimed, and deeply valued by God without doing anything to gain such grace. Passages like Isaiah 43:1 speak gently: "Do not fear, for I have redeemed you; I have called you by name [I know your essential, truest self], you are mine." Israel belongs to and is cherished by its God.

These particular passages in Isaiah have no sense of legal transaction, contract, or forensic negotiation. Nor do such verses make redemption into a matter of checks and balances. Redemption no longer sounds like something to be negotiated in a courthouse or marketplace or even a temple. There is no reimbursement to God.

Christians often forget that God had been forgiving, offering redemption, and speaking of salvation for hundreds of years before Jesus lived. In Isaiah's time, what God was saying so simply and tenderly through the prophet was; "I love you. I have chosen you. I will give whatever is necessary to take care of you." But even then, the divine message was tinged with the perception of a bargaining God: "I give Egypt for your ransom, Ethiopia and Seba in exchange for you" (Isa. 43:3b). Yet, in spite of the bargaining aspect, the implication comes through clearly: "I will sacrifice for you! I, God, will pay the price."

If there is a price to be paid for healing and reconciliation, it is prepaid by God, even before we sin. Surely God knows what to expect of us and has always been prepared. Any price is paid within God's own being. God, always pervasively present in time and space, does not have to invade earth to settle accounts. Reinhold Niebuhr expresses that very understanding. God's attitude, God's response to the world's evil and human sin is settled within God's being. God requires nothing from the human side except our thirsty receptivity. Our alienations from God, others, and self are solved *within* God. Niebuhr writes:

> The good news of the gospel is that God takes the sinfulness of man into himself, and overcomes in His own heart what cannot be overcome in human life.[185]

The good news of the Gospel had been spoken before Jesus arrived, but people, generally, had not consciously heard it. It took Jesus' life and death to awaken humankind to a new and expanding awareness. Jesus made an unforgettable imprint upon history and, Christians believe, opened to us awareness of the More, both here and beyond. We are offered healing, forgiveness, freedom, inclusion, and reconciliation: all that salvation is.

What Does God Ask?
We have every reason to ask if God has need to be "satisfied." Must God be recompensed for all of our evil and error before saving grace is given? Surely the Almighty Lord of heaven and earth is not that needy or that small. In one sense, we can neither pay nor give anything to God, since all we have has been given to us by God. Psalm 50 proclaims:

> I am God, your God....
> I will not accept a bull from your house,
> for ... all that moves in the field is mine....
> If I were hungry, I would not tell you:
> for the world and all that is in it is mine.
> Do I eat the flesh of bulls,
> or drink the blood of goats?
> Offer to God a sacrifice of *thanksgiving*.

The psalmist, speaking for God, taunts human beings for their gross misunderstanding of the Divine. The Creator of heaven and earth does not crave, need, or use blood. Neither shed blood nor death of a victim can erase the human tendency to sin. Nor will they gladden the heart of God or be useful to any human being, except for the priests for whom slain animals provided food.

Surely nothing can pay for sin. Nothing can make up for evil. It can only be repented (radically turned away from) and forgiven by transformative grace. Only grace can save. Only grace can offer us new hearts. One does not have to pay for salvation if it is a gift. We might have said that Jesus paid the ransom that God imposed (Matt. 20:26-28). But we now recognize that God does not impose ransoms or sell salvation. God does not barter for our love. We cannot earn heaven. Nor can we earn God's love. True love is not bought. It is simply given. We respond by receiving, loving God back, and by giving God's love away.[186]

Consequences to Being A Christian

There are consequences to being a Christian. A contemporary spiritual director, Monseigneur Michael Chester, writes, "The crucifixion of Jesus was the supreme expression of God's love for us. Our expression of love for God and others entails a similar crucifixion."[187] "Unless a grain of wheat falls into the earth and dies, it remains just a single grain; but if it dies, it bears much fruit. Those who love their life lose it, and those who hate their life in this world will keep it for eternal life" (John 12:24-25 NTP-IV).

I have been challenged by the possibility of personal crucifixion most of my adult life. It is a shocking awareness that most people would prefer to ignore or reject. Yet it is unavoidably true that many sensitive individuals throughout history have experienced this reality. They have accepted torture and death as a result of sharing their insights and risking daring words and actions. Because they stood out as different from those around them, they were considered to be "the other."

Those who band together in the hierarchy of relationships and power, often perceive someone who is unusual to be a threat, an enemy, or a barrier to attaining the group's desires. It is likely that an individual chosen for a job or given recognition is someone who will not challenge the status quo. Perhaps that person will even enhance the authority of those in charge rather than challenge it from inside the system. Such an insecure and selfish *modus operandi* among those in dominance always has been found throughout the professional world, in society, and in the church.

Yet, there are times when those unique individuals who are willing to live as their true selves (as the Prodigal finally did and as many martyrs and heretics did), could enlighten and strengthen us all. We are not necessarily called to be mavericks, to dare the dangerous, or to live outside an affirmative circle. But we certainly must be called to support those who do, if we believe they are right and their insights valuable. Yet too many of us lack courage. To save ourselves, we abandon those who have a greater vision. Then they truly are alone!

In being a Christian, we often may be brought to the place where God asks us to allow ourselves to be vulnerable for the sake of others or for the values we hold dear. We may defend someone whom our friends loathe. We may noticeably disagree with a powerful group's opinion at the risk of our job or our place in society, especially if we are not yet in a position of prominence. It may be at great cost to us, that we show compassion to a destitute person whom others scorn as worthless.

Crucifixion is not something we seek. It can result from what we choose to do in trying to be true to ourselves or to encourage others or to live in solidarity with them. In the process, we may lose something valuable in earthly treasure, relationships, or influence. Like Jesus, we may well be aware beforehand that rejection might ensue.

Why do some seek to maim or destroy the life God has given them? God does not ask for martyrdom. In early Christianity, and even up through medieval times, there were devoted people who yearned to be martyrs. To begin to understand them, we need to know that the word *martyr* means *witness*. Just as Jesus was witnessing to the depth and compass of God's love by accepting the crucifixion he could have avoided, so the early martyrs, by their witness, publicized the love of God in Christ. Others sought torture and death as their gift to God. They believed that it would prove their devotion. But God already knew.

Certainly, there is no need to cause self-punishment, which tradition has termed "mortification" and is almost a self-crucifixion. That, in itself, is disrespect for our own person, over which God has given us primary responsibility. To seek more deprivation might even weaken or destroy the life God has given us to use for good. As Evelyn Underhill made quite clear: "We do not look deliberately for crosses, but accept, without hesitation, those that come to us."[188]

Assessment

After Gustav Aulén died in 1977, a memorial was written mentioning his great work: *Christus Victor*. Aulén's third way of understanding the concept of atonement (mentioned above) was described by author Bernard Ehrling: "Rather than satisfaction of the righteous demands of the law calling for punishment of the sinner, this whole legalistic structure of the God-humanity relationship is put out of function and replaced by a God-humanity relationship based not on law, but wholly on love and forgiveness."[189]

It seems that Ehrling is more clear than Aulén was. But Aulén, himself had written elsewhere, "[Christ's] sacrifice is ... the sacrifice of divine love itself. [It] affirms that there is no limit to the self-giving of divine love."[190]

We have been forgiven *before* earthly justice "can have its day in court." The separations between us and others are mended and our own spirits are healed by the experience of that forgiveness and supportive love. We are offered release from bitterness toward others and even from our greatest temptation: our own self-hate. We can be inspired to receive God's life, which is Spirit, and then, as a privilege, pass it on. Evelyn Underhill would point out our primary need: "We must receive before we can transmit."[191]

Christ's Blood As God's Love

Often, our words in worship say that we are saved by the blood of Christ. Instead, we need to proclaim that we are saved by the love of God *through* the self-offered Christ. As his blood poured down upon the ground, God's love poured out through him. Consequently, we may argue that Jesus had to die in order for us to live. It is closer to the truth, though, to say that Jesus died in order for us to live more fully, knowing we are beloved.

It is not the act, ritual, or blood, all by themselves, that heal us. That would be magic. It is the grace of God's love alive and incarnate in the act, ritual, and blood that makes us whole. Jesus' death was the extreme of love, love to give life, not an appeasement of God's wrath. God needed Jesus to make saving love real, obvious, and experienced on the earthly, human plane.

Because Jesus loved people deeply, genuinely, and empathetically, we know he suffered for them. Often they rejected the love he offered.[192] But his love must also have been exalted, exciting, joyous, and inspiring. And surely he laughed often. He saw further than the rest of us could, perceiving God's triumph past the pain. His sorrow was terrible and real, but it was endured, knowing that pain, itself, was not his purpose, nor was it to be his end. Throughout much of the life of Jesus, God's self was sacrificed – given away joyously – for our good. Jesus has shown us that God's healing love is both an objective and subjective reality. It is offered *to* us, *for* us, *in* us, and *through* us. That love is our salvation in this present moment and through all eternity.

Chapter 10

FROM ANIMISM TO TODAY
Spirits to Holy Spirit

Without consciousness, we would not know that we are alive, that we are selves, or that there is a God. Religion would not exist without a sense of the sacred so often spoken of as spirits or Spirit. Without a conscious relationship with his Father and knowledge of his tradition, Jesus would have had no concept of his mission and would not have preached or healed or been crucified. And, without consciousness, we would have no impulse to worship, to care about others, or to create a theology. But we *are* conscious, and therefore, we can be awake to the presence of God and aware of meaning and worth in our own lives and the lives of others. Because we are conscious, we can rethink the meaning of Jesus' death.

The effectiveness of any life is dependent upon how each person responds to his or her own time. Someone like Jesus could not have existed or been recognized in the Paleolithic Period. He was effective because of when he lived. Donald Baillie, with whom I am often of one mind, expressed the importance of the timing of Jesus' life:

> God was continually pressing through into human life in every age, so far as man would allow, and the reason why the Incarnation did not take place earlier is because man was not sufficiently receptive ... God cannot go faster with His revelation than man will let Him.[193]

Before History

Before there was a Yahweh or an Elohim, and before the gods of Greece and Rome, Mesopotamia and Egypt, India and the Far East, something preceded religion. That something must have been consciousness. By attempting to interpret artifacts and understand myths emerging from prehistoric times, we can surmise that religion was an early human creation. It appears to have been constructed as a response to what was most real and powerful, pervasively present, and yet transcendent to all else: a kind of unseen life.

We can conceive of a time when consciousness, as *we* know it, did not exist. People were alive, but had no sense of individuality or identity. There were no words for "I," "you," "they," or "God." There were no words at all.

In the history of humankind, there must have been a first awakening, a striking awareness that one's self existed as well as other selves and other things. Such an experience would have been the beginning of consciousness, the first recognition that each person is a separate being, that there is an other, and that, perhaps there is a Great Other.

In the time before remembered history, we can only assume that those very early people, like other animals, had instincts and all their senses. Past the most basic safety and survival instincts, they also must have had feelings of attraction, relationship, and ownership. Their world would have included sex, procreation, children, family, and tribe with only the most minimal recognition of differentiation between the self and others. But at some point there had to be more. Eventually there had to come a strong sense of the mysteries of life, of all that nature displayed, of human relationships with animals and the need for plants; indeed, the need for each other.

Awe must have been a part of their experiences of storms, of sunrises and sunsets, of the stars in changing patterns, of plant growth, and of beauty. Fear would have been part of life too, for what was there to protect them from what they could not comprehend? Surely there was an intuition of something greater than they. It was probably, for a very long time, only an emotional experience, a vague impression, making no sense because they could not express it in thought or words. Often, they must have felt weak and overwhelmed as they experienced so much that was real, but unexplained, and especially, undifferentiated.

However, over time, a simple self-consciousness would have developed: an awareness of relationships with everyone and everything. Eventually, there was an awakening to the uniqueness of one's own self. When the stunning realization of individuality finally came, so did the need for a name, and individuals recognized each other as unique persons. Everyone and everything needed names. That naming was the beginning of language, and, simultaneous with the development of language was the inception of thought. Language and concept cannot exist apart. One writer estimates that words and thoughts appeared together 300,000 years ago.[194]

Those first experiences of conscious thought, reasoning and naming must have been profound. Those early minds would have been filled with myriad suppositions, superstitions, and finally questions about all they could not know for sure! Were those first experiences of consciousness anything like ours as we look at the heavens, wondering how many living worlds might exist beyond our present knowledge? Are we too on the edge of new awakenings?

At some point, primitive people would have come to a sensibility of the life force, the power within everything that could breathe or bleed. In all that grew, that evolved from seedling to flower or fruit or to new living beings, the animate force they experienced seemed to be present and pervasive. Anything that grew and changed had life. They found it everywhere.

Primitive people were engulfed in an ocean of life, the same ocean in which we also live. They must have felt almost helpless to deal with it. Yet, in the long, gradual formation of human cognizance, there came the emerging awareness of something many first called *spirit* or *breath*. By the time Hebrews saw themselves as a people, they recognized this spirit or breath as the Source of all, and they named it the Holy.

Today, many assumptions about the earliest human societies come from the few aboriginal tribes still left on earth. But, as the American religious philosopher Robert Wright, notes, we cannot assume that today's aborigines are "crystalline examples" of the early hunter-fisher-gatherers of 14,000 years ago. That was the time, numerous scholars believe, that might have seen the inception of religious consciousness, the time when a kind of history began.[195]

The Birth of Spiritual Consciousness

Turning to the birth of spiritual consciousness across the world and across time allows us to set the Judeo-Christian narrative into the larger story. While there is not much we can know about these beginnings from a scientific point of view, numerous scholars have delved into what logically can be presumed.

My own thought on the evolution of spiritual consciousness has been much informed by the research and perceptions of Michael J. Barnes and the American sociologist Robert Bellah.[196]

"Religion," says Barnes, is "a human response to mystery."[197] At first the product of an infant consciousness, religion seems to have been present in the early stages of history as a world-wide phenomenon. It is reasonable to place the dawn of religion in the time period of awakening self-consciousness. This instinctive awe of the unknown would have been a "fuzzy" kind of mentality, surely resulting from being overwhelmed by what could not be effectively confronted or managed. It can be assumed that over time there developed within more and more people an instinctive awareness of what we now call 'the Holy" or what is known generically as *God*.

There could hardly have been a sense of love in such a response, for love is a relatively recently experienced phenomena in religion, and it is personal. It was probably impersonal *power* that impressed earlier people, a breathtaking, living, pervasive power affecting their lives in ways they could not predict. The sentient awareness of something greater and more potent than the self, in and behind nature, seemed inescapable.

From Spirits to Gods and Sacrifice
Today we call this first type of spiritual consciousness *animism*, a word derived from the Latin *anima* – the term for breath, life, soul, or the vital principle. In 1871, the Englishman Edward Tylor who created the term, wrote that to primitive humans, the "ghost soul, [a] vapour, film, or shadow," was the "cause of life and thought in the individual it animates."[198]

Animistic societies evidently thought those spirits had to be appeased, cajoled, and bargained with in order to keep them from harming human beings. As a result, early worship probably was based on sacrifice, and the essence of early sacrifice was payment for protection and other favors.

According to Tylor, the concept of a particular spirit in each thing finally gave way to the idea of a god for each species of spirits, and thus *polytheism* became the norm for a while.[199]

Barnes' approach to polytheism suggests that when people began to believe there were beings more powerful and more transcendent than spirits, they referred to them as "gods." Conceived of as further away than spirits and much more powerful and fearsome, the gods were thought of as possessing human qualities. They were thought to get angry or to be jealous and unforgiving, at least periodically. They also could seem playful and childlike. No one could trust the gods because they were fickle and undependable. Sacrificing to them resulted from fear, insecurity, and distrust. A sense of trust in those gods probably could not have been imagined.

But eventually there did come the belief in gods who protected humans yet required allegiance in return. They were considered to be local divinities, belonging to a particular people or tribe. Conflicts occurred between people who were committed to different gods. Worshippers had to follow *their* god alone in order to be considered loyal to the tribe and to remain unthreatened by godly vengeance. Gods were perceived as capable of incredible violence, and the violence thought to originate in them was accepted as justice by everyone. The god with the most power was assumed to be right and to be true, as in the story of Elijah and the priests of Baal told in the first book of Kings. Fear of godly power must have resulted in human commitment to a single god for the sake of self-preservation. Nature was not blamed for tragedies, but the gods – thought to control nature – were. Perceived godly power and human fear held primitive religions together.

Not all gods were seen as equal, however. A hierarchy of gods developed in people's minds with a "high god" above them all. The high god ruled over all people and all the other gods. To recognize each god while worshipping only the one seen as superior is known as *monolatry*. The high god ruled over all people and all the other gods.

In the tale of Elijah and the priests of Baal (I Kings 18:20-40), for example, the old prophet tried to force the Israelites into a choice between Yahweh and Baal. He taunted them, almost sneering: "How long will you go limping with two different opinions?" Yet Elijah never seemed to be completely successful. For Israel, however, the belief in one's own god as distinct from others finally became strong. Prophets spoke of "the God of Abraham, Isaac, and Jacob." The Israelites spoke of "our god" and "yours." It was much as someone today might respond to a statement about God by challenging: "Do you mean Yahweh or Allah or Brahman?" even if the speaker is referring generically to God as inclusive of all cultural particularities.

But in the days of polytheism and monolatry, religions could be amorphous, collecting followers of other gods because people were insecure as to which god really had the most power. Sacrifices to and worship of Baal, Molech, Ashtoreth, and others were not at all unknown among the Hebrews. Some Hebrew child sacrifices were doubtless to the god Molech. According to Exodus 32, Yahweh commanded that for sacrificing at the altar of the Golden Calf in Moses' time, the wavering Hebrews be punished by the sons of Levi. The Levites obeyed by slaughtering three thousand of their own brothers, sons, friends, and neighbors, thus warning everyone against unfaithfulness to the selfsame Yahweh for ages to come.

Israel finally chose Yahweh as their own, and, at the same time, they saw themselves as "the chosen people," for even in the days of the Exodus, God had said to them: "I will take you for my people, and I shall be your God" (Exod. 6:7). They belonged to Yahweh. Eventually, not just awe, law, and obedience bound them, but love appeared between Israel's God and *his* people. We hear of it in the Psalms and in the later prophets. Israel was privileged and came to understand that with that privilege came a responsibility to share what was theirs, to offer it to others.

It is at this point that we might see the effects of belief in a hierarchy of gods as presented in Hebrew scripture. Yahweh was supreme among Hebrew worshippers, proclaiming a law that would guide them, and claiming Israel as his own beloved and chosen people. According to the book of Exodus, Yahweh, in giving the Ten Commandments, proclaimed either "You shall have no other gods *before* me," or "You shall have no other gods *besides* me." If the true intent of those words was *before* me, it would mean that even Yahweh recognized the reality of other gods, so long as he was considered superior and was accorded primary allegiance and power. If the sentence were read as no other gods *besides* me, the text would have to have been written in the days of monotheism or at least edited in those times.

Finally, within a few hundred years of each other, cultures across the known world began confirming the reality of one supreme, sacred

Spirit or one God. In sociological terms, that incremental awakening can be described as an arc that had moved from animism to polytheism to monolatry and, finally, to monotheism.

While reading scripture, it is essential to keep this gradual change in mind. Our theology did not come to us ready-made. These layers of growth could not have been simultaneous happenings. One cannot read the Hebrew Bible and recognize the same God throughout because no one can perceive God as destructive, wrathful, and war-like while teaching peace and forgiveness through Jesus. Nor can one conceive that a jealous or self-concerned God, more like a person than a god, would be full of self-giving, even sacrificial, grace as offered on the Cross.

I do not consider the existence of these different gods to have been a "changing of the guard" within religious history. If there always has been one ultimate God, one source of life and love, the difference, as set forth in Chapter 3, was a change in human perception of that supreme being. Although we have seen through the glass of history darkly, let us hope and believe our sight has now improved. Only in growth toward God can early concepts be replaced with insights more patient and wise, more compassionate toward human pain and sin, and more inspiring and encouraging. Only in recognizing the Holy Spirit as the Spirit of Love could the Cross have meaning. The Cross was not a power play. It did not invoke God's prestige or validate God's honor. The Cross was not obedience to Law. The Cross was a living expression of Love incarnate and utterly self-giving.

Finally: Monotheism

With *monotheism*, came the realization that there had to be one ultimate power, one transcendent reality upon which all life depended and from which all life came. At first, and even until today, followers of varying religions have believed that there is only one God, but it is *their* God who is the One. It seems to me that there are few who realize that one God can be known by many names and assumed, by different believers, to have varying characteristics. This One "is above all and through all and in all" as Ephesians 4:6 proclaims.

The period of time in which monotheism appeared was designated as the First Axial Period by Karl Jaspers in *The Origin and Goal of*

History.²⁰⁰ Centered in 500 BCE but extending from 800 to 200 BCE, the period saw a transformation of consciousness in China, central Asia, and the eastern Mediterranean. This is also the time when most of the Hebrew Scriptures seem to have been written.

The idea of one God as the ultimate Lord of all appeared in several places within that period. In Israel, the concept of Yahweh was transformed from the God of the Israelites to the God of everyone. That same realization appeared in India where the Ultimate Reality of the philosophers became personally known as Brahman, the only God, described in a trinity of ways and thousands of manifestations and characteristics. Monotheistic consciousness won out in Persia where the twin forces of evil and good seemed as close as brothers in an eternal conflict. There, too, the one called Ahura Mazda, who represented goodness and light, finally became acknowledged as supreme.

Jaspers writes: "In this age were born the fundamental categories within which we still think today, and the beginnings of the world religions, by which human beings still live, were created."²⁰¹ Writing about Jaspers' thought, Ewert Cousins points to "the eastern Mediterranean [where] the Jewish prophets – Elijah, Isaiah, and Jeremiah – were effecting a transformation of Judaism from an emphasis on ritual observance to individual moral consciousness." Cousins noticed, as have we, that "the Jewish prophets preached to the people that it was not animal sacrifice that pleased God, but a pure heart." It is sacrifice – the change in its status and kind – that he sees as a pivotal point in religion and in human history.²⁰²

Other Monotheisms

Although there has been general agreement among scholars that the above assumptions are well founded, the British author Karen Armstrong has noted that one scholar, Wilhelm Schmidt, published a theory in 1912 that there had been a primitive monotheism before people had begun to worship a number of gods. His book, *The Origin of the Idea of God*, speaks of one creator and governor of the universe. It states, however, that the sense of a real presence of this god faded away and the idea of a pantheon of gods emerged as a replacement.²⁰³

There are scholars who think there was monolatry in Egypt during the reign of Amenhotep IV in the 14th century BCE. But the preponderance of information, thus far, claims that time as a brief period of monotheism, five hundred years before the Axial Age began. If so, it was the first appearance of monotheism in history. During his 17-year reign (1379-1362 BCE) Amenhotep IV instituted a religion in honor of the deity Aton, whose visible aspect was the solar disk, and changed his own name to Akhenaton, meaning "servant of the Aton." Thereafter, it was Aton alone – as supreme god and creator – whom he worshipped in the full light of the sun and whom he called upon all Egypt to revere. Previously, the priestly class had served multiple gods, above which was the high god, Amen-Ra. Because they wielded more power than did the Pharaoh, it may have been that one of Akhenaton's purposes in radically changing Egyptian religion was to destroy the positions, enormous power and prestige of the priests. But when Akenaton's seventeen-year reign ended with his death, the former priests tried to erase all signs of the religion he had begun. Thus polytheism moved to monotheism and back again in less than twenty years.[204, 205]

Cosmic Consciousness

In 1901, a book entitled *Cosmic Consciousness* was published by Richard Maurice Bucke, a Canadian doctor whose medical expertise was insanity. He wrote about an extraordinary state of mind which he claimed was experienced by some of the greatest spiritual leaders of history, as well as by himself and some few others whom he named. In the state of Cosmic Consciousness, a person experiences the oneness of the Universe and a strong sense of the Whole; the pervasive presence of God; love as the basis of the Cosmos; and freedom from a sense of sin and the fear of death. One of Bucke's most important points makes clear that when something unusual occurs in human experience, when a particular sensitivity or genius is seen for the first time, it appears in only one person, then a few. Eventually, however, it is found through most of the human race. Bucke believed that Cosmic Consciousness, at some time in the future, would be a "regular attribute of adult humanity."[206]

From a spiritual point of view, this is an awesome perspective, because, if it happens to be positive, it heralds greater maturity and inspiring insight. But Bucke does not deal with the obvious question of increasing confusion or evil. We have seen throughout history that any movement, whether useful or destructive, life-giving or life-destroying, begins with just one person or with a minority that *infects* those around them. The infection continues until a large mass of people permits and eventually fosters a growing spirit that affects the direction of history thereafter. One might wonder what would have happened if the crowd greeting Jesus on Palm Sunday had been the same as that which Pilate queried regarding Jesus' fate? Or, if they were the same people, what type of spirit infected them six days later, and why did they yield to it?

The Future: More Evolution?
The most obvious question at this point is: "Where are we going from here?" I will mention the predictions of two forward-looking people.

One of the two was an Italian Cistercian monk known as Joachim de Fiore. Born about 1130 or 1135, he died sometime in 1201 or 1202. He was founder of a group of hermits who became a Florensian Order. His theology of the Trinity was condemned by the Fourth Lateren Council in 1215. But he also proposed a theory of the three ages of humankind that has been remembered. Joachim's ages are: the Age of the Father, which began with the creation of the world; the Age of the Son, which began with the life of Jesus; and the Age of the Holy Spirit, which he felt would commence after his lifetime, beginning in 1260 CE. What would the Age of the Holy Spirit be like? Joachim believed it would give birth to "the church of the Spirit." Do you think we are living in that hoped for age?

If such an age had come to pass, would we not be realizing that the Holy Spirit is God, as Jesus is quoted as saying to the woman at the well in John 4:24 (see Chapter 5)? That could mean that the disagreement on this issue between the Eastern Orthodox and Western churches would finally cease. The two bodies still have not agreed on whether the Holy Spirit proceeds from both the Father and the Son (as the West contends) or simply from the Father (as Eastern Christianity teaches).[207] If "God *is* Spirit," as Jesus said, this is not an issue.

If we consciously understood and experienced the truth that the Being of God is Spirit, we would not be calling on God to send the Holy Spirit as though it is not already here. The Holy Spirit is already cramming every nook and cranny of the world. That is the first job of the Spirit: to be the Presence that is present! But the Spirit will never force itself upon our consciousness, no matter how deeply we sink into evil or tear apart our world. We can be filled with the Spirit if we are willing to pay attention, a matter of some dedication and discipline, which a disciple might expect. God, as Spirit, is completely self-giving. When we ask for the coming of the Spirit, let us understand God's coming as a *renewal*, a greater infilling of the life without which no one has ever lived.

If de Fiore was at least correct in seeing the period after Christ as belonging to the Holy Spirit, we would not refer to the Spirit as coming *again* as though it had gone away and we needed an infusion of Spirit. Instead, we would intentionally be open to its presence. It would be a time when people finally a*waken* to the magnificent presence of the Spirit already among them, empowering them to passionately reach out to those they could uniquely help.

Another prophet who pointed to a future evolution of consciousness in the Church was the twentieth century German theologian, Karl Rahner, who died in 1984. His thought, in many ways, was fresh and sometimes visionary. Probably the outstanding Roman Catholic theologian of his time, Rahner wrote of the "transcendental existential," which simply means the immanence of the transcendent God. In other words, we could say that the God we often feel above and beyond us is also experienced as being right where we are, even inside us. When we speak of the Holy Spirit in our midst and in our minds and hearts, that is what we mean. This is very much a theology of mysticism.

In fact, Rahner believed that the Church of the future would be a mystical church. He wrote: "*The Christian of the future will be a mystic or he will not exist at all.*"[208] Those are strong words. But Rahner's explanation is simple and sensible. He states that mysticism is not some esoteric phenomenon but "a genuine experience of God emerging from the very heart of our existence." Furthermore, he states that human beings do not discover God from knowing theology, but from personal experience, and that experience is the basis of spiritual conviction.

Such statements reinforce what we have said above: that both spirituality (the experience of the Holy Spirit) and theology (the explanation of the experience) are both deeply important and need each other. But theology should first be built upon an experience of God and then a cultivated relationship with God, without which theology would be hollow.

Mysticism As Personal Relationship With God and Others
Mysticism deals with the inner essence of things and people. It is concerned with our deepest values and with truth. Kierkegaard wrote a small book on this subject, a work rarely mentioned in expositions of his thought. Known as *Purity of Heart*, its signature statement is: "Purity of heart is to will one thing." I perceive that one thing to be *knowing the will of God* (the opposite of Eve's assumed purpose long ago). When I suggested that interpretation to the man who translated the text from Danish into English, he smiled at me sweetly and said something like: "Uh-*huh*!" Perhaps he wanted to keep it as a bit of an enigma. Although he was a professor, I never considered him loquacious![209]

Mystical experience (which all people may sometimes taste) involves the desire of all life to be in *union* with God. Many consider union to be the ultimate fulfillment at the end of the spiritual path. I do not think it is. "My cup runs over" is a far better perception of our spiritual horizon, and the horizon is never the end. If we are in union with God, we *will* run over, provided we are well and unhindered. In fact, we will leak!

Mysticism is not a spiritual quest for the sake of the ego, nor is it self-actualization or the gaining of a splendid identity. It is loving God so much that one's whole self, one's whole life, is given as much as possible to loving, receiving, and sharing God. The self is necessary as a tool, an instrument of God, and must not be a distraction from that which matters most: receiving the gift of God's very self. Whether we become a bishop or a martyr or a famous Christian speaker is not the issue. To receive God's healing love and then to share it for the healing of the world seems to me to be all that matters now.

Mysticism looks for and sees the unseen in the seen, the extraordinary in the ordinary. It is frequently behind the inspiration and creativity of artists, wonderful counselors, healers, and others who draw forth hidden beauty.

All Christian systematic theology courses should include a correct understanding of mysticism. These courses usually deal with God, Christ, the Holy Spirit, and relationships with God and people through mediums such as the Church, prayer, and worship. They also deal with morality: goodness, and sin. Sin was defined by Augustine and the most famous Augustinian monk, Martin Luther, as *incurvatus in se* or as humanity curved in upon itself.[210] In other words, sin is self-centeredness, selfishness, "me first."

Mysticism, however, is a movement from self-centeredness to selflessness because of love of God and others. But if our goal is to be selfless, we will always be self-centered. That is an excellent way to make our own spiritual attainment the god of our lives. Yet, if we live to learn truth and to love and serve God, we may attain usefulness on earth.

Buddhism, which rarely mentions God, speaks a great deal of Nirvana, traditionally explained as a state of *blowing out*, or extinguishing, a desire for temporal things and for satisfaction of personal needs. It teaches that the spiritual call is to move from the self to *no-self* or from the Ordinary Self to the True Self, a term I prefer. No-self can be interpreted as the self annihilated and is even taught in those terms by some. Regardless, that hyperbole is used to mean *selflessness*, a focusing beyond the self and its desires.

This is an important teaching, but it can be misinterpreted as has much similar Christian writing. The danger here is to interpret such instruction as promoting irresponsibility and flight from the world God loves. The other danger, which was very real in medieval Christianity, is to denigrate the self as a stumbling block to goodness or to see the self as evil, or at least as separating us from God. I grew up with the latter understanding, and so did many of my graduate students now in religious vocations. Assumed to be true and therefore, accepted, it became a destructive self put-down and not at all what I now passionately believe is the will of God.

Without the self, we cannot live with practical effectiveness. It is a necessity and a tool of responsibility and response in the world. We have nothing to give to God or to others if we cannot give ourselves.

The mystical path is shared by all major religions in the world. It is the heart of each of those religions. And every one of them says the same thing: progress is moving from self-centered ego to selflessness, or better, to love. It is moving away from fixation on one's possessions, power, and prestige toward the simple and heartfelt love of God and, thus, love of people who are in God's image, no matter how wretched they are. True saints, whether canonized or not, are those who live that kind of truth. I am convinced that we have more true saints than we realize, and more than a few hidden mystics.

Mysticism is simply spirituality in an intense form. And spirituality, from my point of view as a theologian and teacher of spirituality, is the very heart of the Church's life. Spirituality is an experience of and relationship with God resulting in responsive life. Theology is a theory about that *experience*. Therefore neither spirituality nor its more intense form in mysticism should be viewed as extraneous to the life of the Church or to theology. They are its foundation. It is possible to have a wonderful spirituality without much of a theology. But it is not possible to have significant, genuine theology without spirituality. Such a theology would be empty. It would be only someone's opinion, with little connection to truth.

I doubt that Rahner's prediction – that Christians of the future will be mystics – will be taken as a goal for the Church at large. Most people will probably never hear of it. However, if mysticism were understood for what it really is, the Church would recognize it as simply the *living* continuation toward the goal God set before us in Christ long ago: self-giving love through the power God has given us.

Looking Back and Then, Ahead

Certainly a child's understanding of God and relationship with God changes as that person matures. It is a type of personal evolution that Luther once said would continue at least until death. He wrote: "This life is not health, but healing; not being, but becoming; not rest, but exercise. We are not yet what we shall be, but we are growing toward it. The process is not yet finished."[211]

We who have lived within the Judeo-Christian strain of faith have moved, almost without realizing it, from boldly singing "The Lord is a man of war!" (Exodus 15:1-3) to Jesus' appeal to "turn the other check" (Matt. 5:39) and his passionate pleading to go out into the roads and lanes to compel the poor, crippled, blind, lame, and everyone left over to come to the banquet of God (Luke 14:21-23). We have moved from perceiving God as the one who commands Joshua to "slaughter all that breathes," including infants, to one who is known first of all as Savior, that is, healer. Believers once perceived God as having hardened Pharaoh's heart and closed his ears to Moses' plea. We are told that, in one night, God killed all of Egypt's first-born sons and later drowned the entire Egyptian army. But we have moved to the perception of God as loving little children, opening the ears of the deaf, healing those whom society had discarded, eating with the despised and disenfranchised, and reaching out to calm troubled waters – all through Christ. This is an enormous change in spiritual perspective.

The only God there is, the God of all people – even though called by different names and comprehended and worshipped in manifold ways – has been known throughout history and experienced in cultures far different from each other. The one God surely must be an inclusive Spirit who wills healing and eternal life for every living soul. That one God must be the Spirit of Love, waiting to be perceived and claimed, the One who will open hearts and awaken minds to recognize what must be true.

Isaiah 2:4 forecasted that someday swords will be beaten into ploughshares and there will be no more war. What a vision to hold onto! We are still waiting for such consciousness to fill the world. It will not arrive, of course, without our participation. It cannot fill the world if *we* are the piece that is missing.

If we use Jesus' experience and perception of God as a means of better understanding the God of all people, it becomes clear that human beings have truly misunderstood and maligned God since the beginning of history, often without realizing the terrible consequences to their own faith or its destruction. The consciousness of the human race has been mired in a false understanding, conceptualizing God as limited by human traits, both good and bad. Some of us are still at that point today. Others believe they and their God are unique and superior. They do not realize *their god* is only their perception of the one God and that God is far bigger than what we can imagine or perceive.[212]

Early in these pages we noted a growth in understanding among those in Jesus' time who felt strong and secure in their faith. They had the

Law, knew it, and tried to follow it. They believed that they already possessed God's complete revelation. Attempting to be faithful to what they knew, and with all their devotion, they refused to investigate more deeply. They could not know that future prophets would challenge them to the core but, also would offer relief from certain restraints and limitations of the Law. They had no idea a man called Jesus would come, not to abolish all law and leave them bereft of the security of thinking themselves righteous, but to turn law and even justice into instruments of love.

Now, two thousand years after Jesus lived and died, it is fascinating to observe the difference that he made in human understanding of what God was like and what God's dream was and is for us. I believe that a great deal of Jesus' teaching is still not generally understood, nor has it been interpreted well in terms of how it applies to his followers. But I believe that what he said about his own mission describes the call given us.

> Whoever believes in me, believes not in me but in the one who sent me. And whoever sees me sees the one who sent me.... I have not spoken on my own, but God who sent me has indeed given me a commandment about what to say. ... What I speak, therefore, I speak just as God has told me (John 12: 44-45, 49-50 NTP-IV).

The miracle of Jesus is that he unconditionally gave over his heart, will, and life to become God's wholly committed instrument on earth. By offering himself in life and in death, he lived and died as the embodiment of God's gift of grace. If enough of us are willing to think of our lives as God's gift, to be used in freely offered love, the time in history in which we live could be transformed. We are challenged to live true to our call, whether it leads to crucifixion or joyous fulfillment. Through God's love in us, many individuals and much of society can be healed. That healing is salvation and true fulfillment, here and now, "on earth as it is in heaven."

The Next Step in Human Spiritual Evolution

To become a Christian in the days of the early church was certainly a definitive change in human consciousness. Some died for their faith. Some became inflamed with the Gospel. Is all of that past? It is not. Today's Christian martyrs are more numerous than they have ever been, even in past days of devastating, historic persecution. I have no doubt that today the Spirit is teaching in new ways what it has not yet been successful in laying upon our hearts. Nor do I doubt that the Spirit will ever stop teaching.

In the twentieth century, James Fowler clarified the stages of faith from earliest childhood to the end of life. His thoughts have been a revelation to my younger college students who often expressed, when they entered my class, that they already knew all there was to know about religion. But in one session with Fowler's thoughts, they began to see life and their study of religion as never ending and always expanding and exciting.[213] Other scholars, too, have shown how growth in faith is strengthened or stultified in every life. Lawrence Kohlberg, Erik Erikson, Evelyn and James Whitehead, Brian Hall, Benjamin Tonna, Abraham Maslow, and numerous others have led the way for many. We can continue to learn from them.[214]

I believe that the next great step in human spiritual evolution will be in accepting that we are called to be like Jesus. We are called to accept and treasure God's claim upon us to be a servant in whom God will be glorified (Isa. 49:3). We are asked to allow the Holy Spirit to live in and through each of us, for each human being is meant to be an instrument of the Spirit's transforming power.

We have been asked:
>to let God love us deeply,
>to face and claim our true identity as the called of God,
>to be one of the few with real courage,
>to dare to live what we believe.

We have been asked to see beyond the ordinary
>and the obvious to find real truth.

We have been asked to question anything
>that does not say "God is love."

Chapter 11

THE BIG QUESTION
and
God's Great Intention

"Are you saved? he asked earnestly. It was the caretaker at my host church who voiced the question. I was, to put it mildly, surprised. I had gone to Puerto Rico for a week of teaching Receptive Prayer, and then, on Sunday evening, to offer my *Life of Christ* in song and narration. Evidently he had learned that not everyone who "talks the talk" knows on an experiential level, what they are talking about. As Jesus taught, not everyone who says "Lord, Lord!" is necessarily "saved." The caretaker intended to find out if I was authentic!

That was not the time to say: "And what do *you* mean when you speak of being saved?" Instead, I waited a minute, walked over to where he stood, looked into his earnest eyes and quietly said: "Yes. And I'm grateful!"

He pushed on: "Do you speak in tongues?" "No. I sing instead," I replied. "If God takes over in anything we do, I think it can be done through any means we offer and God chooses. But I sure can tell where it's coming from!"

I had never experienced such an encounter in my retreat or concert ministries. I was taken aback. But later I thought of Matthew's counsel: "When they deliver you up, don't worry about what you should say, for the Spirit will tell you then and there. The Spirit will speak through you." (This is my free translation of Matthew 10:19.) Not until that moment had I ever thought of the response I gave that day.

Saved

Saved. This whole book has been about salvation.

What did being saved mean to the caretaker? It does not mean the same thing to everyone. For my parents, it meant loving, with all their might, the One who first loved them. They suffered for it, but their suffering was borne within the experience of God's sustaining love. They felt gloriously privileged to speak of that love all their lives. I love God too, and I *do* believe that I am saved in a way I have not mentioned yet. In spite of all my inadequacies and fears, I know God personally. While I was a little child, God waited for me inside my heart until I knew the Spirit and grew in knowing. It first came when I was alone and quiet in my room, reading my Bible. I imagined that I was present where Jesus was. I watched him and listened when he spoke. Something in me said: "Listen! Some of his words are for you too." So I did listen in the silence, and it seemed filled with a gentle enveloping energy. The silence and I were alive. And God became real.

Using Receptive Prayer in complete silence – knowing that I was within the Spirit's presence – has guided my life far more than any other contact with God. I have been physically healed more than once, both instantly and over time. Often, but not always, I have known what to say in challenging situations. I have had the great privilege of helping people die because, in Receptive Prayer, they found themselves with the One they could trust, One in whose life-giving presence they could live forever. I have experienced God singing with my voice so that I, the singer, was filled and also moved in worship. God says simply: "If you're frightened, just do what you already know to do, and I will do the rest."

Fear, insecurity, another's arrogance, and imperfect knowledge have kept not only me, but everyone, from being God's perfect vessels. Fear is the worst. Its power can destroy any noble intention. And there is another spiritual requirement that has made a misery of many lives: the call to be perfect. "Be perfect as God is perfect" means "Grow up. Be mature." I have lost my adolescent belief that we are called to perfection, and have replaced it with the strong sense that all that is asked of anyone is to love God and to love others as wisely as possible with God's love.

But the question here is this: Is knowing and loving God "being saved?" I think so. What could be better? My understanding of salvation has continued to grow, but life after death has always been part, and a *big* part, of salvation for me.

Jesus said: "I *am* the Way." For me, he is the Way. Why? Because he embodied it. He embodied God's truth. He embodied God's life. He embodied God's saving love. And those who are touched by him live by the grace of that continuing experience. In some measure, they begin to embody that grace themselves. And I believe that no one can "come to the Father" but by Jesus' way: receiving and living by the Spirit and the gifts God offers. We can learn to live what we believe, to embody what we believe, even though our success is always partial.

Inconceivable as it may seem, Jesus predicted in John 14:12 that those of us who trust God's power will accomplish as much and even more than he did! Yet, when we are receiving the Spirit, God can do what earth needs done by using the brains and bodies, talents and time, and firing the passion of those who love God's world. And I do mean *firing*.

One of Luther's finest works is *The Freedom of A Christian*, which he wrote when he was thirty-seven. There he states that when iron is touched by fire, it glows as they become one. Just so, the Spirit, the Word of God, gives itself to the soul, and the soul is transformed. It becomes burning hot and glows.[215] Oh, yes, the iron is still iron, just as we are still human. Were the fire far removed, we would be just iron again. But when iron and fire remain close together, when we and the Spirit are one, we really are different in a very important way. We are alive and we know it! As Paul saw it, *we have become new creatures* (II Cor. 5:17). Our appearance may be the same, but our essence, which is our true name, our basic nature, has certainly changed.

We will not always be consciously in touch with the Fire. If we were, we might burn out, as some have done. Sometimes we forget, or we need to take a break from the passion of inspiration and the work of living what we believe. We do not always glow, nor do we want to.

When people have been touched to their core, either by trauma or by love, the neuron pathways in the brain permanently change. Only a similarly deep experience, repeated or carried on long enough, will change them back again.

We cannot, for instance, send young minds and hearts to the horror of war and expect them to come back the same. People cannot be on a drunk for weeks and return to the way they were.

And none of us can live long in the fiery presence of the Spirit and not be changed for the better. Because of being touched by the inspiring love of Mother Teresa as she cared for the poor, sick, and orphaned in India, more than a million people around the world could not help but join her Missionaries of Charity."

I believe that the Spirit is omnipresent: around us *and* inside us, permeating us. It is knocking on every door within us, not just waiting on the outside to get in, as some paintings imply. In my first years of teaching, Karl Rahner, together with Thomas Aquinas, taught me that "God is the core of our being."[216] Scholars call that Transcendental Thomism, and Rahner calls it the *supernatural existential*.[217] That simply means that if God is where we are, "God is both inside and outside of us or there's a hole in God!" as my physician, Dr. Lloyd Grumbles, once exclaimed.

If Spirit fills the universe, there is no place where God is not present, even though we may be unaware. The Spirit speaks to us objectively and subjectively. It seeks our sensitivities, confronts our attitudes, and sometimes breaks through old negatives. Its voice can be so soft that it comes only as a holy whisper. As Elijah discovered, it can seem to be the silence itself, not just *in* the silence. When we are caught by its winsome wonder and receive it, even for a time, we cannot help but love back the One who loves us. Then we receive an energy, a power, just as Jesus predicted.

Jesus was very clear in John 14:16-17 when he disclosed that the Spirit, which had been *with* the disciples, would now be *in* them. What a difference! Luke also said: "And when the Holy Spirit has come upon you, you will receive power" (Acts 1:8). He did not mean power *over* people such as the Napoleons and Hitlers have craved. He meant power *for* people. Those who heard the good news were to witness, not only with their mouths, but by the Spirit flowing from their hearts!

If the final blessing of salvation is "going to heaven when we die," we all must wonder what heaven is. Is it a place? A dawning of increased consciousness? I believe it is the magnificent awareness of the pervasive Presence of the life of God, the Spirit permeating everything. Therefore it can be and is on earth as well. John, the gospel writer, tells of Jesus praying to his Father the night before his crucifixion and saying: "And this is eternal life, that they may know you, the only true God, and Jesus Christ whom you have sent" (John 17:3).

That night, Jesus had withdrawn to be alone. The sleepy John was several feet away and probably could not hear Jesus as he prayed. Furthermore, sixty years later, it is not likely that John would have remembered Jesus' exact words, even if he really had heard them. But

John understood, perhaps better than the others, the message he wrote nineteen times in his gospel. Throughout that book, the "good news" comes through as it does nowhere else: Jesus declares that he can say and do nothing without the Father who speaks and acts in and through him (John 14:10). With all my soul, I believe that is what it means to know and love God.

We began this book with Jesus' declaration to the woman at the well: "God is Spirit," the Spirit of Life, for the very essence of Life is God. God is Being. As long as there IS anything, it will be because God IS, because God was, is, and eternally will be "I AM."[218] To be aware of God as Spirit, to have a personal relationship with this everlasting source of Life, to be able to receive it and to let it live through us: "*This is eternal life.*"[219] *This is salvation.*

Jesus' primary purpose may not have been to take people to heaven. This planet, which is our home now, is meant to be filled with awareness of the Holy. But the hardest thing for most of us to comprehend and accept is that it is *we* who are called to be filled with the Spirit who will make life holy. Unbelievable as it may seem, *we are called to be like Jesus.*

Have we been brainwashed to think we can not be like Jesus? Do we consider it arrogant to think that we could be other christs? Or are we simply scared stiff? We do not want to be crucified! The presence of self-giving love in the midst of a "me-first world" has almost always been destroyed. To be like Jesus, to be another christ, is too much of a challenge to those without that vision. Appreciating other people or other points of view, which "in" groups have purposely ignored, is simply not generally comprehended and certainly not accepted. Once a noble life has passed on or an opportunity to serve is no longer possible, the situation is different. The noble people and their fervor are something wonderful to discuss, but no fun to be! It is incredible how we allow God-inspired passion to die. It simply disappears when there is no soul that catches the Spirit.

Until we face the truth, we will miss the message of Jesus. When, instead of saying that Jesus was the Son of God, as Christians did in the first three centuries, we change to Nicean wording naming Jesus as "God, the Son," we have trapped Jesus' message in an idea born three hundred years after his death, affirmed fifty-six years later, and argued through years of heated, contentious debate.

It is questionable whether Jesus' unique identity can ever be understood or explained with human logic and human words. Dogma has been dignified and authenticated by churchmen who not only did not know how to describe what is beyond us all, but who, just like us, simply did not know and could not comprehend it.

It did not occur to them to attempt to write doctrine that was open-ended toward mystery. They apparently thought they had to have an answer for everything and tried to answer the biggest questions in the world: What is God like? Who was Jesus? Was Jesus God, or like God? In what way was he a connection to God? How was his life special? In the end, what was his life about? Why was he crucified? Why are we sure he lives today? All in all, what does any of this have to do with the Holy Spirit?

If we say that Jesus was God and, therefore, we cannot be like him, we can ignore everything he said about the Spirit in us as it was in him, doing the work of God. I doubt that anyone thinks God asks us all to be crucified as Jesus was, but I do believe that God would invite us all to live as Jesus lived. Jesus spent the latter part of his life trying to reveal God and showing us how to do the same. He dared to let God live through him. He asks us to follow. We have no excuses. *God is not limited except by human limitations.* Jesus could die. We can say "No" to the Spirit.

Spong writes: "Jesus ... reveals the source of love, and then he calls us to enter it."[220] I cannot tell you how many of the wonderful writers I continue to read have come to that same conclusion. Can we see what they see? Are we awake? Do we care? Do we dare?

It can be frightening to speak for the Lord – or to become the eyes or hands or feet of God. I sometimes pray: "Help me to think like you do!" What would happen if, like Frank Laubach, we would play his Game of Minutes? We would try to see with God's eyes and perceive with God's mind once a minute, all day long, every day.[221]

When I am dying, I hope to remember those with whom I have shared my life. I want to be aware and joyfully grateful for their presence in my days. They have meant everything to me! *They have given me God's life through their love.* I know now that there also will be many I can name to whom I have tried to offer what my friends have given me. There will be those with whom I have attempted to share the life that is in me, those with whom I have tried to stand, facing what is real, and offering love, encouragement, and support. To die still sharing God's love in my heart for others, while fully receiving the Spirit's incredible invitation to greater love, is the way I hope to experience that further journey within eternal life.

What would it take for each of us to seriously accept the challenge to be a force through which the Spirit flows? What would it take to consciously work with the Spirit to create the Kingdom of God "on earth as it is in heaven?" What would it take to increasingly sense how to do God's own work for God, to follow the example of Jesus, who came to do one *thing*: "to give life abundantly"? The work of the Cross will never be done.

> God was, in Christ, reconciling the world unto God
> not counting the people's trespasses against them,
> and entrusting the message of reconciliation to us.
>
> II Cor. 5:19 (NTP-IV)

EPILOGUE

There is a voice that says:
"I have put my hand upon you.
It is you I want to call.

Leave all the noise outside you.
Let go of all the wants inside.
For a moment, let all your needs
be set aside.

Now, in the silent, sacred space
you have discovered,
you may be centered, focused,
and at peace.

Feel the life *move* within your body.
Notice power coming *into* you,
every time you breathe.
Hold the breath … and then … watch!
Power flows *from* you
as breath flows out.
It never stops.

The breath flows in again.
With every inhalation
you are filled and filled with grace.
It comes
without your asking.

You are deeply moved.
You are deeply grateful.
You … are … alive!

Listen. Listen.
Whether to
sound or to silence
outside or within,
to silence behind *all* sound.
Someone, some need, is speaking
to the treasure that is in you.
The call is yours to claim.

It is the God of Jesus
you experience as Spirit
who will show us what to do
and who to be.

It always will be the Spirit who teaches
how to look into the eyes and see the heart,
how to touch the heart and teach the mind
how to heal through love and listening,
inclusion and encouragement.

Can there be anything more important
than to know God, who is Spirit:
Jesus' God?

The Spirit asks:
"May I have your whole being
to do what you alone can do
in a way unique,
appropriate for you?"

Before you answer, you may ask
the question once made popular
because it could not be more pertinent:
"What would Jesus do
if he wore my shoes?"

You might be surprised.
You may be able to do some things even better
than could he!
Remember what he said:
"Greater things (than you have yet perceived) …
are now yours to do,
"because I am going, and I leave it up to you."[222]

What is our call?
Some of us know,
and we are living it with passion.
Others of us must wait to recognize
where we best belong.

But one thing is important:
while we wait, we love.
We may not realize
we are following our call already.
For now,
the people and the tasks around us
are our call!

Perhaps we have not recognized
the simplest labor
can reveal the greatest truths
and offer the holiest of inspirations.

Often what we do will seem not good enough.
We may feel that we have failed.
But no one fails who lives in love.
No one fails
if they give away
the best that they can share:
thinking clearly, loving with their all.

We need not announce
that our work is a way to love.
We need not explain
that our words voice our compassion.
We need not say
that the well-being of the people whom we serve
is our purpose and our passion.
The Spirit in our hearts
will speak for itself.

We will share our true identity,
the self we have to give:
that which responds to everyone –
grateful, quiet, and secure,
looking for and drawing out
the soul within their being.

In life that never ceases to be new,
we will dream dreams,
and we will live determined
to do something every day
that helps another to begin again.

Jesus did not go to college.
As far as we can know, he did not travel.
In all probability, for fifteen years or so,
he followed the trade of a carpenter
while thinking, watching, and perceiving
the hearts of people, and
caring for their ordinary needs.

Had he lived today, with different training,
he might have chosen to be an insurance man,
a scientist, an artist – or
just what he chose to be before:
a carpenter.

The Spirit living in him
can live in anyone
and express itself in countless ways.

Were he to come again, who knows?
Might the Spirit that is his life and ours
come as a woman?
Might "he" be "she?"
Might she run for president,
serve an inner city shelter,
be a musician or a mother,
or, at different times,
be all of the above!

The Spirit speaks in many tongues,
with many voices.
The Spirit sings in every heart
and pleads only that we hear.

The Spirit serves.
What we can do,
according to our unique ability,
the Spirit *will* express
in and through our being.

I can never say all that may be said
of how the Spirit lived and died and rose in Jesus.
But I know the Spirit dares to live in me,
in spite of what I cannot do or be,
yet more than *fully* through me.
I have been amazed!

Beware of those who quench the Spirit.
They are not sent by God.
Do not let them say:
"Who do you think you are?"
Those are words inducing fear and weakness,
not humility or modesty or wisdom.

They often will be spoken
in the spirit of jealousy and superiority,
meant to hold you down.
You must not receive the message
if it would lessen
what you can give to others
and give back to God.

There may be times
when the Spirit seems to
leave a heart vacant and used up,
unneeded, unnoticed,
and alone;
when no one asks for us
to share the Spirit,
the essence of the soul.

Sometimes
the fire within us finds
no place to light another flame.
And yet this treasured life,
this burning hope to offer
what we have to give,
must never be abandoned.
No other gift compares.

When the fire is challenged,
it is time to simply do the task at hand,
humbly to offer love
until the embers glow again.

The Spirit will not die!
The fire is deep in everyone:
Its flames of gentle power grow
until it fully lives
right where we are,
until we sing increasingly
the little chant that
lives inside our heads
and accompanies our days.

"Use me. Be me!"
Our spirits sing
as, once again new birth is given
with new trust and joy.

The gospel hidden in the Hebrew scriptures speaks
in this very moment:
"Wake up! Get up! Arise!
The glory of the Lord has risen
in the place where we are standing.
It *rises* … upon you and me,
upon us all!"[223]

This unfathomable More, this Life,
Is All that ever shall be.

ENDNOTES

p. 12   1. Exod. 3:14. This quotation also can be translated as "I will be who (or what) I will be," according to the NRSV footnote and many other sources. I have taken the liberty to say: "who *and* what" since both are true simultaneously. This is helpful regarding use of personal versus non-personal references to God. In one sentence, this text reveals that God who is Being, or Life Itself, is eternal and also both personal and transcendent, that is, more than personal.

p. 13   2. Arnold Toynbee, *Christianity Among the Religions of the World* (New York: Charles Scribner's Sons, 1957). Toynbee authored the comprehensive twelve-volume study entitled: *A Study of History* (London: Oxford University Press, 1934, 1961).

p. 15   3. Frank Laubach, *Channels of Spiritual Power* (Westwood, NJ: Revel, 1954).

p. 15   4. Grace Adolphsen Brame, *Faith, the Yes of the Heart* (Minneapolis, MN: Augsburg Fortress, 1999). See Chapter 4, "Loving With Both Head and Heart," on belief and trust, pp. 51–64.

p. 18   5. Grace Adolphsen Brame, "The Cross: Payment or Gift?" *Perspectives in Religious Studies*, vol. 32, no. 2, Summer 2005, pp. 167–181.

p. 19   6. Raymund Schwager, *Must There Be Scapegoats? Violence and Redemption in the Bible* (San Francisco: Harper and Row, 1987), p. 55.

p. 21   7. Anonymous, *The Cloud of Unknowing*, ed. and intro. William Johnson, S.J. (Garden City, NY: Image Books, 1973), p. 80.

p. 21   8. Henry F. French, former Vice President for Academic Publishing, Augsburg Fortress Publishers, correspondence: May 31, 2010.

p. 21   9. *Cloud of Unknowing*, p. 80.

p. 21   10. Grace Adolphsen Brame, *Receptive Prayer: Prayer Which Nourishes, Heals, and Empowers*, 3rd ed. (Wilmington, DE: Charis Enterprises, 2005).

p. 23   11. "Philo," *Internet Encyclopedia of Philosophy #10*, ed. James Feiser and Bradley Dowden: http://www.iep.utm.edu/philo (accessed 7 February 2010). Philo, a Hellenistic Jew, attempted to explain Hebrew theology in Greek philosophical terms.

p. 23   12. Leonard Swidler, "Goddess Worship and Women Priests," in *Women Priests: A Catholic Commentary on the Vatican Declaration*, ed. Leonard and Arlene Swidler (New York: Paulist Press, 1977), p. 174. Leonard Swidler wrote that the term *Elohim* is derived from names of even more ancient gods: *El* and *Eloah*, masculine and feminine names for two gods said to have a court of female and male lesser gods, the Elohim. *Elohim* was later chosen as a name for the one God.

p. 23   13. E. O. James, *The Cult of the Mother Goddess* (New York: Praeger, 1959), pp. 180, 177, quoted in Swidler, *Women Priests*, p. 174. "The divine was first worshipped as female...." [In the] "early Paleolithic Period [the pre-historic

Stone Age], there was no male god. Furthermore, in the following Neolithic Period, goddess worship increased."

p. 23 14. Cuthbert A. Simpson, "Exegesis on Genesis," *The Interpreters' Bible*, vol. 1 (New York: Abingdon-Cokesbury Press, 1952), p. 485.

p. 24 15. Brame, *Receptive Prayer*, pp. 37, 38, 49, 78.

p. 24 16. Ibid. pp. 145–48.

p. 24 17. Ibid. pp. 38–39.

p. 25 18. Grace Adolphsen Brame, *A Manual of Receptive Prayer: For Study, Practice, and Retreats*, 2nd ed. (Wilmington, DE: Charis Enterprises, 2006).

p. 29 19. John 14:28.

p. 29 20. Jurgen Moltmann, *The Crucified God* (San Francisco: HarperSanFrancisco, 1991), p. 208. "Christ is the visible revelation of God's being … in the reality of [the] world."

p. 29 21. John 14:6.

p. 29 22. Ibid.

p. 29 23. John 14:12.

p. 30 24. Acts 1:8.

p. 30 25. John 15:16.

p. 30 26. John 14:12.

p. 31 27. Brame, *Faith*, pp. 71, 72.

p. 31 28. Romans 11:29.

p. 36 29. Schwager, p. 55.

p. 43 30. St. Augustine, *De gratia et libero arbitrio (On Grace and Free Will)*, is one of eight writings on grace by Augustine (Washington, DC: The Catholic University of America Press, 1968).

p. 43 31. *Webster's New Twentieth Century Dictionary of the English Language*, Unabridged, 2nd ed. (Cleveland: William Collins Publishers, 1979).

p. 43 32. McBrien, *Catholicism*, p.158. "Nature mean[s] human existence without grace, but at the same time as radically open to, and capable of receiving, grace."

p. 44 33. "There Is A Green Hill Far Away" can be found in many older hymnals including *Service Book and Hymnal*, Lutheran Churches Cooperating in The Commission on the Liturgy and Hymnal (Minneapolis, MN: Augsburg Publishing House and Philadelphia: Board of Publication, LCA, 1958), p. 77.

p. 45 34. John C. Dwyer, "The Implications of Tillich's Theology of the Cross for Catholic Theology," in *Paul Tillich: A New Catholic Assessment* (Collegeville, MN: Liturgical Press, 1994), p. 74.

p. 45 35. Dwyer, p. 86.

p. 45 36. Dwyer, p. 87.

p. 46 37. Anselm of Canterbury, "*Cur Deus Homo*," in *St. Anselm's Basic Writings*, trans. S. N. Deane, intro. Charles Hartshorne (LaSalle, IL: Open Court Publishing Co., 2001), pp. 191–301. Anselm was exiled by each of two kings of England for not consecrating priests invested by the kings. While exiled he wrote this famous treatise.

p. 46 38. Gerard S. Sloyan, in 1994, then professor at Temple University, pointed out the ambiguity caused by the lack of punctuation accompanying the title of *Cur Deus Homo*.

p. 46   39. Roger Haight, *Jesus, Symbol of God* (Maryknoll, NY: Orbis Books, 1999), p. 230.

p. 46   40. *Anselm of Canterbury*, Hopkins, p. 139.

p. 47   41. Dwyer, p. 78.

p. 47   42. Dwyer, p. 74. "*This 'satisfaction/reparation/compensation/atonement' theory of the Cross is not Pauline* (although it has often been given a pseudo-Pauline pedigree), and it might seem strange that, in the absence of any real foundation in Paul's writings, it has assumed such a prominent position in dogmatic theology manuals and has been able to exercise such a destructive influence on liturgy and devotional life." (emphasis added).

p. 47   43. *Anselm of Canterbury*, vol. 1, ed. and trans. Jasper Hopkins and Herbert Richardson (New York: The Edwin Mellen Press, 1974), p. 139.

p. 49   44. Peter King, "Peter Abelard," *The Stanford Encyclopedia of Philosophy* (Fall 2008 ed.), ed. Edward N. Zalta, (Stanford, CA: Stanford University): http://plato.stanford.edu/archives/fall2008/entries/abelard. The respected monk, Bernard of Clairvaux (much beloved by Martin Luther), was against Abelard's explanation of the Trinity and his attitude toward reason. This encyclopedia claims that the Council of Sens was influenced by a kangaroo court set up by Bernard to meet at the same time as the Council of Sens. Abelard was then briefly silenced by the Pope.

p. 49   45. Robin Maas and Gabriel O'Donnell, O.P. *Spiritual Traditions for the Contemporary Church* (Nashville: Abingdon Press, 1990), p. 12.

p. 49   46. A Monk of the Orthodox Church, *Orthodox Spirituality* (Crestwood, NY: St. Vladimir's Seminary Press, 1978), p. 75. This author is now known to be Lev Gilet.

p. 51   47. Gerald O'Collins, S.J. and Edward G. Farrugia, S.J., "Christocentrism," *A Concise Dictionary of Theology* (New York/Mahwah, NJ: Paulist Press, 1991) "A systematic focusing of all theology and devotional life on the person and work of Jesus Christ."

p. 53   48. I Thess. 5:17.

p. 53   49. O'Collins and Farrugia, *Dictionary of Theology*, p. 165. "Original sin ... the loss of grace and the wounding of nature suffered by our first parents, which affected all later generations [which] inherited ... the sinful condition into which all human beings are born.... *Eastern Christianity has ... no theology of original sin.*" (author's emphasis)

p. 53   50. See St. Thomas Aquinas, *Summa Theologica*, trans. Fathers of the English Dominican Province (Westminster, MD: Christian Classics, 1981), vol. 2, question 81, art. 1, p. 953. "[T]he semen, by its own power, transmits the human nature from parent to child, and with that nature, the stain which infects it."

p. 53   51. Paul Tillich, *Systematic Theology*, 3 vols. (Chicago: University of Chicago Press, 1951–1963), vol. 1, p. 12. "The ultimate concern is unconditional, independent of any condtions of character, desire, or circumstance. The unconditional concern is total: no part of ourselves or of our world is excluded from it; there is no 'place' to flee from it." Ref. Psalm 139.

p. 53   52. Toynbee, p. vii. Toynbee refers to "man's self-centered worship of himself."

p. 54   53. Annemarie Schimmel, *Mystical Dimensions of Islam* (Chapel Hill: University of North Carolina Press, 1975), pp. 190, 171. Islam's similar understanding (regarding the heart, in this case) is that we are born to be "mirrors of God," but the mirrors have become dusty and rusty. "The mirror in which God reflects Himself ... has to be polished ... until all dust and rust have disappeared and it reflects the primordial divine light." Nevertheless it can be cleaned and renewed. In Islam, to remember God is to pray, and praying "polishes the mirror of [the] heart so that it becomes pure enough to reflect God's beauty."

p. 54   54. French, correspondence cited.

p. 54   55. Tillich, *Systematic*, vol. 1, p. 259.

p. 59   56. French, correspondence cited.

p. 60   57. Toynbee, p. 22. The general understanding is that God is a personal term as well as a biblical one, whereas *Ultimate, Original,* or *Eternal Reality* is employed more frequently by philosophers and is broader and more objective. It is possible to use both, with the intent to express the personal as well as the transcendent. The term, *the Impersonal*, infrequently employed, simply refers to what has been referred to by mystics as "the God beyond God," that is, indescribable and nameless. That means the God beyond explanations and emotional attachments. Toynbee writes: "[That] presence ... that is spiritually greater than [the human being] in personal terms, reveals itself as god, and in its impersonal facet, as absolute reality."

p. 60   58. Toynbee, p. 17. "Plato means by 'myth' a form of expression to which one turns when the resources of the intellect have been exhausted and yet one still has something of immense importance and significance which one must express somehow."

p. 61   59. Martin Luther, "Sermon for the Sunday after the Feast of the Circumcision, January 4, 1540," in *Luther's Works*, Weimar ed. (WA), vol. 1, chap. 49, p. 9. A more complete form of the statement is: "Faith is the yes of the heart ... a confidence on which one stakes one's life." It is this declaration upon which my previous book, *Faith, The Yes of The Heart*, was written.

p. 65   60. The story is told more fully in *Faith, the Yes of the Heart*, pp. 55–56.

p. 66   61. Matthew Fox, *Original Blessing: A Primer in Creation Spirituality* (Rochester, VT: Bear and Co., 1983). Fox is one writer who deals well with these concepts.

p. 68   62. John Shelby Spong, *Jesus for the Non-religious* (San Francisco: HarperSanfrancisco, 2007), p. 2.

p. 70   63. Fritjof Capra, *The Tao of Physics* (Boulder, CO: Shambala Publications, 1976).

p. 73   64. John Meyendorf, *Byzantine Theology* (New York: Fordham University Press, 1979), p. 40. The bishops' ecumenical Council of 1170 dealt with the distinction of Christ's humanity from his divinity. Meyendorf writes: "The Council of 1170 reaffirmed once again the decisions of Chalcedon and Constantinople II about the divinity of Christ, [in essence] united with a real and active humanity ... created, depictable, and mortal.... Divinity is certainly greater ... than such humanity."

p. 74   65. Pastor Judith Van Osdol contributed this insight regarding the Syro-Phoenician woman who, in telling words, reminded Jesus that "even the dogs eat the crumbs that fall from the master's table" (Matt. 15:27).

p. 75   66. "Christians Without A Prayer," *Wall Street Journal*, Dec. 24, 1996. Also Nina Shea, *In the Lions' Den* (Nashville: Broadman and Holman Publishers, 1997), p. ix.

p. 76   67. Richard Wurmbrand, *Tortured for Christ* (Bartlesville, OK: Voice of the Martyrs, Inc., 1968), p. 34.

p. 76   68. John Shelby Spong, *A New Christianity for A New World* (San Francisco: HarperSanFrancisco, 2001), p. 140.

p. 77   69. Voice of the Martyrs, Bartlesville, OK, also has a monthly magazine bearing the name of the organization. The magazine covers current martyrdom throughout the world.

p. 78   70. Toynbee, pp. 18–19. The full quotation is found later, in the quotation section of this book.

p. 79   71. I John 4:8.

p. 79   72. Schwager, p. 55.

p. 81   73. Tillich, *Systematic*, vol. 1, p. 285. "Not everyone is prepared to accept saving grace."

p. 85   74. Anselm of Canterbury, "Proslogion," "The Ontological Argument," *Philosophy of Religion*, 2nd ed., ed. George L. Abernethy and Thomas A. Langford (New York: MacMillan, 1968), pp. 170-174.

p. 85   75. *Pseudo-Dionysius Areopagite, The Divine Names and Mystical Theology*, trans. and intro. John D. Jones (Milwaukee, WI: Marquette University Press, 1980), pp. 209–222.

p. 86   76. *The Koran, interpreted* trans. Arthur J. Arberry, sura (chapter) 2:109 (New York: Macmillan, 1955), p. 42.

p. 88   77. Coventry Patmore, "Magna Moralia, xxii", in *The Rod, the Root, and the Flower*, quoted in Evelyn Underhill, *Mysticism: A Study In The Nature and Development of Man's Spiritual Consciousness* (New York: E. P. Dutton, 1961), p. 199.

p. 88   78. Tillich, *Dynamics of Faith* (Chicago: University of Chicago, 1957), pp. 41–54. The concept also appears throughout his *Systematic Theology*.

p. 88   79. Huston Smith, *The World's Religions* (San Francisco: HarperSanFrancisco, 1991), p. 128.

p. 89   80. Luther, *Works*, WA, vol. 7, p. 337, trans. William Lazareth. See Brame, *Receptive Prayer*, p. 119.

p. 89   81. James H. Fowler, *Stages of Faith* (San Francisco: HarperSanFrancisco, 1981).

p. 89   82. Martin Luther, *Lectures on Romans*, WA, vol. 56, p. 70, and *Lectures on*

Galatians (1519), WA, vol. 2, p. 496.

p. 90 83. I am indebted to Pastor Brady Faggart, Greensboro, NC, for this story.

p. 90 84. Johann Heermann, "Ah, Holy Jesus," trans. Robert Bridges, *Service Book and Hymnal*, (Minneapolis, MN: Augsburg Publishing House and Philadelphia: Board of Publications, LCA), p. 85.

p. 94 85. This is the venerable translation of the Authorized King James Version of the Bible, commissioned by King James I of England and published in 1611.

p. 94 86. *nephesh*, James Strong, S.T.D., LL.D., *A Concise Dictionary of the Words in the Hebrew Bible*, with their Renderings, #5315: http://www.heraldmag.org/olb/contents/dictionaries/SHebrew.pdf (accessed 10 July, 2010). A "breathing creature ... [with] animal vitality," a person [having] desire, pleasure, lust, etc.

p. 94 87. *ruach*, Jeff A. Benner, Ancient Hebrew Research Center (©1999-2007): http://www.ancient-hebrew.org (accessed 10 July, 2010). The *ruach* is wind following a prescribed path. "A man's wind is not just a spiritual entity within a man, but ...his character."

p. 94 88. *Rua ha-odesh*, *The Jewish Encyclopedia*: http://www.jewishencyclopedia.com (accesed 10 July, 2010). The Rua ha-odesh [*Ruach ha Kodesh*] is, literally, the Holy Spirit. Transliterations vary in spelling and diacritical markings.

p. 95 89. This explanation is the basis for my books on Receptive Prayer.

p. 100 90. Meyendorf, *Byzantine Theology*, p. 11.

p. 100 91. Richard McBrien, *Catholicism*, 3rd ed., (SanFrancisco: HarperSanFrancisco, 1994), pp. 441, 1238. To Arius, Jesus was "the Son of God, the highest of creatures, greater than us, but less than God.

p. 100 92. McBrien, *Catholicism*, pp. 289–290.

p. 101 93. John Meyendorf, *Byzantine Theology*, pp. 32–41.

p. 103 94. The Trinity, seen as three different modes of God's relationship to us and activity among us, is termed *modalism*. It has largely been held in disfavor by Christian theologians but seems to be increasingly accepted today, probably because it makes so much sense.

p. 104 95. McBrien, p. 131.

p. 105 96. C. S. Lewis, *Mere Christianity* (New York: Macmillan, 1977), p 49. Lewis says: "Goodness is, so to speak, itself: badness is only spoiled goodness. And there must be something good first before it can be spoiled." In *Letters to Malcolm*, he further writes: "Every sin is the distortion of an energy poured into us." *Letters to Malcolm: Chiefly on Prayer* (Boston: Houghton Mifflin Harcourt, 2003).

p. 106 97. Brame, Faith, p. 117. Thomas Aquinas noted that God possesses infinite, absolute power (*potentia absoluta*) but chooses not to use all of it for the sake of human spiritual growth. Then, God ordains God's own self-limitation or *potentia ordinata*. Here, the old image of God as parent is appropriate. To very small children, a parent can be overwhelmingly powerful, all-wise, and authoritative. It is sensitive love in a parent that knows when to stop crossing the street with growing children, when not to help them with their homework, and when not to give them many of the things that children desire.

p. 106 98. *The Koran Interpreted*, trans. Arberry, p. 302. Sura (chapter) 17, verse 1, only touches upon the intriguing story of the Prophet's one-night journey – the *Mi'raj* (ascent) to the presence of Allah. Leaving from Jerusalem on the back of a winged white horse named Barak, he is said to have ascended to the seventh heaven and the throne of God. There he was given *salat*, the pattern of daily prayer to be done as "remembrance of God" five times a day. On his journey upward, he passed through six ascending levels toward the throne. Most levels were watched over by a Hebrew prophet, but in the fourth were Jesus (considered a prophet by Islam) and the Gospel writer, John. (The title of Islamic scripture may be spelled as Qur'an or Koran.)

p. 106 99. The Nicene Creed.

p. 106 100. Charles Haddon Spurgeon, "There Is No Place Where God Is Not," in *The Treasury of David* (Charleston, SC: BiblioBazaar, 2008), p. 168.

p. 107 101. For a non-academic and insightful book on the Holy Spirit, see Elizabeth Barberi, *Matter of Spirit* (Salisbury, CT: Spiritual Understanding Network, 2004).

p. 107 102. John Redtail Freesoul, *Breath of the Invisible* (Wheaton, IL: Theosophical Publishing House, 1986), p. 86.

p. 107 103. C. S. Lewis, *The Case for Christianity* (New York: Macmillan, 1979).

p. 109 104. Brame, *Faith*, p. 136.

p. 110 105. Donald M. Baillie, *God Was In Christ* (New York: Charles Scribner's and Sons, 1948), p. 197.

p. 111 106. Baillie, p. 191. Baillie comments: "We … speak of an eternal Atonement in the very being and life of God…. God's reconciling work cannot be confined to any one moment in history." p. 191.

p. 111 107. "What Wondrous Love Is This?" North American Folk Hymn, 19th century, in *Evangelical Lutheran Worship* (Minneapolis, MN: AugsburgFortress Publishers, 2006), p. 666.

p. 111 108. Søren Kierkegaard, *Works of Love*, trans. Edna and Howard Hong (New York: Harper and Row, 1962), p. 320.

p. 112 109. Tillich, *Systematic*, vol. 1, p. 235. "The being of God is *being-itself.* The being of God cannot be understood as the existence of *a* being alongside others or above others." (author's emphasis)

p. 114 110. In both Mark 10:45 and Matthew 20:28, Jesus is quoted as saying: "The Son of Man has come not to be served, but to serve, and to give his life as a ransom for many."

p. 114 111. Peter Schmiechen, *Saving Power: Theories of Atonement and Forms of the Church* (Grand Rapids, MI: William B. Eerdmans Publishing Co., 2005).

p. 114 112. Gustav Aulén, *Christus Victor* (New York: Macmillan, 1969).

p. 116 113. I would like to suggest J. Denny Weaver's *A Non-Violent Atonement* (Grand Rapids, MI: William B. Eerdmans Publishing Company, 2001) as one which people may read to grasp a bit of the scope of what scholars have been thinking.

p. 119 114. T. H. Gaster, "Sacrifice and Offerings, O.T.," *The Interpreters' Dictionary of the Bible* (Nashville: Abingdon Press, 1962).

p. 119 115. Ibid., pp. 148, 149.

p. 119 116. E. O. James, *Sacrifice and Sacrament* (New York: Barnes & Noble, 1962), pp. 19, 26, 27, 89.

p. 119 117. James, p. 61.

p. 119 118. Toynbee, pp. 42, 43.

p. 120 119. The first exile of Jews to Babylon was in 598 BCE and the major exile in 586 or 587. Cyrus stopped it by an edict in 538, but many Jews did not leave until the second temple was finished in 515. For some people, the exile might have lasted for forty-eight years, but, for others, it could have gone on for eighty-three to one hundred years or more.

p. 120 120. James, p. 70.

p. 120 121. Rolland E. Wolfe, "Micah," *The Interpreters' Bible*, vol. 6. It has been confusing to many people reading Hebrew scriptures to understand the meaning of "passing [their] sons through the fire."

p. 120 122. Ibid.

p. 120 123. I Kings 16:30 counts Ahab as the most evil of all of Israel's kings up to that time. After marrying Jezebel, Ahab built a house of worship for the god, Baal, as well as erecting an asherah, a sacred pole at which people worshipped the Amorite and Canaanite goddess Asherah.

p. 120 124. Biblical references include Deut. 18:10; Lev. 18:21, 20:2-4; II Kings 23:10, 32:35.

p. 122 125. Gaster, pp. 147–159.

p. 126 126. Gerhard Forde, "For You?" in *The Lutheran* (April 1996).

p. 128 127. Origen, a Christian Greek, at first had great theological power in the church, serving as director of the catechetical school in Alexandria, Egypt, for twenty-one years and then was founder and head of a similar school in Caesarea, the Roman capital of Palestine. The catechism is the set of basic theological beliefs of each church, but differs according to denomination.

p. 128 128. Aulén, pp. 103, 104.

p. 128 129. James, p. 120. James says that the forensic idea of paying a ransom to the devil was "generally accepted with some modification by ... St. Hilary of Poitiers, St. Augustine, Gregory the Great, St. Leo, and their successors such as St. Bernard of Clairvaux and Peter the Lombard."

p. 128 130. Mary B. Cunningham and Elizabeth Theokritoff, *The Cambridge Companion to Orthodox Christian Theology* (Cambridge: Cambridge University Press, 2008), p. 104. The term, "devil," (*diabolos* in Greek) often is defined as "slanderer" or "backbiter." But it also can mean "divider," a term that means the opposite of "reconciler."

p. 129 131. "Anthony," *The Oxford Dictionary of the Christian Church*, ed. F. L. Cross and E. A. Livingstone (New York: Oxford University Press, 1997), p. 80. After giving away all he owned, Anthony lived on the Outer Mountain at Pispir from 285 to 310. There he counseled those who came to him and, it is said, fought demonic forces in the form of wild beasts. In 310 he moved, for greater solitude, to the Inner Mountain near the Red Sea. He is especially well known because of his biography, *The Life of Antony*, usually ascribed to Athanasius of Egypt.

p. 130   132. Cunningham and Theokritoff, p. 169. The authors have made this famous phrase somewhat inclusive by writing: "He became human so that we might be made divine."

p. 130   133. Paul was describing sanctification when he wrote II Corinthians 3:17-18.

p. 130   134. Luther, *Works*, WA, vol. 45, p. 582; WA, vol. 24, chaps. 14–16, *Sermons on the Gospel of St. John*, ed. Jaroslav Pelikan, trans. Martin H. Bertram (St. Louis, MO: Concordia, 1961), p. 78.

p. 130   135. Meister Eckhart (1270–1327), a Dominican monk, is often thought of as Christianity's finest mystic. He was charged with heresy. Although interrogated and treated harshly, he died before the issuance of a papal bull in 1329, condemning 28 of his propositions. Probably the deepest misunderstanding about his philosophy was in terms of *henosis* and *theosis*. (Diacritical markings for the two words differ between East and West.) When Eckhart said: "The eye with which I see God is the eye with which God sees me," he meant that, in a state of union with God, one sees with God's eyes, by the influence of the Holy Spirit. He was not claiming identity with God.

p. 131   136. Aulén, p. 96.

p. 131   137. "atonement," *Oxford Dictionary of the Christian Church*, 3rd ed., ed. E. A. Livingstone (Oxford: Oxford University Press, 1997).

p. 131   138. *A Scholarly Miscellany*, ed. Eugene Fairweather (New York: Macmillan, 1970), p. 282.

p. 132   139. Aulén, p. 96.

p. 132   140. Ibid.

p. 133   141. Tillich, *Systematic*, vol. 2, pp. 178, 179.

p. 133   142. Tillich, *Systematic*, vol. 2, p. 171. "In this formulation of the doctrine of atonement, any relation to [the human being] is completely lacking. A cosmic drama ... happens above man's head.... It is the experience of the love of God which precedes ... the conquest of existential estrangement."

p. 133   143. Cunningham and Theokritoff, p. 98.

p. 134   144. Ibid.

p. 134   145. S. Mark Heim, *Saved from Sacrifice: A Theology of the Cross* (Grand Rapids, MI: William B. Eerdmans Publishing Company, 2006), p. 4.

p. 134   146. Cunningham and Theokritoff, p. 98.

p. 134   147. Martin Luther, *The Shorter Commentary on Galatians*, as quoted in Aulén, p. 106.

p. 135   148. Evelyn Underhill, "The Dark Night of the Soul," in *Mysticism* (1974), pp. 380–412.

p. 135   149. This is such an important statement that I cannot forget it and do not want to omit it. Yet I no longer remember where to find it in *Luther's Works*. I would appreciate knowing the reference if anyone will pass it along.

p. 136   150. Edgar M. Carlson, *The Reinterpretation of Luther* (Philadelphia: The Westminster Press, 1948), pp. 69, 56.

p. 136 151. Kierkegaard took on this theological challenge. His *Works of Love* must have been so-called intentionally. He was showing, as Luther said, that love produces good works. The mistake to be avoided is doing good works in order to "get something," to be blessed, or to gain eternal life. Good works for selfish motives versus those done joyfully or sympathetically for others was the point.

p. 136 152. Aulén, p. 116.

p. 136 153. Aulén, p. 127.

p. 136 154. *Saint Augustine: On Free Choice of the Will*, trans. Anna S. Benjamin and L. H. Hackstaff (New York: Macmillan, 1985), p. xviii. The *felix culpa* or "fortunate fall" or "happy fault" is part of the totality argument that says if we were to look at any event as a whole, we would find no evil or sadness.

p. 136 155. "The Easter Proclamation," usually sung by a cantor on Easter eve. Why these lines have not been removed from the Proclamation is a mystery. Have we simply been careless, or do we still think that way?

p. 137 156. The response to too many films and articles has been to fasten on the specific instigators or perpetrators, completely forgetting Christ's stated purpose to "give life abundantly" (John 10:10), thus to heal, free, and bind up wounds (Luke 4:18).

p. 137 157. Isaac Watts, "When I Survey the Wondrous Cross, no. 185, in *The Hymnal for Worship and Celebration* (Waco, TX: Word Music, 1986).

p. 139 158. Toynbee, pp. 21, 43.

p. 139 159. See Introduction.

p. 140 160. Yvonne Sherwood, "Binding-Unbinding: Divided Responses of Judaism, Christianity, and Islam to the 'Sacrifice' of Abraham's Beloved Son," *Journal of the American Academy of Religion* (Dec. 2004): pp. 821–862.

p. 140 161. Vol. 2, sura 37:99-113.

p. 140 162. Sherwood.

p. 141 163. The plural forms of *midrash* and *tafsîr* are *midrashim* and *tafarsîr*. The terms mean, respectively, "to seek" and "to reveal."

p. 141 164. Muqtadar Kahn, in lecture to clergy in Wilmington, Delaware, on April 22, 2010, shared this traditional story.

p. 143 165. "*do ut des*," James T. Bretske, S.J., ed., *Consecrated Phrases: A Latin Theological Dictionary* (Collegeville, MN: The Liturgical Press, 1998). Bretske says that *do ut des* is "positively a *quid pro quo* (q.v.) in which one does something in order to receive something from another; negatively, a sort of *lex talionis* (q.v.), a getting even or taking revenge."

p. 144 166. Evelyn Underhill, *Worship* (New York: Harper and Brothers, 1936), p. 48.

p. 145 167. I no longer know where this information can be found, but would appreciate information about it.

p. 146 168. Evelyn Underhill, *The Mystery of Sacrifice* (London: Longmans, Green, and Co., 1938), p. 20.

p. 148 169. Hebrews 10:5 quotes the first of these lines in reference to Christ.

p. 148 170. Brame, *Faith*, p. 136.

p. 148 171. Martin Luther, "Lectures on Romans," in *Works*, vol. 25, p. 435.

p. 148   172. Martin Luther, "Preface to the Epistle of St. Paul to the Romans, 1522," in *Martin Luther: Selections from His Writings*, ed. John Dillenberger (New York: Doubleday & Company, Inc., 1961), p. 33.

p. 149   173. "redemption," *The Oxford Dictionary of English Etymology*, ed. C. T. Onions (Oxford: Clarendon Press, 1966).

p. 149   174. Tillich, *Systematic*, vol. 2, p. 170.

p. 149   175. "salvation," *Jesus Living in Mary: Handbook of the Spirituality of St. Louis de Montfort* (Litchfield, CT: Montfort Publications, 1994): Eternal Word Television Network, 1998: http://www.ewtn.com/library/montfort/Handbook/Salvatio.htm (accessed 4 July, 2010).

p. 150   176. Douglas Harper, "salvation," "saved," "safe," *Online Etymology Dictionary*: http://www.etymonline.com (accessed 4 July, 2010).

p. 150   177. Tillich, *Systematic*, vol. 2, pp. 166, 170. "The original meaning of salvation (from *salvus*) [is] '*healed*....' Healing means uniting what is estranged, giving a center to that which is split, overcoming the split between God and man, man and his world, man and himself."

p. 150   178. Evelyn Underhill, "Sanctity: The Perfection of Love," in *The Ways of the Spirit*, comp., ed., and intro. Grace Adolphsen Brame (New York: Crossroad, 1991), p. 68.

p. 150   179. "Israel," *Webster's Geographical Dictionary* (Springfield, MA: G. and C. Merriam Co., Publishers, 1949). After the death of Solomon (c. 933 BCE), the ten northern Hebrew tribes of Israel seceded from the union and became the Northern Kingdom or Israel. The two southern Hebrew tribes chose to be known as Judah, and its people were called Jews. After being conquered by Assyria in 722 BCE, the Northern Kingdom was weakened and disappeared, becoming known as the lost tribes of Israel. Only Judah and the Jewish people were left. Thus it is correct to call *their* ancestors Hebrews, not Jews.

p. 154   180. "salvation," Alan Richardson, *Interpreters' Dictionary*.

p. 154   181. John 17:3.

p. 154   182. "atonement," C. L. Mitton, *Interpreters' Dictionary*.

p. 155   183. Michael Barnes, *In the Presence of Mystery* (Mystic, CT: Twenty-Third Publications, 1984), pp. 87–152.

p. 157   184. The Rev. Richard Stazesky first introduced me to this wonderful insight. It is the clearest story I know that shows the difference between the meaning of redemption and salvation.

p. 158   185. Reinhold Niebuhr, *The Nature and Destiny of Man*, 2 vols. (New York: Charles Scribner's Sons, 1943), p. 53.

p. 159   186. I was moved recently when I asked a new retiree what she was going to be doing with her time. With a light in her eyes, she answered: "I want to give myself away!" She has always done much of that, but now she feels that she can do it more freely and wholeheartedly.

p. 159   187. Chester P. Michael and Marie C. Norrisey, *Arise: A Christian Psychology of Love* (Charlottesville, VA: The Open Door, Inc., 1981), p 108.

p. 161   188. Underhill, "Sanctity: The Perfection of Love," in *Ways*, comp., ed., and intro. Brame, p. 67.

p. 161   189. Bernhard Erling, "Gustaf Aulén: A Life Well Lived," *The Christian Century* (April 1978), p. 424.

p. 161   190. Gustav Aulén, *The Faith of the Christian Church*, trans. Erich Wahlstrom, (Philadelphia: Fortress Press, 1973), p. 206.

p. 161   191. Underhill, "The End for Which We Were Made," in *Ways*, comp., ed., and intro. Brame, p. 136. This is repeated in "Inner Grace and Outward Sign," p. 176.

p. 162   192. See Luke 13:34.

p. 163   193. Baillie, p. 148, 149.

p. 165   194. Richard Maurice Bucke, *Cosmic Consciousness* (New York: E.P. Dutton and Company, Inc., 1969 ed.), pp. 27–33.

p. 165   195. Robert Wright, *The Evolution of God* (New York: Little, Brown, and Company, 2009), p. 17.

p. 166   196. Robert Bellah, "Religious Evolution," *American Sociological Review*, 39 (1964), pp. 348–74. Also see summary of his views in Barnes, pp. 3–5.

p. 166   197. Barnes, p. 1.

p. 166   198. Edward Tylor, *Primitive Culture*, vol. 1, p. 400, quoted in Wright, *The Evolution of God*, p. 13. Wright, a philosopher of religion, says: "Tylor is credited with a doctrine which became a pillar of social anthropology – the 'psychic unity of mankind,' the idea that people of all races are basically the same, that there is a universal human nature."

p. 166   199. Wright, p. 14.

p. 170   200. Karl Jaspers, *Vom Ursprung und Ziel der Geschichte* (Zurich: Artemis, 1949), pp. 19–43.

p. 170   201. Ewert H. Cousins, *Global Spirituality Toward the Meeting of Mystical Paths* (Radhakrishnan Institute for Advanced Study in Philosophy; Madras, India: University of Madras, 1985), p. 11.

p. 170   202. Ibid.

p. 170   203. Karen Armstrong, *A History of God* (New York: Ballantine, 1993), p. 3.

p. 171   204. *Standard Dictionary of Folklore, Mythology, and Legend*, ed. Maria Leach and Jerome Fried (New York: Funk and Wagnalls Company, 1949).

p. 171   205. Ibid., p. 90. A debated suggestion exists that Amenhotep IV, or Akhenaton, was actually Moses' Egyptian father. Furthermore, through the influence of Moses, who was monotheistic and said to be a priest of Aton, Yahweh became known as the principal god and, finally, the only God of the Israelites.

p. 171   206. Bucke, pp. 45, 61–82.

p. 172   207. O'Collins and Farrugia, p. 79. O'Collins and Farrugia say that the *filioque* phrase, "and the Son," has "often been considered the greatest point of difference separating east and west."

p. 173   208. Karl Rahner, *Theological Investigations*, vol. 20 (Baltimore, MD: Helicon Press), p. 149.

p. 174   209. My friend, the Quaker Douglas V. Steere, learned Danish simply to translate this work into English. Of partially Danish extraction, I consider the language most difficult and admire Steere enormously for his integrity.

p. 175 210. Ewald M. Plass, *What Luther Says*, n. 6 (St. Louis: Concordia Publishing House, 1959), p. 824. This is a comment by Plass, describing Luther's theology.

p. 176 211. Martin Luther, *Works*, WA, vol. 7, p. 337, trans. Lazareth. Quoted more extensively in Brame, *Receptive Prayer*, p. 119.

p. 177 212. Anselm of Canterbury, "Proslogion," pp. 170-174. Here Anselm says God is beyond the scope of human comprehension, and, in this case, he was right.

p. 179 213. James H. Fowler, *Stages of Faith* (San Francisco; Harper San Francisco, 1981).

p. 179 214. Chester P. Michael, "Different Levels of Faith," in *An Introduction to Spiritual Direction* (New York/Mahwah, New Jersey, 2004) p. 99. The book includes a summary of the approaches of most of these psychologists.

p. 182 215. Martin Luther, *Three Treatises*, "The Freedom of A Christian" (Philadelphia: Fortress Press), p. 284.

p. 183 216. McBrien, *Catholicism*, p. 131. McBrien, discussing both Aquinas and Rahner, says: "The Word of God is not just some message given from some heavenly perch, but rather, it *is* God. And this is the distinctiveness of Jesus' preaching, namely, that God is present to us, not as some abstract power, but as the core of our being (what the Scholastics called 'uncreated grace'). God enters into the very definition of human existence."

p. 183 217. *Karl Rahner, Theologian of the Graced Search for Meaning*, ed. Geffrey B. Kelly (Minneapolis: Fortress Press, 1992), pp. 43, 98, 109, 113.

p. 184 218. We repeat the essence of Exodus 3:14, including the sense of the fullest translation possible.

p. 184 219. John 17:3.

p. 185 220. Spong, *New Christianity*, p. 142.

p. 185 221. Frank Laubach, *The Game With Minutes*, (Syracuse, NY: New Readers' Press, 1953).

p. 189 222. John 14:12.

p. 193 223. Ref. to Isaiah 60:1.

NOTABLE QUOTATIONS ON SACRIFICE AND SALVATION

Edward Schillebeeckx, *Interim Report on the Books of Jesus and Christ* (London: SCM, 1980).

"Pictures and interpretations which were once appropriate and evocative can become irrelevant in another culture. Or within our present culture, which regards, for example, the ritual slaughter of animals as repulsive, it is highly questionable whether we should go on describing the saving significance of the death of Jesus as a bloody sacrifice made to an angry God who needed it in order to be placated. In modern conditions this is likely to discredit authentic belief in the real saving significance of the death: it goes against all critical and responsible modern experiences." (p. 16)

Marcus Borg, *Meeting Jesus AGAIN for the First Time* (San Francisco: HarperSanFrancisco, 1994).

"**Gustaf Aulén** identified three main understandings of the death and resurrection of Jesus in the history of Christian theology ... The oldest is *Christus Victor*, ... Christ victorious over the powers ... including sin, death, and the devil.... The second ... pictures the death of Jesus as sacrifice for sin that makes God's forgiveness possible.... [The] third understanding portrays Jesus ... as 'revelation' or 'disclosure.' The emphasis is not upon Jesus accomplishing something that objectively changes the relationship between God and us, but upon Jesus *revealing* something that is true. What is revealed is more than one thing. Sometimes the emphasis is upon Jesus revealing what God is like (for example, love or compassion) [or] ... upon Jesus as 'the light' who beckons us home, [or] the embodiment of the way of return, a disclosure of the internal spiritual process that brings us into an experiential relationship with the Spirit of God. Jesus is the incarnation of the path of return from exile.

"Yet ... the priestly story ... has dominated the popular understanding of Jesus and the Christian life to the present day.... [T]he priestly story of sin, guilt, sacrifice, and forgiveness is most commonly the primary story shaping our sense of who we are, our image of Jesus and of what God requires. The image of Jesus as a sacrifice for our sins is a sign of God's great love for us.... But when the priestly story becomes the dominant story or the only story for imaging Jesus, it produces severe distortions in our understanding. [The following paragraph lists some of the six distortions.]

"Believe now for the sake of salvation afterward.... Though the priestly story speaks of God as gracious, it places the grace of God within a system of requirements.... The notion that God's only son came to this planet to offer his life as a sacrifice for the sins of the world, and that God could not forgive us without that having happened, and that we are saved by believing this story, is simply incredible. Taken metaphorically, this story can be very powerful. But taken literally, it is a profound obstacle to accepting the Christian message." (pp. 128–131)

Edgar M. Carlson, The Reinterpretation of Luther (Philadelphia: The Westminster Press, 1948).

"Agape [God's love- is] the definition of God and God's activity." (p. 77)

"The Swedish interpretation of Luther takes radical exception to the interpretation that prevailed within fifty years after his death." (p. 157)

[**Brame:** If this has been true since before Carlson's book was published, why has not the alternate Swedish view been known worldwide? It is obvious that many have ignored and silenced it in favor of prevailing theology. Why have informed Christians allowed it to be silenced? Thinking Christians will not agree with all views, but everyone is entitled to know what they are.

Actually it took much less than fifty years to alter (according to the Swedes) the understanding of Luther's words. The official statement of beliefs entitled *The Formula of Concord* was published in 1580, thirty-four years after Luther died. The Formula's subtitle claimed it was "the Pure, Correct, and Final Restatement and Explanation" of some "Articles from the Augsburg Confession on Which for Some Time There Has Been Disagreement." Its subtitle also claimed the Formula had "Resolved and Reconciled" those opinions. From my point of view in the twenty-first century, they have not been reconciled.

People want to feel secure in their beliefs. There are few who have even conceived of the possibility of open-endedness toward the mystery that is God, to live with the knowledge that we will never have all the "answers." Consequently, they depend upon their chosen theologians to tell them what is "true." Generally, people have ignored their birthright to engage seriously and in depth in matters of theology. We argue about practices, not essence, like the woman at the well. Yet each of us, in the end, is responsible to decide if we agree with professional theologians or with which theologians (that is, with which church or religion) or none at all. Unless we, ourselves, think carefully, we have no adequate reason for our choices. Then we choose based on family custom, authority, training in inherited beliefs, friendliness of a church, its mission to help others, or its effectiveness in addressing public life. Otherwise we ignore the religious and institutional, but not necessarily the spiritual dimension of life.

In introducing the "The Formula of Concord" included in *The Book of Concord*, **Theodore Tappert**, editor, has commented:]

"In the wake of Luther's death (1546) ... a series of controversies about the 'pure doctrine' of the Reformation threatened to split the Lutherans into two camps: an increasingly isolated 'Gnesio Lutheran' party claiming to adhere to the original teachings of Martin Luther ... carried their mentor's thoughts to extremes." (p. 463)

The Book of Concord: The Confessions of the Evangelical Lutheran Church, trans. and ed. Theodore G. Tappert (Philadelphia: Fortress Press, 1957).

[**Brame** notes: The word *gnesio* means "genuine" or "legitimate" or "true," which is self-applied by the more conservative churches. Their views seem to emphasize righteousness, law, authority, power, precise explanation, an acceptance of violence in God, and a deeply negative view of human nature as can be found in different measure in Augustine, Luther, and Calvin, regarding original sin. The *gnesio* view is closer to Lutheran Orthodoxy or what many scholars, mostly outside Lutheranism, refer to as Lutheran Scholasticism.]

Carlson writes: "The Swedish interpretation of Luther... impli[es] definite criticism of the theology of [Lutheran] Orthodoxy.... **Aulén**, the historian among Swedish theologians, ... dealt most comprehensively with the shortcomings of Orthodoxy. Aulén's criticisms may be reduced to two: ... Orthodoxy reverted to the medieval scholastic method.... It also went back to the judicial framework of medieval thought. Justice replaces love as the fundamental fact about God and his relation to men.... Righteousness determines conditions under which love operates" [**Brame** - instead of love determining conditions under which righteousness operates]. (pp. 157–160)

"The important thing about the suffering of Christ is that it was Christ, the full revelation of God, who suffered. The only alternative open to him finally was [his own] death or judgment [of us]. That he chose to die rather than to condemn indicates the sovereignty of God's love. *The conflict between judgment and grace takes place in God himself,* and grace wins out. What happened historically in the cross happens constantly in justification.... The decisive factor in both atonement and justification is the victory of God's love over all that opposes it." (pp. 58, 59) (author's emphasis. Note the similarity here to the statement of **Reinhold Niebuhr**, quoted on page 158.)

"It is customary to view the atonement either in terms of a forensic transaction or in terms of moral influence [**Abelard**].... [But] **Aulén** designates 'the classic view': God defeats the devil, and thereby releases man from ... bondage. God's nature is love, and the atonement is throughout an act of love. Through it, God brings about fellowship between himself and men on the basis of his grace." (pp. 58, 59)

Douglas John Hall, *The Cross in Our Context* (Minneapolis, MN: Fortress Press, 2003).

"The cross of Christ marks, in a decisive and irrevocable way, the unconditional participation of God in the life of the world, the concretization of God's love for the world, the commitment of God to the fulfillment of creation's promise." (p. 35)

"The theology of the cross ... is not that God thinks humankind so wretched that it deserves death and hell, but its redemption is worth dying for.... [If the meaning of the atonement was clear] under the aegis of this assumption, instead of being taken over lock, stock, and barrel by **Anselmic** sacrificial theory (as happened to the whole of Western Christendom), we would not have Christian feminists and humanists who find the cross of Jesus Christ an obnoxious and ethically dangerous symbol." (p. 24)

"[There is] an astonishing persistence of the Latin or Anselmic/Calvinistic theology of atonement. Much of the West got stuck in this theory – and it still is." (p. 130)

"The brutal death of Jesus of Nazareth is not to be attributed to some heavenly blueprint intended to make up for the guilt of the race, *à la* Anselm. It is not God's vindictiveness, God's 'plan.' It is the work of human beings who are entirely and accurately representative of human behavior whenever and wherever the spontaneous and unmotivated love of God comes close enough to them to judge their unloveliness and sham ... [t]hat Jesus was 'delivered up according to the definite plan and foreknowledge of God' (Acts 2:23) ... should not be equated with straightforward manipulation from on high.... God's sovereignty never abandons the dialectic of grace and freedom.... That Jesus Christ was crucified was no more the direct will and plan of God than that a million innocent children should have been slain in the Holocaust.... Only after (the events of Holy Week) – but only then – faith is allowed to see the hand of God in this human tragedy. 'He maketh even the wrath of men to praise him' (Ps. 76:10 KJV)." (p. 103)

J. Denny Weaver, *The Non-Violent Atonement* (Grand Rapids, MI: William B. Eerdmans Publishing Company, 2001).

"The God of dispensationalism is a violent and vengeful god who overcomes evil and violence with greater violence. The God of Revelation is a God who overcomes nonviolently through the Word, which is Jesus Christ." (p. 33)

[**Brame:** Weaver cites Michael Hardin* and Loren Johns** on the subject of sacrificial language in **Hebrews**:] "**Hardin** writes ... that 'the mediating function of Jesus is not compared to that of the sacrificial lamb but of the high priest. Jesus is not so much offering as offerer.' .... In rejecting sacrifice – 'the religion grounded in violence' ... [a]nd in doing the will of the Father, Jesus models 'Christian life as self-offering....' This giving rather than the taking of life 'is a fundamental reorientation....' **Johns** emphasized: 'Hebrews treats Jesus' death as exemplary rather than substitutionary.' And **Raymund Schwager** contends: 'In Hebrews 10:1-18 and its use of Psalm 40:6-8 there is a repudiation of the sacrificial hermeneutic.... Christ quotes Psalm 40:6-8 ... about God not desiring sacrifice.... The writer of Hebrews notes ... that [Christ] abolishes ... [the law] in order to establish ... [God's will]....' Hebrews puts in Christ's mouth words that abolish the sacrificial system and replace it with obedience to the will of God." (pp. 62–64)

***Michael Hardin,** "Sacrificial Language in Hebrews: Reappraising René Girard," in *Violence Renounced*, ed. W. M. Swartley (Telford, PA: Pandora Press, 2000) pp. 107, 114, 115.

****Loren J. Johns,** "'A Better Sacrifice' or 'Better Than Sacrifice'? Michael Hardin's 'Sacrificial Language in Hebrews,'" in *Violence Renounced*, p. 121.

*****Raymund Schwager**, *Jesus in the Drama of Salvation* (New York: Crossroad, 1999), p. 183.

Karen Armstrong, *A History of God* (New York: Ballantine Books, 1993).

"Human sacrifice was common in the pagan world. It was cruel but had a logic and a rationale. The first child was often believed to be the offspring of a god, who had impregnated the mother in an act of *droit de seigneur* (the right of God). In begetting the child, the god's energy had been depleted, so to replenish this and to ensure the circulation of all the available *mana* [force, power], the firstborn was returned to its divine parent. The case of Isaac was quite different, however. Isaac had been a gift of God but not his natural son. There was no reason for the sacrifice, no need to replenish the divine energy.... It had only been a test." (p. 18)

***A Scholastic Miscellany,* ed. Eugene Fairweather** (New York: Macmillan, 1970).

"In opposition to the Anselmian model, Abelard reasons that since human beings were incapable of paying an infinite debt to God, the purpose of the incarnation must not be the payment of anything to anyone. Rather, he understands the incarnation to be the ultimate revelation of God's love for humanity: 'To us it seems that we are justified nonetheless in the blood of Christ and reconciled to God in this: that by his extraordinary grace exhibited to us, in that his son assumed our nature, and by teaching us by word and example, persevered until death, he draws us closer to himself through love.'" **Peter Abelard**, "Exposition to the Epistle to the Romans," in *Miscellany*. (p. 282)

"In the Abelardian view, reconciliation between God and human beings – that is, atonement – is brought about by love, the love of God that Jesus the Christ perfectly embodies. This love is so potent that when human beings encounter it, we are actually inspired to emulate it, to love God as Jesus loved God, and to love one another as Jesus loves us. The event of atonement, then, is an event of creative love: God created the universe out of love; God became incarnate in Jesus out of love; and in and through the incarnation, God elicits from human beings a responsive love. The example of divine love, says Abelard, has this result: 'That our hearts should be enkindled by such a gift of divine grace, and true charity should not now shrink from enduring anything for him....' Jesus is the perfect embodiment of God's love for humanity. And in his unwavering devotion to God, Jesus is the perfect example of humanity's love for God." (p. 282)

Rebecca Ann Parker, *Proverbs of Ashes*, with Rita Nakashima Brock (Boston, MA: Beacon Press, 2001).

"What happens when violent realities are transubstantiated into spiritual teaching?... Tragedy is renamed a spiritual trial, designed by God for [a person's] edification. God becomes the sender of torture, who injures us then comforts us – a perverse love." (p. 44)

"**Leonardo Boff**, in *Passion of Christ, Passion of the World*, writes: 'This is the sense in which Christ was the sacrifice par excellence. He was a being-for-others to the last extreme. Not only his death, but his whole life was a sacrifice: it was wholly surrender.... Sacrifice is self-donation: the total gift of life and death.'" [quoted in Parker, n.p.] (p. 42)

Roger Haight, *Jesus, Symbol for God* (Maryknoll, NY: Orbis, 1999).

"Jesus reveals something that has been going on from the beginning, before and outside of Jesus' own influence." (p. 422)

John Hick, *The Metaphor of God Incarnate: Christology in a Pluralistic Age* (Louisville, KY: Westminster John Knox Press, 2005).

[**Brame**: Hick presents two theological approaches about salvation. I will refer to them as view A and view B in order to be clear. However, please note his following comment first.]

"One can find much the same language somewhere within each [viewpoint]. Nevertheless, their basic tendencies move in different directions, one guided by a transactional-atonement conception and the other by a transformational conception of salvation." (p. 114)

A. "The term 'atonement' ... in its broad, etymological meaning, at-one-ment, signifies becoming one with God – not ontologically [in being] but in the sense of entering into a right relationship with our creator, this being the process or state of salvation." (p. 112)

B. "But in its narrower sense atonement refers to a specific method of receiving salvation, one presupposing that the barrier to this is guilt. It is in this context that we find the ideas of penalty, redemption, sacrifice, oblation, propitiation, expiation, satisfaction, substitution, forgiveness, ransom, justification, remission of sins, forming a complex of ideas which has long been central to the Western or Latin development of Christianity." (p. 112)

"It was generally accepted by [early] Christian writers and preachers that the human race had fallen through sin under the jurisdiction of the devil and that the cross of Christ was part of a bargain with the devil to ransom us." (p. 114)

A. "Jesus' death was of a piece with his life, expressing a total integrity in his self-giving to God (p. 132).... We can say that the broader sense has been more at home in the Eastern or Greek development of Christianity and the narrower in its Western or Latin development. (p. 112)

B. "In my view it would be best ... to restrict the term 'atonement' to its narrower and more specific meaning.... Salvation requires God's forgiveness.... [The] atoning act is a transaction analogous to making a payment to wipe out a debt or cancel an impending punishment.... I am going to argue that in this narrower sense, the idea of atonement is a mistake; although of course the broader sense, in which atonement simply means salvation, is vitally important." (pp. 112–113)

A. "The idea that guilt can be removed from a wrongdoer by someone else being punished instead is morally grotesque.... God's insistence on the blood, sweat, pain and anguish involved in the crucifixion of God's innocent Son now seems even to cast doubt on the moral character of the deity." (pp. 119, 123)

A. "**Auguste Sabatier** wrote that Jesus' passion and death 'was the most powerful call to repentance that humanity has ever heard, and also the most operative and fruitful in marvelous results. The cross is the expiation of sins only because it is the cause of the repentance to which remission is promised." (p. 129)

A. "**E. P. Sanders** ... says 'The forgiveness of repentant sinners is a major motif in virtually all the Jewish material which is still available from the period [of Jesus' lifetime]....' Within contemporary Protestant thought there has come to be a widespread acceptance of the idea of a free divine forgiveness for those who truly repent." (p. 128)

B. and A. "[T]he Latin view *to be saved* is to be justified, i.e., relieved of guilt, by Christ's sacrificial death ... the Orthodox view to be in process of salvation is to be responding to the presence of the divine Spirit and thus gradually moving towards a radical new re-centering with the divine life." (p. 130)

"The sacrifice of animal or human blood pointed, in a crude and inadequate way, to the much deeper sacrifice of the ego ... in becoming a channel of divine grace on earth.... The real meaning of Jesus' death was not that his blood was shed ... but that he gave himself utterly to God in faith and trust. His cross was thus a powerful manifestation ... of the divine kingdom in this present world, as a way of life in which one turns the other cheek, forgives one's enemies 'unto seventy times seven', trusts God even in the darkness of pain, horror and tragedy, and is continually raised again to the new life of faith.... [This] has a moral power that reverberates beyond any words that we can frame to express it." (p. 132)

Bart D. Ehrman, *Misquoting Jesus* (San Francisco: HarperSanFrancisco, 2005).

"It is a striking feature of Luke's portrayal of Jesus' death.... That he *never*, anywhere else [than Luke 22: 17-19] indicates that the death itself is what brings salvation from sin.... Jesus' death for Luke ... drives people to repentance, and it is this repentance that brings salvation." (pp. 166–67)

John Shelby Spong, *A New Christianity for A New World* (San Francisco; HarperSanFrancisco, 2005).

"This human Jesus seems to possess his life so totally that he can give it away without fear. The freedom that marks this man becomes so frightening to those who are not free – and who cannot admit that they are not free – that they rise up in anger to destroy the life-giver. The cross, to me, stands for this destruction which still goes on in religious disputes. The cross does not represent a sacrifice required by a blood-seeking deity; it rather reveals the ultimate portrait of the threatening power of love that is present in the life of this victim. Even when Jesus walked what later came to be called 'the way of the cross,' and even when the threat of death became the reality of death, still the bearer of this gift of life discovered that nothing could finally destroy the life he possessed. As this Jesus succumbed to the power of those who could not abide his call to enter 'the new being,' to grasp a new and radical sense of freedom, he still was able to give his life away. The gospel picture of Jesus portrays him as giving life to others even as he died." (pp. 138–39)

Spong begins by speaking of Jesus and then continues: "When the being of that person is so real that he enhances the being of those around him, then that person is seen as an enabler of life, a source of being for others. Being is always beyond the person who manifests it. It does not originate in any of us; it simply flows through us. It is a gift that comes from beyond ourselves; it is not our possession. Like life, it is found in all the created order. We are rooted in it, grounded in it, recipients of it, bearers to others. It relates us beyond ourselves to ... a God thought of not as a person, but as the source of personhood, the God defined as ... that presence or power in which 'we live, and move, and have our being'" (Acts 17:28). (p. 142)

"Life cannot be given away until life has been possessed.... Jesus first reveals the source of life, and then he empowers us to enter it." (p. 139)

John Shelby Spong, *Sins of Scripture: Exposing the Bible's Texts of Hate to Reveal the God of Love*, (San Francisco; HarperSanFrancisco, 2005).

"Christianity ... validates violence because it attributes to God's punishment of Jesus salvific themes; and not surprisingly, it validates our own violence, since when we abuse others we are only acting after the example that God has set for us." (p. 172)

"Our struggle to survive, which manifests itself in radical self-centeredness, is not the result of original sin. It is a sign of emerging consciousness. It should not be a source of guilt. It is a source of blessing. We do not need to be punished. We need to be called and empowered to ... give ourselves away freely in the quest for an even deeper sense of what it means to live. Jesus did not die for our sins. Jesus demonstrated in an ultimate way that it is by giving that we receive and by loving that we enhance life.

"Guilt, judgment, righteousness, orthodoxy, creedal purity: these are the products of a religion of control in which we hide in fear. They are attempts to build security. None of these boundary marks is life-giving. All are methods of seeking righteousness when that for which we yearn is love." (p. 174)

"To be 'saved' does not mean to be rescued. It means to be empowered to be something we have not yet been able to be." (p. 179)

Gary Wills, *Papal Sin* (New York: Doubleday, 2000). Comments on René Girard's *Violence and the Sacred*, trans. Patrick Gregory. (Baltimore: Johns Hopkins University Press, 1977).

Wills' understanding of **Girard** is: "[This] universal trait of sacrifice is meant to placate – to flatter and, at the same time bribe – an appropriately violent set of gods. Envious rivalry ... leads to and is assuaged by concentration on a foe (or its surrogate), on whatever must be destroyed that the people might live. After that, the state is made the guardian of the violence that articulated its structure in the first place.... The community builds itself around a shared enmity and seals its bond by a sacrifice of the object of its fear." (p. 303)

"[There is a] harmony of hate that blossoms from sacred violence. They have still to learn that when Jesus says one can only follow him by taking up the cross (Matt. 10:38), this means meeting the violence of the world with unresisting love. Only this willingness frees one from the dominance of the power system called Satan." (p. 305)

"Girard's most radical assertion is that Jesus is not a sacrifice. His Father is not one whose aggressions need to be bought off. Jesus is not an item of barter in the exchange system set up by sacrifice. God does not accept victims. He sides with the victim against its slayers, reversing the whole logic of placation. The prophets of Israel had moved toward the insight that God does not want sacrifice, but Jesus turns their hesitant questioning of the system into confident assertion of its irrelevance. This is clearest in his opposition to the Temple activities that all revolved around sacrifice. His 'cleansing' of the Temple was not an attack on peripheral abuses like money exchanges in the forecourt. He is rejecting the validity of sacrifice as an avenue to God – a view of the episode that Raymond Brown finds John's text capable of bearing. 'Do not make my Father's house a house of barter' (John 2:16). The commerce in victims is ended." (pp. 305–306)

"Yet it is this very act of scapegoating – the Satan system of condoned violence – that is being condemned. The lying patterns collapse when triumph over the victim becomes a triumph of the victim.

"Girard makes it clear why the triumph of Christ is a struggle with Satan. Jesus lets the violence of the world system defeat itself on his dying body – instead of this being a sacrifice to a vengeful God, it is a paradoxical defeat of the torturer. The fallen world of satanic resistance to God causes the final violence, not any placatory act demanded by the Father. The only sacrifice by Jesus is his offering of his innocent body to the fury of the sacrificial system that is being canceled. This was exactly the position of Augustine. In an early work, he opposed the ransom theory of Christ's death, the theory that Jesus was a substitute who accepted the suffering that the Father wanted to inflict on others – as if the Father could find satisfaction in causing pain: 'The Lord's was obviously not a death of ransom but of restoration (*dignitatis non debiti*).'" (p. 307)

"The sacrificial system, just as in Girard's work, is the devil's discipline – 'oppressing life with a claim to purification by rites and sacrifices that insult God.'" (p. 307)

"This [future] church would not restrict the priesthood to men. In fact, it would not restrict the priesthood to priests – to magicians of the Eucharistic transformation. It would not deprive whole communities of their own priests rather than relax a code of celibacy never imposed on the apostles." (p. 310)

"[In the first Vatican Council ... it] was not only the faithful, the critical, the questioning, who were excluded from that Council. The Spirit was excluded. None of the Council's distinguishing characteristics – secrecy, coercion, deception – is a characteristic of the Spirit. The old system of sacrifice was brought back, the one canceled by Christ on the cross – only here the believers were sacrificed to an idol, to the papacy. Pius IX stood not for all-speak (*parrh sia*) but for non-speak (*ourh sia*), for blind subjection, not liberation in the Light, the Light who enlightens everyone who comes into the world" (John 1:9). (p. 310)

"But where can this church of the Spirit be found? Not in some imagined purity of the past. There were no good old days of the faith apart form what faces us today. There was betrayal and bitterness in the clash of Paul with Peter, Peter with Paul, as in the betrayal of both men to Nero. Then where is the church of Pentecost, that original feast of multilingual multiculturalism? It is anywhere the Spirit breathes freedom into a Christian community – where peacemakers are at work, where Sister Prejean is telling people that capital punishment is revenge and not a Christian action, where Daniel Berrigan is caring for those stricken with AIDS, where people unite to help the helpless, where Philip Berrigan is telling us that no one has the right to build weapons that can destroy the world." (p. 311)

Jaroslav Pelikan, *Luther, the Expositor: Introduction to the Reformer's Exegetical Writings* (St. Louis, MO: Concordia Publishing House, 1959).

"Luther had to give detailed attention to the sacrifices described and prescribed in the Scriptures.... This exegesis brought him to the observation that the word 'sacrifice' had been used in the Scriptures to designate two distinct types of action.... A 'sacrifice of atonement' was an action by which the favor of God was secured; its relation to the favor of God was that of cause and effect. A 'sacrifice of thanksgiving' ... came from a person who already stood in a reconciled relation to God; its relation to the favor of God was that of effect to cause." (p. 238)

[**Brame**: If Pelikan is correct, it would mean that Luther had missed the fundamental and inspiring *root meaning* of atonement. That meaning, as noted in Chapter 7, is that atonement is a reconciliation, an *at-one-ment*, between God and human beings, with others, and within ourselves. Pelikan's definition here is of propitiation or payment. This secondary meaning is a widely used, but profound misunderstanding of the term. What Luther is really contrasting are the same two views of sacrifice that were pointed out in Chapter 6 above.]

[**Pelikan** continues:] "Since the basis of patriarchal religion was a covenant of grace with God, the patriarchs recognized that their sacrifices were not a means of appeasing God's wrath or of winning His favor but only a means of expressing gratitude to God and of bearing witness to God's grace given in the covenant. But when others saw the patriarchs offering up their sacrifices and then also discerned that the patriarchs stood in a special covenant with God, they concluded that the sacrifices were the basis of the covenant, and God was gracious to the patriarchs because of sacrifices. Imitating the actions of the patriarchs, rather than their faith, the Gentiles thus became pagans." (p. 239)

Arnold Toynbee, *Christianity Among the World's Religions* (New York: Charles Scribner's and Sons, 1957).

"[A]s we look at the conduct of the totalitarian neo-pagan faiths, we shall find, I fear, that their conduct has been inspired by one vein in the Christian and Jewish tradition of conduct – I mean, the vein of fanaticism and intolerance which one can see if on looks back on the history of all the Judaic religions: Islam, Christianity, and Judaism itself. It is a spirit which does not hesitate to try to inculcate its doctrine and practice by persecution.... This sort of fanaticism was not a feature of the primitive, pre-Christian form of paganism.... I think it has been inherited by post-Christian neo-paganism from Christianity and Judaism, and I think its ultimate inspiration is one of two Christian and Jewish conceptions of God which, as I see it, are incompatible with one another.

"Christianity and Judaism have one vision of God as being self-sacrificing love – God the merciful, the compassionate, according to the Islamic formula – and another vision of God as being a jealous God. I know that this is a very controversial subject, and I think some psychologists, and many theologians, would contend that the two concepts, though they may seem incompatible, are in truth, inseparable from each other. But these two visions of the nature of God seem to me, at any rate, to be irreconcilable, and the presence of both visions side by side in the common tradition of Christianity and Judaism and Islam has produced in these three Judaic religions an inner contradiction, which, I should say, has never been resolved. One can also see, I think, that this duality of vision is reflected in a duality of conduct. The jealous god's chosen people easily fall into becoming intolerant persecutors. The worshippers of the god who is love – God the merciful, the compassionate – try to act on the belief that their fellow creatures are their brothers, because they are all God's children. These two conflicting elements in the Judaic religions will keep on confronting us." (pp. 18, 19)

Garth R. Thompson, *The Most Important Virtue: A Sermon on Luke 2:1* (privately published, December 27, 2009).

"Suffering and sacrifice will automatically be part of anything we have a passion for." (p. 5)

"God is enfolding *all* ... people in salvation. Our job is to help them *realize* that enfolding." (p. 4)

INDEX OF PERSONS
(outside Scripture)

("n" refers to endnote number)

Abelard, Peter – 48, 49, 131-132, 134, 213
Akhenaton (Amenhotep IV) – 170-171, n 205
Amen-Ra – 171
Anonymous author of The Cloud of Unknowing – 21, n 9
Anthony, first known solitary – 128, n 131, n 132
Anselm of Canterbury – 41-48, 85, 131-133, 136, 177, 211, n 37, n 40, n 43, n 74, n 212
Aquinas, Thomas – 48-49, 53, 128, 183, n 50, n 53, n 203
Armstrong, Karen – 170, 213, n 203
Athanasius – 129
Augustine of Hippo, Aurelius – 43, 136, 146, 175, n 30, n 154
Aulén, Gustav – 114, 128, 131-133, 136, 161, 208-211, n 112, n 128, n 136, n 139, n 140, n 152, n 153, n 193

Baillie, Donald – 110, 163, n 105, n 106
Barbieri, Elizabeth – 107, n 101
Barnes, Michael J. – 155, 166-167, 205-206, n 183, n 197
Bellah, Robert – 148, 166, n 196
Berrigan, Daniel – 221
Berrigan, Philip – 221
Boff, Leonardo – 214
Borg, Marcus – 208-209
Brame, Grace – 15, 18, 21, 24-25, 31, 65, 106, 109, 148, 155, 161, 195-196, n 4, n 15, n 18, n 27, n 60, n 97, n 104, n 170
Brown, Raymond – 219
Bretzke, James T. – 143, n 165
Brunner, Emil – 136
Bucke, Richard Maurice – 165, 171, n 206
Buddha, the – 88, 111, n 79

Capra, Fritjof – 70, n 63
Carlson, Edgar M. – 136, 209-211, n 150
Constantine – 100
Cousins, Ewert – 170, n 201
Cunningham, Mary B. – 128, 133-134, n 130, n 143, n 144, n 146

Desert Fathers/Mothers – 128,
Dwyer, John – 42, 45, 47, n 34, n 35, n 36, n 41, n 42

Eckhart, Meister – 130, 203
Enlightenment theologians – 136
Ehrling, Bernard – 161, n 189
Ehrman, Bart D. – 217
Erikson, Erik – 179

Faggert, Brady – 90, n 83
Fairweather, Eugene – 131, 213
Farrugia, Edward G. – 47, n 47
"Fathers of the Church" – 136
Forde, Gerhard – 122, n 126
Fox, Matthew – 66, n 61
Fowler, James – 89, 172, 179, n 81, n 213
Freesoul, John Redtail – 107, n 102
French, Henry – 21, 59, n 8, n 54, n 56
Francis of Assisi – 145, n 167

Gaster, T. H. – 119, 122, n 114, n 115, n 125
Girard, René – 219-221
Gospel writers – 54, 67
Gregory of Nyssa – 128
Gregory the Great, Pope – 41, 128
Grumbles, Lloyd – 183

Haight, Roger – 46, 197, n 39
Hall, Brian – 179
Hall, Douglas John – 211-212
Hardin, Michael – 212
Harper, Douglas – 150, n 176
Heerman, Johann – 90, n 84

Heim, Mark – 134, n 145
Hick, John – 214-217

Irenaeus – 129

James, E. O. – 23, 119-120, 128, n 13, n 116, n 117, n 120, n 129
Jaspers, Karl – 169-170, n 200
Joachim de Fiore – 172
Johns, Loren J. – 213

Kahn, Muqtadar – 141, n 164
Kierkegaard, Søren – 111, 136, 174, n 108, n 151
King, Peter – 44, n 44
Kohlberg, Lawrence – 179

Laubach, Frank – 15, 185, n 3, n 221
Lewis, C. S. – 105, 107, n 96, n 103
Livingstone, E. A. – 131, n 137
Luther, Martin – 61, 89, 114, 128, 130, 132-136, 148, 175-176, 182, 185, 209-210, 221-222, n 59, n 80, n 82, n 134, n 147, n 171, n 172, n 211, n 215
Lyman, Mary Ely – 71

Maslow, Abraham – 179
Maas, Robin – 49, n 45
McBrien, Richard – 43, 100-101, 104, 183, n 32, n 91, n 92, n 95, n 216
Meister Eckhart – 130, n 135
Melancthon, Philipp – 83, 132-133
Meyendorf, John – 73, 100, n 64, n 90, n 93
Michael, Chester P. – 159, 179, n 187, n 214
Monk of the Eastern Church, A – 49, n 46
Muhammed, Prophet – 86, 95, n 97

Nero – 220
Niebuhr, Reinhold – 158, n 185
Norrisey, Marie – 159, n 187

O'Collins, Gerald – 51, 53, 172, n 47, n 207
O'Donnell, Gabriel – 49, n 45
Origen – 128, n 127
Onions, C. T. – 144, n 173

Patmore, Coventry – 88, n 77
Philo Judaeus – 23, n 11

Pius IX, Pope – 220
Plass, Ewald M. – 175, n 210
Prejean, Sister Helen – 221
Pseudo-Dionysius – 85, n 75

Rahner, Karl – 173, 176, 183, n 208, n 217
Richardson, Alan – 154, n 180

Sabatier, Augustine – 216
Sanders, E. P. – 216
Schillebeeckx, Edward – 208
Schimmel, Anne-Marie – 54, n 53
Schmidt, William – 170, n 203
Schmiechen, Peter – 114, n 111
Schwager, Raymund – 19, 36, 79, 212, n 6, n 29, n 72
Shea, Nina – 75, n 66
Sherwood, Yvonne – 140, n 160, n 162
Simpson, Cuthbert A. – 23, n 14
Sloyan, Gerard – 46, n 38,
Smith, Huston – 88, n 79
Spong, John Shelby – 76, 184, 217-218, n 62, n 68, n 220
Spurgeon, Charles Haddon – 106, n 100
Steere, Douglas – 174, n 209
Stazesky, Richard – 157, n 184
Strong, James – 94, n 86
Swidler, Leonard – 23, n 12, n 13

Tappert, Theodore – 210
Theologians (early) accepting forensic approach – n 129
Theokritoff, Elizabeth – 128, 133-134, n 130, n 143, n 144, n 146
Tonna, Benjamin – 179
Toynbee, Arnold –13, 53, 60, 78, 119, 139, 222-223, n 2, n 52, n 57, n 58, n 70, n 118, n 158
Thompson, Garth – 223

Tillich, Paul – 53-54, 81, 88, 112, 149, 150, 154-155, n 51, n 55, n 78, n 109, n 141, n 142, n 174, n 177
Tylor, Edward – 166, n 198

Van Osdol, Judith – 74, n 65
Voice of the Martyrs – 77, n 69

Underhill, Evelyn – 135, 144, 146, 150, 161, n 148, n 166, n 168, n 178, n 188, n 191

Watts, Isaac – 137, n 157
Weaver, J. Denny – 116, 212-213, n 113
Whitehead, Evelyn and James – 179

Wills, Gary – 219-221
Wolfe, Roland E. – 120, n 121, n 122
Wright, Robert – 165-166, n 195, n 199
Wurmbrand, Richard – 78, n 67

INDEX OF SUBJECTS AND PERSONS IN SCRIPTURE

("n" refers to endnote number)

Abandonment – 92, 159-160
Abraham and Isaac – 140-142
affirmative/attachment way of life – 66
agape – as definition of God - 209
Agnus Dei – 125
   – new text - 126
Ahura Mazda - supreme god in Zoroastrianism – 170
Allah (lit. "the god") – 95
androgeny (both sexes) in God, and more – 23
animism ("breath," "life," or "soul") in all life – 163, 166
anointing – 69, 115
Anselmic, Latin, Western sacrificial theory – 208-209, 211-212, 215-217, 220-221
   (see Anselm in Person Index)
   (see priestly law)
anthropomorphism – (def) 59, 79, 83-87, 97
appearance of truth – 145
argument vs. discussion – 14
Arianism – 100, n 91
asceticism (in training) – 144-145
atonement (as at-one-ment) –
   - as reconciliation – 154
   - as transactional – 215
   - as transformational – 215
   - as non-violent – 116, n 113
   - eternal (Baillie) – n 106
   - Luther's understanding – 221
   - making amends – 154
   - recreating relationship – 215
authors, in Bible – 65, 67
authority – 12, 19, 64, 68, 71, 94, 96, 138
awakening – 31, 48, 94, 158, 164, 193
awareness, living in – 158 (see consciousness)
availability to God – 75

Belief - intellectual, theological, statements, creedal – 17, 21, 99
   - as explanation of experience – 73
   - lived – 65
   - unbelief – 64, 90
blood – 42-43, 47, 68, 70, 115, 139-144, 143, 158, 161, 208, 213, 216, 217
Brahman – Hindu Ultimate Reality – 170
breath, God's – 65, 69, 94, 165, 187
   (see Spirit as breath)
Buddha (the "Enlightened One"), Buddhism – 88

Call, to everyone – 30, 31, 67, 187-189
capacity for God – 54
capital punishment – 221
celibacy – 220
chosen, to be – 30-31, 63
Christ - two natures – 99-100
christ, a - all called to be – 30, 48, 184-189
Christianity - uniqueness, exclusivity – 16
church today – 49
church and state – 100
coincidentia oppositorium (unity of opposites) – 66
commitment – 13
consciousness - 24, 31, 57, 77, 158, 163
   - cosmic - Bucke – 171
   - loss of –92
   - of life force – 165
   - pre-consciousness – 164
   - self-consciousness – 164
   - spiritual consciousness – 24, 163-179
   (see awakening, awareness)
contradictions - in scripture – 12
   - in faith – 12
cor ad cor - heart to heart, human/divine relationship – 24
Councils - Nicea, Chalcedon – 98-99
courage – 179 (see taunts)
Creation as salvation – 153
Creation myths – 58, 65, 66
creed - personal, lived – 26
   - Apostles' and Nicene – 98-99

cristocentrism – 51, n 47
- displacing God – 51
- in creed, liturgy, prayer – 51
Christus Victor, Aulen – 208
Cross, the -
- as gift – 35, 42
- as God's self-giving through Jesus – 169
- as life-giving – 35
- as necessary? – 36, 136
- as payment – 35
- as revelation of affirmative love from God – 20, 159
- Eastern Orthodox view - Holy Spirit recenters life – 215
- Western/Latin view - justification = guilt relieved – 215
Crucifixion, the
- as God's plan – 211-212
- effect on human heart – 43
- God is the issue – 19
- personal – 159-160, 185
(see salvation/Jesus'death)

Dark nights of the soul – 135
death -
- as seed of life – 159
- my death – 184
- itself does not save – 217
defense of God – 17
denial of God – 67
desire for God – 21
desire, perverse/self-centered – 53
detachment – 40, 66, 83, 155
Devil - ransom to – 40, 42, 128-129, n 130
- as evil personified – 40
- stories about – 41
dogma – 184
disenchantment with church – 11, 14-16
distractions/ interruptions – 63
doubt – 14, 61, 62, 65, 68
do ut des – (I give so you give) 143, n 165
disbelief – 15
docetism – 101
dying, in Receptive Prayer – 181

Easter Proclamation (the *Exultet*) as forensic – 136, n 155

Easter Vigil – 129, 133-136
Elijah – 167
Elohim - as God – 23
embodiment - (def.) essence in form – 71
- expressed in Jesus – 29, 131, 178
- expressed in a living person or thing – 72
- of Way, Truth, Life – 29
- ultimate revelation of God's love - (Abelard) – 213
empowerment for good – 218
epigraph - paradigm saying in book – 28, 33
eschatology , realized - the end times experienced now – 108
essence – 64, 72, 76
eternal life - as consciousness of God – 22, 183
- as relationship with God – 22
evil
- as the warping of God's power – 105-106, n 96
- inside and outside person – 14
- personified as Eden's snake – 40, 51
- defeated within individual – 134
evolution
- as natural growth in living things – 84
- future spiritual – 172
- of knowledge – 80
- of law – 77
- of perception of God – 11-13, 68-69, 70-71, 80, 90, 169
- of practice – 11, 170
- of theology – 11, 19
- resistance to, fear of – 82, 83
exclusivity in Christianity – 16
Exile, the - to Babylon – 120, - n 119
experience -
- before consciousness – 164
- central to spirituality – 13
- in my shoes – 188
- of God – 21, 72, 73
- of the Cross – 36
- returning as a "she" – 191
- then and now – 191
experiment – 67, 71
explanation - as theology – 14-15
- as squeezing God – 16, 59, 67

Facts
- as objective, observable – 63, 65, 67, 71, 72

faith
- (def.) trust in relationship – 52, 60-61, 67- 68, 73, 81
- as action of given will – 44
- as depending upon God – 152
- as personal choice – 14
- consequences – 159
- in authority of others – 12
- in the Church – 97
- inherited – 97
- of writers of scripture – 65
- other faiths – 11, 16-17
- uninvolved – 97
- while confronting questions 15

failure – 189
faithful, the – 11
fear – 31, 164, 181, 185
- of God's power in us – 31

felix culpa (happy fault) – 136, n 154
filioque phrase - "and the Son" – n 207

First Axial Period - centered in 500 BCE – 169-170
- appearance of monotheism – 169
- attitude toward sacrifice changed history – 170
- Elijah, Jeremiah, Isaiah – 170
- Judaism's move from rituals to moral consciousness – 170

forgiveness -
- as God's intention – 36
- and healing – 17, 53
- God's forgiveness through Jesus – 44, 51, 53, 55
- of self – 44, 52, 112
- of enemies – 52, 76, 111
- possible without the Cross? – 41
- without requirements – 111

forensics of justice – 42, 83, 134
form criticism – 70
"Formula of Concord" and *Book of Concord* – 210
free will, choice, responsibility – 83,151
- no free will – 151
"fully God and fully man" – 99

Gelassenheit – (def.) 114 and 146,139-148
gift - giver pays – 43, 52
giving life – (John 10:10) - 123
giving ourselves to God – 44
gnesio Lutheranism – 210
God
- (def.) "is Spirit" (John 4:24) – 17, 75, 87
- allegiance to – 142
- as absent – 83
- as an accountant – 50
- as androgynous (including both sexes) and more – 23
- as Being itself, Life - "I AM, Was, and Will Be" – 12, 21, 112, 184, n 1, n 109
- as core of human being – 104
- as changing – 19, 71
- as Creator – 12, 83
- as El, Elohim – 23, 139, n 12
- as empowering – 152
- as faithful – 67, 68
- as Father of Love for all – 12
- as female – n 13
- as fickle – 86, 151
- as god of war – 12, 80
- as guide, not ruler – 153
- as healer (savior) – 67
- as hearing prayer – 125
- as holy – 166
- as immanent – 35, 65, 87
- as jealous – 222
- as Jesus' parent and ours – 29, 35, 75
- as judge – 133
- as Life-Giver – 51
- as Love – 20, 35, 46, 67, 161, 179
- as manipulative – 123, 151
- as More, the – 27, 58, 86, 88
- as pervasive, permeating, surrounding, – 68, 83, 223
- as planning the Cross – 36, 211, 217
- as power – 166
- as self-sacrificing – 222
- as selling salvation – 159
- as sovereign – 150, 152
- as tempter, manipulator of history – 85
- as transcendent – 35, 65
- as Ultimate Reality – 85
- as undefinable – 16, 86, 87

- as unfaithful – 71
- as violent and angry – 35, 80, 208, 212
- as Yahweh – 70, 170
- defense of – 17, 20
- definition, personal, impersonal –16, n 57
- God's condemnation – 113
- God's Great Intention – 48
- God's honor – 41, 45, 47, 79
- God in control – 122, 155
- God's kingdom on earth – 154
- God's moral character – 216
- human perception of – 19, 68-72, 185
- in heaven – 155
- needing placation – 208
- two conflicting views – 222
- visible in Christ – 17

God beyond God – (beyond human conception, definition, or explanation) – p 198, n 57 (see mysticism)
God *in* Christ and us – 17, 50, 110-115, 162
God paying God's self – 113
gods - beyond spirits – 166, 167
- allegiance to – 167
- Baal, Molech, Ashtoreth – 168
- hierarchy of – 167
- high god - monolatry – 167-168
- Mot, god who died to give life to earth – 139
- "no other gods before (or) beside me"? – 168
- sons of gods – 139
- tribal – 167
good works – 136, n 151
gospel writers – 54, 67
grace - as essence of God – 133
- as life-giving gift – 35
- Augustine's views – n 30
- has no law but love – 50
- no requirements for – 27, 111
- prevenient (coming first) – 46, 42
- theology of g. inconsistently applied – 46
- through humans – 15
- undergirding all life – 49
- undeserved love – 47
gratitude – 125, 144
Great Schism, the (E. Orthodox/Roman Catholic - 1054 CE) – 129
growth – 14, 84, 89 (see evolution)
guilt – 42, 50, 90

Hagar (Mother of Ishmael/Arabs) – 141
Hannah (Mother of Samuel) – 139-140
healing – 12, 35, 43, 71, 97, 107, 113, 118, 135, 147
healing - as salvation – 55
heaven – (consciousness of God) 22, 57, 183
- as God's gift – 144
Hebrews (book of) – 136
Hebrew people vs Jews – n 179
henosis (union with God) – 130
history – 63, 66
hokmah (wisdom) – 23
Holy Spirit (see Spirit)
homoiousios - similar essence – 99
homoousios - same essence – 99
honesty (nakedness) in prayer – 21
honor
- God's – 41, 47, 76, 84, 117, 118, 119, 131, 169
- as responsibility – 63

Idol
- (def) – 56
- Ahab – 120, n 123
Image of God - as human capacity to relate to God – 22-24, 51-53
- as Jesus – p 22
- as irreparable – 53
imagination – 64, 69
inclusion – 17, 70
indulgence (payment to shorten time in purgatory) – 144
- Jesus as greatest indulence payment in history – 144
inspiration - (breathed into by God and inhaling Gods breath) – 82
- human receptivity to God's life – 67, 81, 87, 93
- of scripture – 19
instruments of God - tools, channels, voice, work – 17, 118, 178, 179
insulting God – 43, 48, 84, 220
interpretation – 64
intervention of God – 123

intuition – 69
Ishmael – 141
Islam – 40-141, 56, 106, 140, 141, n 53,
    n 162, n 163, n 164, n 98

Jesus
  - as divine, God the Son – 58, 100, 184,
      184, n 64 (see *homoousios*)
  - as door to eternal life – 16
  - as embodiment of Life, Truth, Way,
      grace – 29, 64, 71, 178, 208, 214
  - as example of God's perfect love
      (Abelard) – 214
  - as fully human – 75
  - as metaphor for God – 214
  - as Son of God. – 42, 58, 100, 110,
      113, 119, 184, 200
  - in human shoes – 188
  - returning as a "she" – 191
  - then and now – 191
Jesus'
  - authority – 19
  - choice of Cross – 36, 37
  - humility – 62
  - ordination – 115
  - perception of God – 29, 75, 85
  - relationship to God – 18
Jesus' death – 17, 36, 41, 53, 131, 136,
    162-163, 212, 215, 216, 217
  - as Jesus' sacrifice for forgiveness of
      sin – 208
  - as necessary? – 36, 136
  - as revelation of God – 208, n 29
  - as sacrifice by God for us – 113
  - as victory over power of sin, death,
      devil – 208
  - not a sacrifice to God – 219
  - not God's plan – 211
Jesus' mission – 75, 76
  - to give life (John 10:10) – 35, 90
  - to make God's love visible – 43
  - to reveal God in human terms -
      (embodiment) – 29, 75, 76
  - to speak and act for God – 50, 75
  - to call us to the same – 29
Joshua – 80-81
judgementalism – 151

justice
  - as punishment/retribution – 44
  - as rehabilitation/restoration/grace – 36,
      45, 50, 69, 74, 77, 83, 90, 122,
      133, 134, 147, 149-150, 167,
      178, 210
  - replacing love in theology – 210
justification – 133

Kenosis (self-emptying as related to self-
    giving) – 110-115, 146
Koran, The (Qur'an) – 86, 106, 140, 199, 201
knowing God personally – 22, 72, 91,
    184, 188
knowledge about God – 22, 72, 81, 87

Language – 69, 87, 93
law – 77-78
  - as retributive – 80
  - as Torah – 70
  - as tyrant – 136
  - evolution of – 69
  - expressing God's will – 136
  - God's inner law – 55
  - limiltations – 42, 114
  - of love – 50
  - of prayer – 47
  - scientific – 72
  - Shariah – 80
  - temple – 37, 68, 77
lectio divina – 24
legalism – 161
"*lex orandi, lex credendi*" (the law of paryer is
    the law of belief") – 47
life inside God – 60
limitations of God (by human
    limitations) – 185
literalism – 15, 63, 64
logos (def) the Word – 23
love
  - as a choice – 123, 151
  - as healing – 53
  - as Life – 78, 110-115
  - as loving others to life – 91?
  - not bought – 159
  - of enemies – 77
  - of God for God's self – 21, 184
  - unconditional – 17, 20

"Lord, have mercy!" – 124
losing God – 63, 68
Lutheran Church of Finland – 130
Lutheran Orthodoxy (*gnesio* Lutheranism,
 Lutheran Scholasticism) – 132, 210
Luther's theology - Swedish
 interpretation – 209

Manipulating God – 123
martyr (witness) - current – 160, n 69
meaning – 72
mercy – 80
message of this book – 17
metaphor – (def) 55, 55-58, 64
 in Islam – 56, in Hinduism – 56
miracles – 15, 60
Mi'raj, the – 106, n 98
mission, ours – 63
monotheism – 80, 169
More, the (God) – 58, 88, 193
mortification (see self-crucifixion/
 punishment) – 160
motivation – 124
music – 88
mystery – 13, 73, 164
 - the Great – 89
mysticism – 53, 61, 66, 87, 173
myth - (def) – 59, 58-61, n 58

Naked before God – 21
name(s) as essence – 69, 76
natural law – 152
non-violent atonement – 212

Obedience – 123, 141
offering - giving back God's gifts – 112
opposites - for completion – 66
original sin – 41

Pacifism – 221
participation in symbols – 88
pastors - dealing with faith questions – 11,
 14 -17
Paul, Apostle - Jesus died (not paid) for sin –
 40, 129, 220
payment as concept of law – 134
 (see forensics)
payment before grace offered – 43

payment for crime – 149
payment for grace – 43
payment for sin – 39, 159
payment to Devil – 40
payment to God for salvation – 17, 35-53,
 35, 43, 122, 136
payment *within* God's being - (consequences
 dealt with) – 158, 211
Peaceable Kingdom – 156
perception
 - as basis of belief – 71
 - as evolving – 69
perception (human) of God – 12, 19-20, 35,
 68 - 73, 81, 84
 - Jesus' p. of God – 29, 70,
perfection (def) - maturity – 181
persecution of Christians – 77, 78, 83, 121
pervasive presence – 183
Peter, Disciple – 220-221
pointers to truth – 16, 56-72, 73, 88, 89, 99
polytheism – 166-167
potential, inner divine – 30
power (*potentia*) - from God – 30, 60, 69
 - *potentia absoluta* (God's absolute
 power) – n 97
 - *potentia obedientialis* (capacity to do
 God's will) – n 32
 - *potentia ordinata* (God's self chosen
 limitations) – n 97
 - power over, power for – 15, 153, 183
prayer - as connection w. God – 21, 22, 24
 - affirmative, centering, mantra – 25
 - Receptive Prayer – 21, 24
prehistoric times – 163-164
prevenient grace – 46
pride – 82
priesthood – 220
priestly law – 44, 208, 209
priestly story as obstacle – 209
process – 70 (see evolution)
proof – 73, 145
prophets - (def.) one who speaks for
 God – 31,82, 84
 - and fear – 31, 70, 79, 81, 82
providence – 150
psalms - for worship – 62
punishment,
 - as "acts of God" – 151

- as retribution – 114, 117
- before grace – 122
- capital – 221
- destructive – 39
- earthly, lawful – 80, 90
- everlasting – 35, 37
- godly? – 39, 77, 78, 83, 121
- helpful – 39
- of Jesus – 218
- righteous? – 20, 45
- self- punishment (mortification) – 160

Question, the Big – 180
questions - as caring – 11-15, 25, 68
- essential – 35, 68, 71, 73
- from doubt – 61
- hard, agonizing – 15, 61, 63, 68
- necessary to faith – 15, 71

Ransom (see payment) – 40
- as spiritual insurance – 40
- as punishment – 38
- Augustine's early opposition – 220
- for slave, property – 40
reason – 68
Receptive Prayer – (def) 21, 24, 27, 181
receptivity – 40, 91, 93, 94, 113, 126, 135, 150, 161, n 73
reconciliation - (God's eternal task) – 111, 136, 154
- through Christ
- through us –17, 33
redemption (to buy back or ransom) versus salvation as gift – 149-162
- behind legal justice – 149
- earned – 156
relationship with God – 23, 93
religion, effect on history – 13
- response to mystery – 166
remnant, the – 30
repentance – 155, 217
- as major life change – 155
- before forgiveness – 216
resistance - non-violent – 77
response-ability – 63, 155
responsibility – 20
restoration – 220
retribution – 20, 77,

revelation - (to draw back the veil) – 30, 71, 93, 94, 163
righteousness – 50, 79, 80, 81, 121, 146-147, 151
risking – 159-160, 179
Russia – 15

Sacrament – 88
sacrifice – 116-127, 139-148 (see blood)
- ancient forms – 36, 118
- Anselmic/Western theory-astonishing acceptance – 211
- as giving life – 17, 110-115, 116-127, 140, 147
- as positive act of free will - giving – 144
- as placation, bribery – 219
- as self-denial – 144-145
- Augustine (early) against satisfaction/substitution – 220
- child sacrifice – 119-120, n 121
- commanded by God – 37, 70
- condemned by God – 37, 70, 77, 80, 113, 142
- condoned violence – 219
- destroying life – 116-127
- evolution of – 147
- from fear – 167
- in daily temple rituals – 36
- in love – 223
- insulting God – 220
- Jesus, not a sacrifice – 219
- lambs substituted – 142
- life as sacrifice – 214
- Luther's understanding – 221
- misunderstood – 145
- of Mary and Joseph – 143
- of thanksgiving – 158
- propitiation – 139-144, 147
- questions about – 137-138
- reconstruction of priestly teaching in Anselm – 41, 44
- scapegoating – 219
- transformation – 114
- true sacrifice: ourselves – 148
- two major types - to and for God – 116-128, 139-148, 222
Samuel – 139-140

salvation (from *salvus*, healing) – 55,
   149-150, n 177
   - Are you saved? – 180, 218
   - as God's eternal presence – 48
   - as God "for us" – 153
   - as healing/wholeness, forgiveness,
      freedom, inclusion, reconciliation,
      empowerment, recreation,
      renewal, restoration – 17, 53, 115,
      150,154-158, 162, 174, 176-178,
      n 177
   - as hereafter, eschatological – 154
   - as historical happening – 150
   - as knowing and loving God – 181
   - as present now – 157
   - as renewed, recreated, or restored life –
      153, 220
   - as saved for, not from – 154
   - as saved from danger – 150
   - as saved from sin, loss of God – 150
   - begins within God's heart – 158, 211
   - compared with redemption – 149 -162
   - for a price – 37
   - God pays the price – 157
   - God saves through Christ – 50
   - God's work through people - 156, 162
   - mission of the saved – 156, 184
   - occurs inside us, not just to us –
      134, 162
   theology of salvation (see soterioiology,
   theology of the cross)
Samuel – 139-140
sanctification (lit. "becoming holy"),
   transformation of the human spirit – 50,
   54, 83, 85
Satan and violence – 219-220
satisfaction/reparation (for God's sake, not
   ours) – 42-44, 118, 131, 136, 161, 175,
   215, 220, n 42
savior, human (Hebrew concept) as human,
   not God – 153
scholarship – 68
science – 72
security/survival – 218
self, real – 21
   - "coming to oneself" - becoming
      conscious of true identity (from

self-centered self to God-given
   Self) – 156, 179, 190
self-centeredness – 145, 218, - n 52
self-crucifixion (see mortification) – 160
self-idolatry – 146
self-offering – 146
selflessness – 52
selfishness crucifies – 91
"*simul justus et peccatur*" (simultaneously
   justified and sinning)– 90
sin -
   - as dishonoring God – 41, 47
   - as "missing the mark" – 39
   - as self-centeredness – 51, 52
   - cannot be paid for – 39
   - consequences – 45
   - original – 53, 54, n 49, n 50
   - overcome by God's love – 134
   - not counted – 53, 55, 147
soteriology (see theology of salvation) – 18,
   114, 128 -138
speaking in tongues – 180
Spirit, Holy - (def.) God is – 21-23, 65, 69,
   74, 88, 89, 91-109
   - as breath (*ruach*) – 23 *Ruach ha Qadosh*
      – 89, n 88 (transliterations vary)
   - as Creator – 165
   - as deathless – 7, 193
   - as healing – 107-109
   - as Life-Giver – 7, 60, 65, 104, 109
   - as most important Christian theology
      (pneumatology) – 91
   - as personal – 104
   - as pervasive presence – 7, 183
   - as power – 30, 43
   - as teacher – 188
   - as unrestricted – 91
   - as wisdom (*hokmah*) – 23
   - at creation – 82, 89, 91, 96
   - church of the Spirit – 220
   - excluded in Vatican I – 220
   - in and through persons – 22, 25, 30,
      90, 92, 107, 183
   - in Jesus – 52, 91-109
   - infilling of – 30
   - sharing – 192
spirits – 166

spiritual consciousness – 163-179
- unconsciousness – 30
spirituality – (def) 13, 61, 82, 130
- as self-centered – 137
status quo – 83
suffering v 73, 83, 85, 180, 223
superiority, Hebrew/Christian – 61, 62
supernatural existential, the - (God where we are) – 183
surrender to God – 21, 140-142
symbol (see metaphor) – 71, 72
- as art – 72
- as pointers to truth – 72
- as words – 71
- participation in – 88
synonyms - redemption and salvation used as – 149

Tafsir, tafarsir - Islamic theological interpretive story – 140-141
taunts that weaken – 192
temple – 79, 147, 104, 219
Temple - ritual – 77, 80, 119
Ten Commandments – 152
teshuvah (shuv) - (lit."turning") repentance – 155
tests by God - perverse – 214
thanksgiving – 158
theology - (explanation of experience of God) – 13
- inherently imperfect – 21
- inherited – 12
- of Cross – 17, 18 (see salvation, soteriology)
theologian - E. Orthodox – 47
theology of salvation (see soteriology) – 45, 114, 128-138
- of Apostle Paul – 47, n 42
- of Aulen – Tillich's response 133, n 142
- versus redemption – 149-
theosis – 129-130, n 132
tradition – 62, 68

tragedy – 152
transformation, spiritual – 52, 60,
Trinity, the – 102-104, n 94
trust (see "faith")
truth – 16, 71-72, 179
- as compared to fact – 72
- as essence and meaning – 72
- as God personally present – 99
- in our own words – 35

Ultimate concern – 51
Ultimate Reality – 73, 88
unconscious effect of words – 149
understanding – 15
union with God – 135
unknowing – 21
"Use me! Be me!" – 193

Via affirmativa - (the affirmative way - the way of love and caring attachment) – 66
via negativa - (the negative way - detachment) – 66
victimization by religion – 151
violence (religious) – 218
vocational vows – 137

War
- as holy – 70
will of God as fatalism – 46
women – 22-23
Word, the - *logos* – 23
- living in true theologian – 49
- "of the Lord" – 87, n 216
words, root meaning – 149
worship, unthinking – 125-126
"We *know* you hear our prayer!" – 126

Yahweh - Israel's exclusive God of creation and war – 12
"Yes" - as response to Spirit's call – 31, 193, 59

INDEX OF SCRIPTURE REFERENCES

Genesis 1:1 - 3	65	Creation Stories
Genesis 1:2	89	"A wind from God swept over … waters"
Genesis 1:26	23	"Let us make man in our own image."
Genesis 1:27	22, 23, 85	"In the image of God he created them"
Genesis 2:7	80, 93, 96	"Lord God breathed … the breath of life"
Genesis 22:1-19	140	Abraham's intended sacrifice of Isaac
Genesis 22:16,17	141	Abraham's seed as numerous as stars
Exodus 3:14	12, 195	"I AM who and what I am."
Exodus 6:7	168	"I will take you for my people."
Exodus 15:1-5	176	"The Lord is a man of war!"
Exodus 20:5	152	Effects until third and fourth generation.
Exodus 20:13	119	"You shall not kill."
Exodus 21:23, 24	77	"An eye for an eye…'"
Exodus 22:29	120	"first-born of your sons … give to me"
Exodus 30:11-16	40	Ransom paid as spiritual health insurance
Exodus 32	168	3000 Hebrews killed for Golden Calf incident
Leviticus 18:21	202	Child sacrifice in Israel
Leviticus 20:2-4	202	Child sacrifice in Israel
Deuteronomy 18:10	202	Child sacrifice in Israel
Deuteronomy 32:39	151	"I kill, …/ make alive, … wound and heal."
Numbers 23:19	86	"God is not a man … change his mind."
Joshua 10:40	79	"Slaughter all that breathes!"
I Kings 16:30	202	King Ahab builds for Baal and Asherah
I Kings 16:34	120	Hiel builds Jericho's gates at cost of son
I Kings 18:20	167	Elijah and priests of Baal - Yahweh's trial
II Kings 23:10	202	Child sacrifice in Israel
II Kings 32:35	202	Child sacrifice in Israel
I Samuel 1:28	140	"As long as he lives he is lent to Lord"
Job 34:14,15	104	"If he would take back his breath… all flesh would perish."
Psalm 40:6-8	147, 212	God desires a willing heart, not sacrifice
Psalm 49:7-9	40	Ransom paid to avoid Sheol
Psalm 50:23	48, 158	"Those who bring thanksgiving as their sacrifice honor me."
Psalm 50:21	50	"You thought I was one like yourself"
Psalm 50:13	43	"Do I eat the flesh of bulls or drink …?"
Psalm 76:10	212	God makes even wrath praise God.
Psalm 136 (all)	85	"His mercy endures forever!"
Psalm 137:9	63	Dash enemies' babies against a rock.
Psalm 139:8	105	Even in Sheol, "you are there."
Psalm 139:1-18	62, 106	God's pervasive presence
Proverbs 23:26	148	"My son, give me your heart."

Reference	Page	Quote/Description
Isaiah 1:11-20	68, 147	Offerings are futile - Seek justice,
Isaiah 2:4	177	"Swords will be beaten into plowshares"
Isaiah 5:11	153	"They … come with singing to Zion."
Isaiah 6	106	Isaiah's vision of God on a throne
Isaiah 11:9	156	Earth full of knowledge of the Lord.
Isaiah 30:33	150	"In returning and rest, you … saved."
Isaiah 43:1	157	"Do not fear… I have redeemed you."
Isaiah 43: 3b	157	"I give Egypt for your ransom."
Isaiah 43:11	153	No savior but Yahweh
Isaiah 43:25	53, 147	"I will not remember your sins."
Isaiah 44:21, 22	55	"I have swept away your transgressions"
Isaiah 49:3	179	"You are my servant"
Isaiah 49:6b	156	Salvation to ends of the earth.
Isaiah 51:11	153	"The ransomed … shall return … with singing!"
Isaiah 55:1	37	"Come, buy wine and milk without … price"
Isaiah 55:6, 7	36	"Return … God will abundantly pardon"
Isaiah 55:8	86	"My thoughts are not your[s]"
Isaiah 60:1	193	"Arise! Shine! For your light has come! The glory of the Lord has risen upon you."
Isaiah 61:1-3	157	"The Spirit … has anointed me to …"
Isaiah 65:24	112	"Before they call, I will answer."
Isaiah 66:18-23	156	Universal salvation
Jeremiah 31:33, 34	55	"I will remember their sin no more."
Job (general ref.)	151	Human situation reveals righteousness
Job 34:14,15	104	If God would withdraw God's breath, all humankind would perish.
Hosea 6:6	113	"I desire mercy, not sacrifice."
Micah 6:7	143	"give my body for the sin of my soul?"
Amos 5:21-24	147	Offerings unacceptable - Justice instead
Matthew 3:11	37	"I baptize you with water for repentance"
Matthew 5:17	77	"I come not to abolish, but fulfill law"
Matthew 5:21-42	19	"You have heard it said …. But I say—"
Matthew 5:38, 39	75, 176	"Turn the other" cheek.
Matthew 5:43,44	75	"Love your enemies,"
Matthew 5:45	96	"God sends rains upon righteous and …"
Matthew 9:13, 12:6, 7	77 113, 147	"I desire mercy and not sacrifice."
Matthew 10:19	107, 180	The Spirit speaks through you when most needed.
Matthew 10:36	75	One's foes will be one's family
Matthew 10:38	219	"He who does not take his cross … is not worthy of me."
Matthew 12:6	77	"Something greater than the temple is here."
Matthew 15:24	75	"I was sent only to lost sheep of Israel"
Matthew 15:27	75	"Even dogs eat crumbs from master's "
Matthew 20:28	37, 159	"The Son of Man came … to give his life a ransom for many."
Matthew 23:27	62	"Pharisees … like whitewashed tombs"
Matthew 23:37	80	"Jerusalem … kills prophets"
Matthew 25: 31-46	84, 106	The Last Judgment - Sheep and goats

INDEX OF SCRIPTURE REFERENCES 239

Matthew 25:40	105	Giving "to the least, gives to me,"
Matthew 26:39	141	"Not what I want, but what you want."
Matthew 26:52	80	Those who take the sword perish by sword
Matthew 27:46	92, 139	"My God, …Why have you forsaken me?"
Matthew 27:54	113	"Surely this was the son of God!"
Mark 5:35	135	"Your faith has made you well."
Mark 8:34-37	144	"Deny themselves - take up their cross"
Mark 10:18 (Matt. 19:17)	51	"No one is good but God alone."
Mark 10:45	37	The Son came … to give life as ransom.
Luke 4: 1-30	92	Jesus' temptations/ statement of mission
Luke 4:18, 19	13, 157	Christ's perceived mission
Luke 5:12-26	43	Jesus heals a leper and a paralytic
Luke 11: 1-4	44	Teaching of the Lord's Prayer
Luke 12:29-30	135	"Your Father knows what you need."
Luke 13: 34	206	"O Jerusalem, … stoning those … sent"
Luke 14:21-23	177	Poor, crippled, blind, invited to feast
Luke 15:11-32	156	The Prodigal Son
Luke 21:33, 34	80	Jerusalem kills prophets
Luke 22:17-19	217	Words at the Last Supper
Luke 23:34	111, 137	"Father, forgive - they do not know"
Luke 23:46	93	"Into your hands I commend my spirit."
Luke 5:20-26	38	Healing of the paralytic = forgiveness
John 1:12	115, 137	Power to those who received/ believed
John 1:18	54	"No one has ever seen God."
John 2:16	219	"my Father's house [is not one] of barter."
John 3:16	37, 111, 141	"God so loved the world … he gave his only begotten son, … eternal life."
John 3:17	15, 113, 126, 141	Christ came to save, not to condemn
John 4:24	74, 86, 92, 172	"God is Spirit"
John 10:10	38, 130	" I came that they may have life … abundantly"
John 12:24	159	"Those who love their life lose it."
John 12:31	40	"The ruler of this world … driven out"
John 12:44-45	178	"I speak as God has told me."
John 13:34	137	"Love one another as I have loved you."
John 14:2	58	"In my Father's house are many rooms."
John 14:6	29, 182	"I am the way, the truth, and the life"
John 14:10	9, 52, 102, 184	"I do not speak on my own authority… the Father … within me … works"
John 14:12	29, 107 189, 207	"Greater works … will you do … I go."
John 14:28	29, 73	"The Father is greater than I."
John 14:16-17	104, 183	"The Spirit dwells with … will be in you."
John 14-17	29-31	Jesus final discourse with disciples
John 14:28	29, 196	"The Father is greater than I."
John 15:4,5	38, 61	Abide in me as I abide in you."
John 15:16	30, 115	"I have chosen you … bear fruit."
John 15:20	121	"If they persecute me, … persecute you."
John 16:2	84	"Those who kill you think they … worship"
John 17:3	2, 183, 205, 207	"This is eternal life, to know thee"

Reference	Page	Quote
John 18:11	80	"Am I not to drink the cup the Father …"
John 18:36	153	"My kingdom is not of this world."
John 19:7	51	"He ought to die because he has claimed to be the Son of God."
John 20:22	125	"Receive the Holy Spirit."
John 21:17	107	"Feed my sheep."
Acts 1:8	30, 183	"You will receive power when the Holy Spirit has come upon you"
Acts 2:23	211	Cross was the "definite plan … of God"
Acts 17:28	218	"In him we live and move and have …"
Romans 7:25	37	"with my flesh, I am a slave to … sin."
Romans 8:26	25	"The Spirit within us prays."
Romans 11:29	31	The gifts and call … are irrevocable
Romans 12:1	148	"Present … bodies … a living sacrifice"
Romans 13:8	113	"Love is the fulfilling of the law."
I Corinthians 3:2	14	"fed w. milk … not ready for solid food"
I Corinthians 3:16, 17	23, 104	"God's Spirit dwells in you."
I Corinthians 13:8-13	127	"Love never ends."
II Corinthians 3:17-18	91, 129	"The Lord is the Spirit" - "We are being transformed."
II Corinthians 4:7	59	"the power of God in clay jars"
II Corinthians 5:17	182	"Anyone in Christ is a new creation."
II Corinthians 5:19, 20	27, 33, 108, 126, 186	"God was, in Christ, reconciling … not counting trespasses … entrusting the message to us."
Colossians 1:15	22	"He is the image of the invisible God"
Colossians 1:19	98	In him all the fullness of God - dwelt.
Philippians 2:5-7	110, 138	Kenosis-letting go in order to give
Philippians 3:4-14	146, 155	Nothing matters except knowing Christ
Philippians 4:6	135	"Do not worry about anything."
Ephesians 2:8	135	"saved by grace through faith"
Ephesians 4:6	169	One above, through, and in all.
I Thessalonians 5:17	51	"Pray without ceasing."
II Timothy 3:16	19, 94	"All scripture is inspired of God."
Hebrews 9:22	117	"Under the law … without the shedding of blood there is no forgiveness."
Hebrews 10:1-18	212	Ancient law versus the given will.
Hebrews 10:4	43	Blood of bulls, goats cannot erase sin
Hebrews 10:5	204	God desires the given will, not sacrifice
Hebrews 10:9b	212	Christ abolishes law to do God's will.
Hebrews 10:14	42	"Christ offered, for all time, a single sacrifice for sin"
I John 1:1-3, 13	111	"That which we have seen and heard we declare to you"
I John 2:20	220	"the Light who enlightens everyone"
I John 4:8, 16b	46, 81	"God is love…. Those who abide in love, abide in God."
I Peter 3:18, 19	106	Christ preaches to disobedient spirits "in prison"

Grace Adolphsen Brame, Ph. D. theologian and professor of spirituality, teaches the Integration of Theology and Spirituality in the Graduate Religion Department of LaSalle University in Philadelphia and formerly taught at Villanova University. She is an author, speaker, retreat leader, a former lay pastor, and a professional singer in opera and concert, having represented the United States in Europe and in the former Soviet Union where her concerts broke the cultural blockade between the two countries. Her books are listed at the beginning of this volume.

>   Web: www.gracebrame.com
>   E-mail: grace@gracebrame.com

Henri Nouwen:
"*Receptive Prayer* is a beautiful book."

Douglas Steere:
"*Receptive Prayer* is magnificent in its insights and the great sanity that shines from it all! Persons would profit greatly by reading this choice book. I personally have given away over 30 copies."

Richard Rohr, OFM:
"Grace Brame's work, reflected in *Faith, the Yes of the Heart* and *Receptive Prayer*, is very fine and very much needed."

John Largen:
"My heart-felt endorsement for the work of Grace Brame, a theologian whose books, retreats, lectures, and singing have so greatly helped to bring the church into a new awareness of its rich spiritual legacy."

Marcus Borg:
"For a wise and insightful treatment of faith ... see Grace Adolphsen Brame, *Faith, the Yes of the Heart*."

Bradley Holt:
"*Faith, the Yes of the Heart*, opens up a neglected landscape of Luther's writing...revisioning the history of the interpretation of Luther..."

Reuben Job:
"*Faith, the Yes of the Heart* should be required reading in every seminary, in the primary library of every pastor, and a companion for everyone on a serious spiritual journey."

Pastor Brady Faggart:
"*The Cross: Payment or Gift?* is a great and important book which we really need. It will transform people's understanding of the Cross and will *feed* so many hearts. – Brame's 'way' is to inform and challenge, encourage and inspire."